LOGISTICS AND TRANSPORT IN A FAST GROWING ECONOMY:

Managing the Supply Chain for High Performance

LOGISTICS AND TRANSPORT IN A FAST GROWING ECONOMY:

Managing the Supply Chain for High Performance

Edited by

JOHN MANGAN AND KEVIN HANNIGAN
Irish Management Institute

With a Preface by
MARTIN CHRISTOPHER
*Professor of Marketing and Logistics
at Cranfield School of Management*

BLACKHALL
Publishing

This book was typeset by
Gough Typesetting Services for
BLACKHALL PUBLISHING
26 Eustace Street
Dublin 2
Ireland

e-mail: blackhall@eircom.net
www.blackhallpublishing.com

ISBN: 1 901657 97 3

A catalogue record for this book
is available from the British Library.

Printed in Ireland by
Colour Books Ltd

Contents

SECTION III
Logistics and Supply Chain Management

Preface

Industry and business is undergoing a significant transformation as we move from competing in predominantly local or regional markets to a much wider global stage. Inevitably as these new markets take shape, significant changes are required in the way in which organisations respond to these new competitive challenges. One of the greatest challenges is in the physical process by which customer demand is met. This is the arena of logistics and supply chain management.

The global marketplace is typified by ever-more demanding customers requiring more reliable delivery in ever-shorter time frames. The winners in these new markets will be those organisations that have recognised the importance of managing the logistics pipeline as a truly integrated process. To become a more responsive organisation requires a different way of managing the physical flow of product from one end of the supply chain to the other.

In the past, it could be argued, companies succeeded or failed on the basis of their own actions. Now it is more often the case that competitive advantage is gained through the way in which an organisation manages the 'extended enterprise', comprising its relationships with upstream suppliers as well as downstream customers. Hence the importance of managing the physical processes of logistics and transportation that link the various players in the chain.

This importance is magnified in the context of the profound change that underlies the remarkable growth of the Irish economy in recent years. In addition, as we look to the future, this growth and change means that greater attention in economic planning must be afforded to managing transportation infrastructure. The principles of logistics are no less relevant in this arena.

Against this background the timing of this new book could not be better. The boardrooms of all our companies need to give much greater consideration to the ways in which logistics and transportation strategies can be developed to gain competitive advantage. The issues and ideas that are addressed in this book have application in every commercial organisation and they warrant the serious attention of managers everywhere.

Martin Christopher
Professor of Marketing and Logistics,
Cranfield School of Management

This book is dedicated to the memory of the late Jim Crowley,
Professor of Transport Policy and Logistics at University College Dublin

Acknowledgements

We wish to thank Barry Kenny, Chief Executive and our colleagues at the IMI for their help and support in the completion of this book. We also wish to thank the President, Chairman and Council of the IMI for their ongoing support for research into the development of best management practice.

Our thanks are also extended to the contributors for the efficiency and expertise with which they produced the various chapters. On their and our own behalf we would also like to extend our gratitude to the numerous practitioners in Irish business who gave generously of their time and experience in the research for this text. We wish to convey a special word of thanks to Martin Christopher, Professor of Marketing and Logistics at Cranfield School of Management, for his perceptive comments on the ideas and materials contained in the text.

We wish to also thank Gerard O'Connor and the staff of Blackhall Publishing for their help over the past number of months.

Lastly, a very special word of thanks to both of our families and in particular to Maeve and Cathal and to Siobhán for their ongoing love and support in this, as in all our endeavours.

Biographical Notes

Dr Sean Barrett
Sean is a senior lecturer in the Department of Economics and Fellow of Trinity College, Dublin. He was educated at University College, Dublin and at McMaster University, Hamilton, Ontario. His specialist areas are public policy and transport and he is author of several books and many journal articles on these topics. He was a director of Bord Fáilte, a member of the Culliton Review of Industrial Policy and of the Review Group on Commercial Harbours. He has been an economic consultant to the European Commission, the OECD, and the European Science Foundation. He is a member of the editorial board of the Journal of Air Transport Management.

James Cunningham
James is a lecturer in the Department of Management at National University of Ireland, Galway. His main area of specialism is strategic management. His research interests include strategic change in the Irish public sector, the role of the strategist in the firm, and innovation in Irish SMEs. His current PhD research is focusing upon the impact of environmental voluntary agreements on corporate strategy in the Irish grocery industry. Prior to joining National University of Ireland, Galway he lectured in the Department of Business Administration at University College Dublin. He has also completed a number of research projects in a variety of industry sectors.

Dr Sean Ennis
Sean lectures in marketing at the University of Strathclyde in Glasgow. His main research interests cover retailing, supply chain management and entrepreneurial marketing. He has published widely in a number of scholarly journals including *Qualitative Market Research: an International Journal, European Management Journal, Review of International Retailing and Consumer Research* and the *Irish Marketing Review.* He is also the co-editor of *Competing from the Periphery,* with Brian Fynes. He received his PhD from Dublin City University and examined the marketing planning practices of indigenous firms in the Irish electronics sector. He is currently completing a book on entrepreneurial marketing which is due for publication in 2000.

Tom Ferris
Tom holds a Masters degree in economics and is a fellow of the Chartered Institute of Transport (FCIT). He is currently Head of Planning at the Department of Public Enterprise in Dublin. He previously worked in the Department

of Finance, the National Economic and Social Council, the B&I Shipping Line, the Irish Co-operative Organisation Society and the Joint Oireachtas Committee on State Sponsored Bodies. Having been President of the Chartered Institute of Transport in 1994 – 1995, he is currently a Member of the Institute's National Council. He is also a Member of the National Council of the European Movement. He lectures in transport planning in UCD and in Corporate Governance at UCC.

Dr Sheila Flanagan

Sheila holds Bachelors and PhD degrees from University College Dublin. She is currently a college lecturer in the Dublin Institute of Technology and holds positions as visiting lecturer with the University of Paris, Sorbonne and the University of Ulster. Prior to this she lectured in the Department of Business Administration at University College Dublin. Sheila has published extensively on tourism and related matters and her recent books include *The Business of Tourism* and *Sustainable Tourism: European Case Studies in how to achieve it*. She has also extensive experience as a consultant in tourism to a variety of bodies in both Ireland and Poland.

Dr Brian Fynes

Brain is a member of the Department of Business Administration, University College Dublin (UCD) and is Senior Lecturer in Operations Management. He is also Director of the Centre for Quality and Services Management at UCD. He has been on the Faculty of London Business School where he was EU *Marie Curie* Research Fellow in the Centre for Operations Management. His research interests focus on the moderating impact of supply chain position on manufacturing (JIT/TQM) practices and business performance.

He has published articles in the *European Management Journal*, the *International Labour Review*, the *International Review of Retail and Consumer Research*, *Supply Chain Management: An International Journal*, *De Qualitate*, the *Irish Marketing Review* and *Irish Business and Administrative Research*, as well as contributing chapters to numerous books. He is co-author of *Flexible Working Lives* (Oak Tree Press) and joint editor of *Competing from the Periphery* (Dryden Press).

Mary Gallagher

Mary is Route Director of Stena Line's Rosslare–Fishguard ferry services. She joined the company in 1989 and worked in the planning department before moving to Holyhead as Passenger and Freight Manager. In 1993 she became Commercial Manager of the Rosslare–Fishguard route from where she moved to Dun Laoghaire in 1998 to become Business Co-Ordinator, Ireland. She moved to her present position in October 1999. Prior to joining Stena Line, Mary worked as a transport consultant and as administrator of the Chartered Institute of Transport in Ireland.

She holds a BA degree in English from University College Galway and a

Master's degree in Transport and Strategic Planning from University College Dublin. She is a Fellow of the Chartered Institute of Transport and served as President of the Institute in Ireland in 1996-1997.

Michael Giblin
Michael holds BA and MBS degrees, and received the prestigious Sir Charles Harvey Award for the latter degree. He is currently Managing Director of Icarus e-Com (Cargo Community Systems-CCS Ltd).

Mr Giblin spent over 25 years with Aer Lingus-Cargo in both Operations and Administration and he held responsibility for Development, Marketing, and Distribution Systems functions. He was Project Manager for network-wide computerisation. He managed the technical development of ICARUS and the setting up of CCS Ltd as the industry owned communications platform with twenty other transport companies, having it approved by IATA as its world pilot site. As Managing Director of Icarus e-Com he has developed the companies multi-modal services to provide e-commerce solutions for the entire logistics, manufacturing and travel sectors, as well as the national electronic Customs clearance service. He is a committee member of the Institute of Logistics and Transport, and a member of the Chartered Institute of Transport and was a winner of its Innovator of the Year Award. He is a member of both the IBEC Transport Council and Telecommunications Services Council.

Orla Gregory
Orla holds Bachelor of Commerce and Masters in Business Studies (Logistics and Manufacturing) degrees from University College Dublin. She is currently a Lecturer in Business Studies at Carlow Institute of Technology where she teaches Logistics, Purchasing and Operations Management. She has also lectured at both University College Dublin and at the Irish Management Institute and has presented papers on logistics research in Ireland and abroad.

Dr Kevin Hannigan
Kevin is Head of Economic Research at the Irish Management Institute. He has previously held positions as an economist with the National Economic and Social Council and with the University of Ulster. He holds primary and postgraduate degrees from University College Dublin and a PhD in economics from Trinity College Dublin. His professional interests centre on Irish economic policy and, in recent years, on the importance of intellectual capital in economic development. In addition to economic analysis, the main focus of his work at the IMI is on the competitiveness of industry and the role of the IMI in enhancing the performance of managers.

John R Harvey
John is Manager, Intercity Accounts and Special Projects with Iarnród Éireann. He is an engineer and has worked on many aspects of the modernisation of the railway in Ireland. He holds a Bachelor of Science (Honours) degree, a Mas-

ters Degree in Industrial Engineering and a Masters Degree in Business Studies, both from University College, Dublin and an MSc (Economics) from Trinity College, Dublin. He is a Member of the Institution of Engineers of Ireland and a Member of the Chartered Institute of Transport. He is currently undertaking research for a PhD in the field of applied transport economics and policy.

John Mangan
John is a Senior Management Specialist in Logistics at the Irish Management Institute and Programme Director of the Institute's BA (Mgmt) Degree Programme. John holds a Bachelor of Science (Honours) degree from University College Cork, a Masters Degree in transport management from Cranfield University, and he is currently finishing a PhD at the University of Wales, Cardiff. His PhD research focused on decision making in logistics. In summer 1997 he was a Fulbright Scholar at the Wallace E Carroll School of Management in Boston College. Before joining the IMI he lectured in the Department of Business Administration at University College Dublin. Prior to this he was Company Secretary of Arramara Teoranta, and he has also worked in the civil service in both the Department of the Marine and the Department of Finance and in both Aer Lingus and Aer Rianta.

Harry McGeehan
Harry is Economist with Iarnród Éireann and was previously a lecturer in the Department of Political Economy, University College, Dublin. He holds a Masters degree in Economics from the University of Essex, is a Member of the Chartered Institute of Transport, and is a graduate of the Institute of Marketing (UK). He has published numerous papers on transport issues, in both Irish and international journals, with particular reference to demand analysis and productivity measurement.

Dr Aisling Reynolds-Feighan
Aisling lectures in transport and regional economics at the Department of Economics, University College Dublin. She holds an MA in Economics from UCD and a PhD in Regional Science from the University of Illinois at Urbana-Champaign, USA. She has published extensively on US and European air transport economics and regulation in international journals such as *Transportation Research A*, *Transportation Research E: Logistics and Transportation Review*, *Journal of Air Transport Management* and *Transport Reviews*. Her book, *The Effects of Deregulation on US Air Networks*, was published by Springer-Verlag in 1992. She has worked as a consultant with the Irish Department of Public Enterprise, the US Department of Transportation, and the OECD, on a variety of air transport policy issues.

Barry O'Grady
Barry is Distribution Systems and Support Manager and Campus Asset Protection Manager in IBM's Dublin Technology Campus. His responsibilities

include distribution systems strategy implementation, finance, business controls, vendor management and security of high value parts in the Campus. Prior to IBM he worked as Logistics Coordinator in Xilinx Ireland where he was responsible for export regulations and logistics. In Intrastat Ireland, the Duty Management division of Walsh Western International, he operated customs duty minimisation regimes on behalf of numerous electronics manufacturing companies in Dublin, Cork and Limerick. Barry holds a Bachelor of International Commerce degree and a Masters in Business Studies (Logistics) degree from University College Dublin.

Paul O'Reilly

Paul works with the Food Marketing Research Group at the National Food Centre, Teagasc, in Dublin. He holds primary and post-graduate degrees from Trinity College Dublin and University College Dublin respectively and was previously a researcher in the Centre for Logistics Studies at UCD. His research interests are in supply chain management and retailing and he has lectured on Food Marketing, Strategic Management and Enterprise Operations in UCD. Paul has also lectured in UCC and Cornell University and has published articles in *Supply Chain Management: An International Journal* and the *International Journal of Retail and Distribution Management*, as well as in various trade publications.

Brendan Ryan

Brendan holds a Bachelor of Commerce degree from University College Galway and a Masters in Business Studies (Logistics) degree from University College Dublin. Brendan is ACCA certified in Accountancy and Finance and he is also IPICS certified. He is a member of the Logistics Institute of Ireland and he is currently 'Head of Logistics' for United Drug PLC in Ireland. He was previously employed in the Irish Defence Forces Logistics Corps and also worked for periods with the Wyeth Medica Pharmaceutical Company and with Walsh Western. Brendan also worked with IBM where he managed the set up of the Distribution and Logistics Operation for the new IBM Technology Campus in Dublin.

Chapter 1
Introduction

Kevin Hannigan and John Mangan
Irish Management Institute

1.1 LOGISTICS AND TRANSPORT IN THE IRISH ECONOMY

One of the major themes in the evolution of business in the 20th century has been the increasing importance, relative to the core activity of the firm, of supporting activities and cost centres. The importance of this development has caused many writers on management to conclude that, in many cases, firms no longer compete on the basis of differentiation of the physical product or the core service produced, but on the basis of associated factors, such as the quality of customer care. Among the most important aspects of this are the ability of the firm to source inputs and to get products to the market in a timely fashion. The globalisation of business and the identification of knowledge as the key competitive factor in modern industries in recent years have further enhanced the importance of ensuring efficient distribution – both upstream (at supplier and factory level) and downstream (at customer level). At this juncture, it appears most probable that these developments have far from run their course, and that the forces that have emerged in recent decades will be intensified further by developments in the new millennium.

Ireland's recent success has brought the importance of these factors into sharp focus. Economic success has been built upon the growth of international trade and the availability of labour force skills. Such has been the rapidity of recent success that Irish output in 1998 was over 60 per cent greater than in 1990 and twice the level of 1986, even when the effect of price increases is removed. However, recent reports from international bodies, and casual observation, make it obvious that, in addition to skill shortages, the greatest threats to continued success in Ireland's economy lie in the unsustainable burdens that rapid growth is placing on the country's transport systems. It is clear that inputs will not be able to increase at a sufficiently fast rate to maintain the recent rate of growth of output. This could compromise Ireland's ability to compete, irrespective of the competitiveness of the economy in other respects.

The reaction and the debate in response to the challenges posed by rapid growth have concentrated overwhelmingly on the need to invest in new transport infrastructure, for example, to build more roads, extend ports and develop airports. In fact, proposals in this regard make headlines regularly. It is estimated that there is currently a backlog of development equivalent to the expenditure of £2 billion in relation to roads alone and that Ireland needs to spend £880 million per annum on transport infrastructure up to 2006 to accommodate projected growth, and that Ireland's ports will need investment of £133 million just to keep up with projected traffic growth. The £4.7 billion for roads and the £2.2 billion for public transport identified in the National Development Plan 2000-2006 reflect this analysis. These are enormous sums for a country such as Ireland, and there will be only one chance to do it right. As a result, it is important that proposals for expenditure are prioritised and that the correct procedures are followed to ensure that the resulting infrastructure is efficient and is appropriate to meet the needs of the economy.

It is undeniable that extensive investment in transport infrastructure is required urgently. However, this is only one element of the solution. Part of the problem arises from the increasing complexity of logistics' systems with firms, operating in a highly competitive global marketplace, striving to reduce manufacturing and total distribution costs while at the same time leveraging marketplace advantage through superior logistics performance.[1] This is particularly the case in Ireland where the size and structure of the economy have changed so fundamentally. In essence, Ireland requires sophisticated management of transport and logistics systems *as well as* modern transport infrastructure.

This book provides an overview of the current state of affairs in regard to logistics and transport in Ireland. It explores the role of these issues in Ireland's economic success and, in particular, it reviews best practice in both transport and logistics in an international context. In doing so, it clearly illustrates that transport and logistics are knowledge intensive operations, the development of which require much more than the provision of fixed capital and infrastructure.

1.2 IRELAND: THE CELTIC TIGER ON EUROPE'S PERIPHERY

The Republic of Ireland, a member of the European Union (EU) since 1973, is an island country in the northwest of Europe, with a population of some 3.6 million people. The island of Ireland comprises both the Republic of Ireland, established initially as a Free State under a treaty with the United Kingdom in 1922, and Northern Ireland, which remains part of the United Kingdom. A feature of the whole island of Ireland is that, since the opening of the channel tunnel linking Britain with continental Europe, Ireland is now the only EU member country without a land link to the rest of the EU. As a result, it is totally dependent on air and maritime transport for external access and egress.

The impact of this dependence is intensified by the importance of external trade to the economy. In recent years a large, mostly export-oriented, manufacturing base has emerged placing a heavy demand on transport and logistics systems. Inward tourism has also grown remarkably in recent years and is now

---

1. The use of the word 'total' is not accidental and is important when referring to distribution costs. The concept of total distribution costs (TDCs) suggests that firms, when considering their distribution strategies, should be concerned not only with transport costs, but should also consider a raft of other costs routinely incurred. These include, but are not restricted to, the cost of capital resources tied up in inventory, customer satisfaction levels with respect to delivery targets and the replication of inventory at multiple stocking points.

a major contributor to the Irish economy. At the same time, Ireland finds itself in the situation of being peripherally located *vis-à-vis* the economic centre of gravity of the EU. The performance of the transport sector within Ireland is also of crucial importance to sustaining regionally balanced economic development and social cohesion. These developments highlight the importance of transport and logistics systems to the Irish economy and set the context for this text.

1.3 OUTLINE OF THE TEXT

A panel of experts, both academics and practitioners, has made a valuable contribution to this text. The chapters have been arranged to provide a logical progression from a general description of the relevant concepts and context of the topic, through to the particular characteristics of transport and logistics in the Irish economy.

Section I sets the scene for subsequent discussions. In Chapter 2 John Mangan of the IMI charts the history of transport and the emergence of logistics and supply chain management and describes the various terms commonly used in the study of associated functional areas. Kevin Hannigan, also of the IMI, describes the phenomenal economic successes of the Irish economy in Chapter 3. This chapter shows that economic success has brought new challenges that provide the background to the issues detailed in subsequent chapters. The development of transport has occurred within a particular and evolving legislative and regulatory environment. This has been created in response to perceived deficiencies in the result that would emerge from a free market approach. In Chapter 4, Harry McGeehan of Iarnród Éireann outlines the economic analysis that provides the rationale for government intervention in the market. The application of this approach is described in Chapter 5 by Tom Ferris of the Department of Public Enterprise who reviews the role played by government and its agencies, both nationally and internationally, in transport and logistics. Sean Barrett of Trinity College Dublin provides a critical review of experience with transport regulation in Ireland in Chapter 6 and illustrates the importance of questioning past solutions in a changing economic environment. Regulatory issues are of considerable importance to transport, and are likely to continue to be to the forefront of discussion in this area in the future. In Chapter 7, Kevin Hannigan and John Mangan of the IMI, and James Cunningham of NUI Galway, examine the environmental impact of transport and logistics systems, a particularly important issue that is increasingly likely to become the basis of regulation.

The first three chapters in section II detail the principal modes of transport. The emphasis is firmly on highlighting the relevant issues as they apply to Ireland. These chapters deal respectively with air transport (Chapter 8, Aisling Reynolds-Feighan of University College Dublin), maritime transport (Chapter 9, Mary Gallagher of Stena Line), and road and rail transport (Chapter 10, John Harvey of Iarnród Éireann). In the final chapter in this section, Sheila

Flanagan of the Dublin Institute of Technology and Kevin Hannigan of the IMI discuss the key role of transport in the development of the Irish tourism industry. Irrespective of the mode of access, this chapter shows that issues of considerable importance in relation to the net benefits of growth arise when the transport supplier is faced with alternating periods of high and low demand. Tourism provides a notable example of this problem, but similar difficulties of capacity utilisation are common in many other industries also.

Section III of the text moves from the specific focus on transport to the broader foci of logistics and supply chain management. Brian Fynes of University College Dublin and Sean Ennis of the University of Strathclyde discuss the role of logistics in manufacturing in Chapter 12. Barry O'Grady of IBM details the role of third-party service providers in logistics systems in Chapter 13 and indicates the extent to which logistics is in the process of undergoing a rapid transformation. In addition to third-party service providers, information technology has been the other principal factor driving the revolution in logistics systems in recent years. In Chapter 14, Michael Giblin of Icarus eCommerce discusses the role of information technology in the supply chain. Logistics is also a vital area in the retail sector and Paul O'Reilly of Teagasc describes the developments that have been taking place in Chapter 15. Finally, Brendan Ryan of United Drug discusses the current and likely future role of e-business in the supply chain in Chapter 16. Each of these chapters ends with a list of further reading and information sources relevant to the subject matter.

Two chapters conclude this book. Orla Gregory of the Carlow Institute of Technology and John Mangan of the Irish Management Institute detail the various sources of information and training in transport and logistics in Chapter 17. They also report on a survey of Irish logistics executives which investigated their current and future skills and training requirements. The final chapter is an overview of the subject of logistics and transport in Ireland by the two editors. This is based on the contributions that comprise this text and illustrates the central role that logistics increasingly plays in achieving competitive advantage at the level of the firm, at industry level and for the economy as a whole. Nowhere is this illustrated better than in Ireland where rapid change has been accompanied by a period of remarkable growth and development.

A wide range of disparate topics is covered in these chapters. This is unavoidable given the scope of the role played by logistics in determining the competitiveness of the economy and the firms located here. At all times, every effort has been made to ensure that the material is directed to, and is presented in a manner that is accessible to, both practitioners and students. In doing so, the contributions of the various authors amount to a detailed and timely discussion of a topic that is of vital importance to the operations of modern firms and the future of the Irish economy.

Chapter 2
Principles and Concepts

John Mangan
Irish Management Institute

2.1 A BRIEF HISTORY OF TRANSPORT: FROM THE CELTS TO THE MARKETSPACE

Ireland has had her fair share of historical events in transport. These include the *Titanic* which berthed near Cobh (formerly Queenstown) on her maiden, and sadly last, voyage; in later decades many of the world's first commercial transatlantic flights were seaplanes which used the Shannon Estuary, while the first duty free shop in the world was opened at Shannon Airport. Transport has played a central role in the economic and social development of Ireland. Traditionally textbooks on transport have defined five modes of transport namely:

- air;
- water;
- road;
- rail;
- pipeline.

The terms *multimodal* transport and *intermodal* transport are often used when considering different combinations of transport modes. Generally speaking *multimodal* transport is a broad term and implies the use of a number of different modes, with or without changing the loading unit, while *intermodal* transport also implies the use of a number of different modes but the loading unit (frequently referred to as an intermodal transport unit or container) does not change.

Subsequent chapters cover the first four modes listed above in detail, but this book will not concern itself with the pipeline mode. A sixth 'mode' is now being suggested, the 'information superhighway'. Today, a growing proportion of communications and commerce takes place electronically and we live in an age where the 'marketspace' has begun to overshadow the traditional marketplace. There are numerous examples representing this new paradigm of the marketspace: videoconferencing is an alternative to travelling to meetings; airline tickets can be booked over the Internet instead of visiting a travel agent; rather than renting a videocassette, a movie may be selected from a pay per view cable TV network. Information and communications technologies (ICT) have revolutionised the efficiency and effectiveness of transport and logistics systems. This theme reappears throughout this book. However, the overall impact, across entire transport networks, which ICT will have on actually reducing the physical transportation of people and freight remains to be seen.[1] Anecdotal evidence suggests, for example, that during the Gulf War many American firms were happy to conduct business using videoconferencing as they risked attacks on American civil aircraft. However, once hostilities ceased, many executives reverted to physically travelling to meetings instead.

Some commentators have suggested that there have been three 'revolutions' in transport, the first being the advent of railways, the second the car, and the third the application of ICT to transport. When reviewing the history of transportation, sea transport was undoubtedly of major importance for many centuries and effectively shaped the direction of world commerce. Ireland itself has an interesting maritime history and has been influenced by maritime trade since the arrival of the Celts from Central Europe in the period up to 150 BC. The next major influx of settlers were the Viking warriors who arrived by sea (mostly from Scandinavia) in the 9th and 10th centuries and built fortified settlements. These included one at the mouth of the River Liffey, establishing it as a centre for maritime trade and giving birth to what is now Dublin, Ireland's capital city. The next wave of settlers were the Normans in 1169, thus effectively beginning some 800 years of association between England and Ireland.

This sequence defined the basis for the development of Ireland's maritime trade which revolved largely around shipping between Britain and Ireland. Unlike the great maritime nations, such as England, France, Spain or Portugal, Ireland never had a large maritime fleet and did not participate in overseas conquests and empire building. Indeed, the domination of maritime trade by flows between Ireland and England was to continue up to and even beyond Ireland's independence from the British Empire. The latter part of the 20th century has seen Ireland increasingly engage in more diverse international trade and particularly since joining the EEC in 1973, it has experienced considerable growth in maritime transportation.

With the invention of the steam engine, railway systems emerged in the 19th century and greatly facilitated both national communications and industrial development in many countries. One needs only look to the considerable role played by the railroads in shaping the United States. An elaborate rail network was also developed covering most of the island of Ireland, but recent decades have seen this network consolidated considerably, with many railway lines, particularly those located in remote peripheral parts of Ireland, now closed. In contrast, there has been reinvestment in suburban rail in the greater Dublin area in recent years in an effort to combat road traffic congestion and an urban light rail system for Dublin is also planned.

The early decades of the 20th century saw widespread production of the motor car, greatly enhancing personal mobility (as well as pioneering the application of some famous manufacturing and inventory management techniques, as will be shown in Chapter 12). However, because of unfavourable economic conditions road transport got off to a comparatively late and slow start in Ire-

---

1. For a good discussion of these issues see Crowley, J., (1998).

land. In more recent years there have been record levels of investment in road infrastructure in Ireland in an attempt to bring the network up to European standards. Disparities, though lessening in recent years, have existed in terms of the quality of the road network in Northern Ireland versus that in the Republic of Ireland due to comparatively much greater investment in the former network, at a time when there was, for a long period, very little investment in the network in the Republic of Ireland.

The 20th century has also seen the proliferation of air transportation and with it the 'shrinking' of the world. Technological developments in the air mode were greatly enhanced by the surges of technological innovation that accompanied the two world wars in the 20th century. Aer Lingus, the national flag carrier for Ireland, was established in 1936. Only in recent decades, however, in line with the global norm, has air travel begun to develop in Ireland, driven in particular by deregulation in the sector in 1986. It would be remiss not to mention the advent of supersonic air travel, and indeed space travel, when discussing the air mode. However the reality is that the economics of the Concorde, and its Russian Tupolev equivalent, are such that aircraft manufacturers have no major plans for the development of commercial supersonic aircraft in the foreseeable future. In Europe, the Airbus consortium is however well advanced in its plans for an extra large ('super-jumbo') jet aircraft; in contrast Boeing is diametrically opposed to the concept and believes the development of such extra large aircraft is not feasible. Interestingly, researchers in the UK are exploring the feasibility of exploiting airship technology for carrying satellites. We will leave commercial space travel to future generations to write about!

2.2 THE TRANSPORT SYSTEM

The transport system comprises the following essential elements:

- Transport infrastructure (which in turn comprises the ways, terminals, units of carriage and units of propulsion).
- Management System (for example, in the case of air transport, an air traffic control system, and safety and commercial regulators, etc.).
- Transport modes and operators.

Advantages and Disadvantages of the Five Principal Modes

Each of the five transport modes has its own unique advantages and disadvantages. Water transportation allows the mass movement of goods and is comparatively cheap but, unfortunately, is relatively slow. Air transportation, on the other hand, is very fast, but expensive. Rail transportation is energy efficient and environmentally friendly, but requires significant initial investment in a line network. Road transport is flexible, fast and allows extensive geographic coverage. Pipeline transport allows mass movement of liquid and gas products and has particularly low operating and unit costs.

When deciding between transport modes two trade-offs are often apparent. There are trade-offs between consignment value and volume (high value consignments can afford more expensive transport solutions), and between cost and time (faster transport modes usually are more expensive). The existence of these trade-offs means that, before exploring both the various improvements in transport efficiency that have occurred and the evolution of logistics and the supply chain concept, it is necessary to consider the economics of transport and develop an understanding of the countervailing forces that determine the outcomes produced by these trade-offs.

Economic Concepts

The costs associated with providing a transport service can be broadly divided into *fixed costs* (associated with providing the transport infrastructure) and *variable costs* (associated with running the actual services). The fixed costs incurred can often be extensive – the Channel Tunnel linking Britain and Continental Europe and the new airport in Hong Kong both cost billions of dollars to construct. In contrast the total co-financed expenditure under the EU aided Operational Programme for Transport on transport infrastructure in the Republic of Ireland between 1994 and 1999 amounted to some IR£2.6 billion. It stands to reason, therefore, that the greater the volume of services that use a given transport infrastructure, the more beneficial it will be to provide and run this infrastructure. This is the concept of *economies of scale*. Dublin Airport, for example, can allocate its fixed costs to a very large volume of users, while some of Ireland's regional airports cannot as they may have as little as one commercial flight per day. The pursuit of economies of scale is usually an important goal of any transport manager.

A second concept worth mentioning is *marginal costs and revenues*. These are the costs and revenues associated with carrying extra freight or passengers. Unlike manufactured goods, which can often be stored for a period of time, transport services are usually highly *perishable*. They are scheduled to operate at a certain time and if seats or freight space are empty on departure, no revenue is earned. In many instances, the marginal or extra costs associated with carrying an extra passenger or unit of freight may be minimal. As a result, any marginal revenue will contribute significantly to the overall profitability of the service. Airlines, for example, may offer last minute discounts on any remaining available seats as a way of earning extra revenue. Finally, there is the concept of *price* or *demand elasticity* in transport. Elasticity refers to the responsiveness of a customer to a change in price. Some customers are highly 'inelastic' which means that significant variations in price may not bother them too much. Alternatively, others may be highly 'elastic', i.e. they are very sensitive to variations to price. This has important implications for pricing strategy in any transport service provider.

2.3 IMPROVEMENTS IN TRANSPORT EFFICIENCY

Recent decades have witnessed a remarkable increase in the globalisation of all forms of business. Many companies now have manufacturing plants outside of their 'home' country. Some of the world's leading companies, such as IBM, Dell, Gateway, Intel, Hewlett Packard, etc., have manufacturing plants in Ireland which import and export components and finished products all over the world. Undoubtedly, the liberalisation of world trade has fuelled this growth with firms increasingly operating in a highly competitive, globalised marketplace. Another key driver however has been the steadily falling cost of transporting goods around the world.

Three contributory factors have been particularly important to achieving this fall in the cost of transporting goods around the world.

1. Reduced transport intensity of freight

In times past, international trade was dominated by bulky raw materials. However, this has changed and finished products, not raw materials, dominate world trade. Some simple examples illustrate this clearly. Compare the value of the various computer products currently being shipped around the world daily with the bulky, low value, agricultural produce shipped around the world a hundred years ago. Agricultural produce, and indeed other comparatively high volume/ low value freight, does still of course traverse the world but, in general, the size and value of the freight which is transported today is very different to that of times past. Higher value freight is better able to 'absorb' transport costs than is low value freight. Hence, we refer to a generally reducing transport intensity of freight. Perhaps the shift is best explained by the shock of the amateur thief who tried to steal a container which stated 'windows' on the outside – instead of containing windows for buildings the container contained a much more valuable consignment, Microsoft windows software.

2. Deregulation of transport

In recent decades the different modes of transport in many countries have been 'deregulated' by governments to various degrees. Sean Barrett explores this trend as it applies to Ireland in Chapter 6, but suffice to say for now that effective deregulation involves removing unnecessary barriers to competition, thus making markets more contestable and enhancing customer satisfaction. The reader need only witness what has happened in the cross-channel air market between Britain and Ireland to see the positive effects of deregulation. As well then as goods becoming less transport intensive, as was shown above, many deregulated transport services have become cheaper and more efficient.

3. Productivity improvements

The concept of intermodal transport has already been discussed in the previous section. Central to this concept is the intermodal transport unit or container. Up to the mid-1950s, maritime freight was all carried on bulk vessels. This began to change, however, when some ship owners began to carry freight containers. Containers can be stacked on top of each other onboard the ship, thus allowing very efficient space utilisation and cargo handling. The advent of containerisation reduced maritime transport costs dramatically and significantly improved the efficiency of maritime transport. Containerisation spread to other modes and various alliances were formed between combinations of transport companies. There were, of course, many other improvements in transportation, for example, in propulsion technologies and the application of various ICTs.

The various productivity improvements in transport systems in recent decades are perhaps best evidenced by the operations of what are called the 'integrators'. These companies (examples include DHL, Federal Express, etc.) make considerable use of ICTs and intermodalism and provide guaranteed, door to door, express transport services (albeit at a premium price) to their customers with service levels which were unheard of in the past. Concomitant however with all of the aforementioned improvements in transport efficiency has been a changing mindset among firms with regard to the management of the entire distribution process. This change of mindset has come to be known as the logistics evolution and with it has come the emergence of the supply chain concept.

2.4 THE LOGISTICS EVOLUTION AND SUPPLY CHAIN MANAGEMENT

'Logistics' was originally a military term used to describe the organisation of moving, lodging and supplying troops and equipment (indeed the field of military logistics is a fascinating one with many military successes attributed to good logistics management). The US-based Council of Logistics Management has adopted the following definition of logistics:

> *Logistics is that part of the supply chain process that plans, implements, and controls the efficient, effective flow and storage of goods, services, and related information from the point of origin to the point of consumption in order to meet customers' requirements.*[2]

The Institute of Logistics and Transport in the UK defines logistics as *"the time-related positioning of resource"*,[2] where the resource can be transport, storage, manufacturing capacity, information, etc. Logistics then involves getting the right product, in the right quantity and quality, in the right place at the

---

2. Both of these definitions were taken from the websites listed in the references and further reading section.

right time, for the right customer at the right cost.

During the decades which followed World War 2, the responsibility for, and management of, inventory in firms was very fragmented. The various functions in which inventory played a key role, for example transportation, warehousing, purchasing and marketing were usually considered by managers to be separate and distinct. However, firms began to realise that cost savings and significant efficiency gains could be harnessed from more integrated and focused management of inventory. As far back as 1962, the famous management thinker Peter Drucker wrote a celebrated *Fortune* magazine article entitled "The Economy's Dark Continent". In this article, he suggested that distribution represented the last frontier for significant cost reduction potential in the firm.

Increased market competition and customer requirements also led to the necessity of seeing improvements in the management of inventory as an essential competitive weapon. In the increasingly competitive, global marketplace, firms began to realise that they could leverage marketplace advantage through superior logistics performance. Cost savings were identified through eliminating unnecessary inventory and 'just in time' (JIT) deliveries became normal operating practice in many industries. Outsourcing became more common, with suppliers playing a more central role for many manufacturers. In more recent years, in particular, competition based on *time*, for example order to delivery time, became a key success factor (KSF) in many markets. These factors then were the drivers behind the emergence of both the discipline of logistics and the concept of the integrated supply chain. The evolution of logistics is illustrated in Figure 1. The various functions that now comprise the discipline of logistics were regarded as separate and distinct, and managed accordingly, up to the 1960s and 1970s. This began to change radically, however, in the 1980s and beyond with firms realising the benefits of integration.

The term 'supply chain management' (SCM) was originally introduced by consultants in the early-1980s and, since then, has received considerable attention. The supply chain is a much wider, intercompany, boundary-spanning concept, than is the case with logistics (Figure 2). Logistics is a subset of SCM and the two terms are not synonymous.[3]

Martin Christopher, Professor of Marketing and Logistics at Cranfield School of Management, and one of Europe's leading thinkers in the area, suggests that the supply chain is the network of organisations that are involved, through upstream (supplier end of the supply chain) and downstream (customer end of the supply chain) linkages, in the different processes and activities that produce value in the form of products and services in the hands of the ultimate consumer (Christopher, 1998). He distinguishes supply chain management from vertical integration – the latter concept implies ownership of upstream suppliers and downstream customers. However, this is becoming

---

3. For a detailed discussion of the definitional distinctions between logistics and SCM see: Lambert *et al.* (1998).

less desirable as a strategy for success because more and more organisations are focusing on their core competencies and outsourcing all other activities. Indeed this growth in outsourcing reflects the more general evolution of relationships between buyers and suppliers from an adversarial model to a more partnership based model. Many of the examples cited in this book evidence such partnership relationships between the various actors in the supply chain.

2.5 CONCLUSION

In almost all markets today, it is difficult to make significant distinctions between many competing product offerings. According to Martin Christopher, marketplace competition is increasingly between supply chains, and not individual firms or their products. He describes a new marketplace of sophisticated and demanding customers, which is volatile and difficult to predict, and where, in order to survive, companies must be responsive. This, then, is the revolution which is supply chain management and which has had a major impact on the Irish economy through the strategic location here of the manufacturing plants of many multinationals as part of their global supply chain strategies. Logistics, and the broader concept of SCM, is then about much more than just transportation. It involves several other critical areas, such as the usage of ICT, the availability of third-party service providers and other supply chain partners, and favourable operating conditions to facilitate supply chain integration.

Today's logisticians (and that includes manufacturers, service providers, academics, consultants and writers on the topic) are a disparate lot with interesting backgrounds. Some have come from a purely transport background, some from materials management, and others have come from marketing. Yet, today, they all speak a common language of logistics and SCM. Indeed, this is well evidenced by the disparate backgrounds of the various contributors to this book. This author is reminded of once seeing a truck on Dublin's M50 orbital motorway with the word 'transport' on its logo blacked out and replaced by the word 'logistics'. Hopefully, this book will show that while transport plays an important role, logistics and SCM are much broader concepts and involve more than just the arbitrary use of terminology.

References and Further Reading

Benson, D, R Bugg & G Whitehead, *Transport and Logistics* (Hertfordshire: Woodhead-Faulkner) 1994.
Button, K, *Transport Economics* (Aldershot: Edward Elgar Publishing) 2nd edn, 1993.
Christopher, M, *Logistics and Supply Chain Management* (London: Financial Times/Pitman Publishing) 2nd edn, 1998.
Christopher, M, *Marketing Logistics* (Oxford: Butterworth-Heinemann) 1997.
Coyle, J, E Bardi & C Langley, *The Management of Business Logistics* (St Paul, Minnesota: West Publishing) 6th edn, 1996.

Crowley, J, "Virtual Logistics: Transport in the Marketspace" *The International Journal of Physical Distribution and Logistics Management* (1998) Vol. 28 (7), pp. 547-574.

Lambert, D, C Cooper & J Pagh, "Supply Chain Management: Implementation Issues and Research Opportunities" *The International Journal of Logistics Management* (1998) Vol. 9 (2), pp. 1-19.

Two particularly useful websites are:

http://www.clm1.org
(this is the Council of Logistics Management website in the United States; it contains a quite useful searchable logistics bibliography)

http://www.iolt.org.uk
(this is the website of the Institute of Logistics and Transport in the UK).

Chapter 3
The Challenge of Economic Growth

Kevin Hannigan
Irish Management Institute

3.1 BEYOND ECONOMIC GROWTH

The strong performance of the Irish economy in recent years has caught the attention of many international observers. This is remarkable given Ireland's experience of an unsustainable boom in the late-1970s and a very weak performance for much of the 1980s. Initially, the recovery in the 1990s was confined to the progressive foreign-owned sector and failed to impact on unemployment. However, it has now spread throughout the economy and employment has grown rapidly.

This performance raises two important questions. Firstly, how should this success be handled to ensure the maximum benefit for the citizens of Ireland? The attitudes and policies of the past, which were more suited to the management of economic failure than to economic success, will be insufficient. Secondly, in what way should our goals and the focus of our policies be redefined to secure sustained economic success now that many of our previous goals have been met? This recognises the fact that rapid growth means that Ireland's resources are being stretched and that supply constraints could make us lose competitiveness. This is seen very clearly in the area of transport where congestion has become a major problem. As with many areas of management, the challenge for logistics is to enable a better use of the available resources. Future growth will increasingly depend on better management of resources and an emphasis on value-adding activities.

This chapter provides the economic background by describing recent performance. It indicates the factors that have led to the remarkable turnaround in Ireland's experience and the issues that will determine future success. Increased capital resources, through investment in infrastructure for example, are required, but this is not the complete solution. Labour and skill shortages mean that a move to higher value-added activity is essential. One important implication is that the process of change in the economy, which has seen Ireland move from a largely agrarian economy to a producer of high technology products, is far from complete. The need for innovation in all areas of economic activity, including logistics, will be just as important for sustaining success as it has been in stimulating recent performance.

3.2 OVERVIEW OF PERFORMANCE

The sustained high rates of economic growth that Ireland has experienced in the 1990s are the most obvious manifestation of our economic success. In the

period 1993-98, Gross National Product (GNP) (a measure of the income available to Irish residents in a particular year) increased by close to 50 per cent in
real terms. The annual rate is expected to slow somewhat in the future as a
result of supply side constraints, particularly a much tighter labour market, but
the economy has the potential to continue to grow at close to 5 per cent per
annum. GNP is substantially lower than Gross Domestic Product (GDP) (a
measure of the output produced in a particular year) in Ireland due to the importance of profit repatriations by foreign firms and interest payments on the
national debt. However, with GDP per capita converging towards EU levels,
Irish living standards are rapidly moving closer to those among our EU partners.

Table 3.1 shows this trend in the Irish national accounts. Increased confidence in recent years has meant that investment and, latterly, consumption
expenditure have been very buoyant. However, the most dramatic growth has
occurred in the foreign traded sector of the economy. This has been sustained
over a considerable period, with the result that it is generally accepted that
Irish exports and the sectors that have contributed to export growth have been
responsible for stimulating the remarkable performance of recent years.

Table 3.1: Annual Real Growth of National Income (per cent)

	1994	1995	1996	1997	1998	1999(f)	2000(f)
GDP	5.8	9.5	7.7	10.7	8.9	7.8	5.8
GNP	6.3	8.0	7.2	9.0	8.1	6.6	5.5
Consumption	4.3	3.7	6.5	7.3	7.4	8.1	7.0
Investment	12.0	22.9	15.9	18.9	16.7	11.5	5.6
Exports	14.7	19.6	11.8	17.0	20.5	15.7	9.2
Imports	15.1	16.1	12.0	16.1	23.2	17.7	10.8

Sources: CSO *National Income and Expenditure* and ESRI *Quarterly Economic Commentary*

Very high unemployment had been the major problem in the Irish economy for
many years. However, although unemployment was slow to respond initially,
sustained economic growth has resulted in a greatly improved situation as shown
in Figure 3.1. Unemployment has fallen from 15.7 per cent of the labourforce
in 1993 to 6.3 per cent in 1999. Long-term unemployment remains high by
international comparison, although it has fallen and accounts for about 50 per
cent of the total. In fact, Irish labour market conditions have now changed to
such an extent that labour shortages are becoming a problem.

In previous years, ease of migration meant that changes in the rate of Irish
unemployment were closely related to changes in the UK. However, the recent
fall in unemployment in Ireland is as a result of very rapid job creation in the

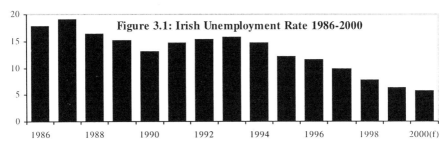

Source: CSO and ESRI (1999)

Irish economy. It is estimated that employment rose by 95,000 in 1998, equivalent to almost 7 per cent of the total. In fact, the buoyant labour market has been accompanied by a rapidly growing labour force as a result of inward migration and rising female participation. Developments in other EU countries suggest that further increases in participation in the Irish labour force are likely.

Employment growth has been widely spread in recent years with private services, which account for 40 per cent of all employment, creating 65 per cent of new jobs. Ireland is also unusual among developed countries in actually increasing the number of jobs in manufacturing in recent years. This has been led by the foreign-owned sector that accounts for close to 60 per cent of output and 45 per cent of employment in manufacturing. The result is that the effects of a rapid decline in agricultural employment have been mitigated by job creation in other parts of the economy.

A much-improved balance on the public accounts has accompanied Ireland's economic growth in recent years. This has facilitated reform of the tax system, overall tax reductions and reductions in the burden of debt. A considerable surplus has emerged on the government's current account, allowing much needed increases in capital expenditure while achieving an overall surplus. This is in some contrast to the situation in the early-1980s where a deficit as high as 15 per cent of GDP was created. This unsustainable situation led to a major build-up of debt, very high personal taxes and a prolonged period of painful adjustment. Public expenditure fell from over 60 per cent of GNP to a steady 45 per cent during this period of adjustment.

Improved management of the public finances in recent years, in addition to strong growth in employment and consumption that have caused rapid growth in tax revenues, mean that the surplus will amount to about 4 per cent of GDP in 1999. This is facilitating a reduction in the Irish Debt/GDP ratio to one of the lowest in Europe. Better management of public finances has also meant that Ireland successfully met the conditions for entry to EMU. These conditions, known as the Maastricht criteria, were formulated to ensure the countries joining EMU were pursuing appropriate economic policies. Ireland's success means that it is not faced with major problems of adjustment in this regard. The key factor in this process has been very buoyant tax revenue receipts. Total revenue is currently growing by about 17.5 per cent per annum. Rapid employment creation and the success of Ireland's approach of using tax policy to promote industrial development are key factors.

3.3 ECONOMIC POLICY

The origins of recent successes can be traced back to 1987 when an economic crisis, as a result of earlier mismanagement, led to a fundamental reassessment of economic policy and the needs of the economy. Six main elements can be identified in economic policy in recent years:

- avoidance of macroeconomic imbalance, allied to a commitment to EMU. The main elements of this were to avoid large government deficits, to keep inflation low and to maintain a stable exchange rate;

- an interventionist industrial policy, built around foreign investment, that aims to modernise the Irish industrial base and create employment. The Irish government has taken quite a big role in promoting Ireland as a location for foreign firms, particularly American firms that wish to have a presence within the EU. A range of initiatives, the most important of which relates to the tax rate on profits, has been used;

- rolling 3-year agreements between the social partners – the government, trade unions, employers organisations and representatives of farming and community interests – on wages, taxation and a wide range of matters related to economic policy;

- investment in the development of human capital at school and college levels through the education system and in later life through financial assistance to firms and individuals;

- the beneficial use of EU transfers obtained under a range of schemes. The most important, in addition to farming-related schemes, are the European Social Fund, which is generally used to aid training, and the European Regional Development Fund, which is used to improve infrastructure;

- a greater emphasis on the promotion of competition in the economy. This has included new legislation, new institutions and various reviews of regulation.

This policy mix is not easily characterised, but two issues stand out. Firstly, intervention, where it has occurred, has been essentially microeconomic, emphasising the need to enhance the international competitiveness of the economy. In other words, the emphasis has been on the need to ensure that markets work efficiently and, where problems arise, to undertake specific, limited interventions. Secondly, the approach has been consistently implemented, with the overall co-ordination of the various elements vital for success. This is not to suggest that the policy mix has been perfect and many areas of the economy retain features that limit competitiveness. However, Ireland has managed to get the overall stance right.

A distinctive and particular feature of the Irish economy that has helped to ensure that the overall policy mix has worked has been a series of successful National Partnership agreements negotiated every 3 years since 1987 between the social partners. Born in an era of economic crisis and a perception of widespread failure, these agreements have evolved from emergency 'recovery' programmes to wide-ranging economic policy agreements. Wage agreements have been the most important and highest profile elements, but the inclusion of a range of commitments – such as no-strike agreements, tax reduction commitments and workplace investments – has resulted in an agreed co-ordination of overall economic policy.

A number of trade-offs have been central to the success of the agreements. The most important of these in recent years has been the commitment of government to reduce income taxes along pre-agreed lines in return for moderate wage increases. The result has been increases in real incomes and job creation. The problem is that while this mechanism has not yet run its course, it is obviously impossible to continue to reduce taxes indefinitely. A more immediate problem is less easily quantifiable and centres on the importance of maintaining realistic expectations to produce beneficial agreements. This was not a problem in the early years of the agreements when stabilising real wages and controlling the rapid increases in unemployment and taxes were prime objectives. However, it means that success brings a new range of problems, the solutions to which may lie outside familiar institutions and policy initiatives.

3.4 Industry in Ireland

In 1960, 40 per cent of employment and 25 per cent of output in the Irish economy was in agriculture. Both figures have now fallen below 8 per cent. When placed in the context of rapid overall employment creation in recent years this change is indicative of the speed of Ireland's industrialisation. Exports have become increasingly dominated by the output of foreign firms. Markets have also shifted with the UK now accounting for only 22 per cent of exports, compared to 37 per cent in 1987, with 45 per cent now going elsewhere in the EU. However, the UK remains particularly important for indigenous firms.

The centrepiece of industrial policy has been the promotion of foreign direct investment (FDI). Over the past decade, the impact of this policy has been improved by a greater concentration on integrating foreign firms into the economy and promoting indigenous enterprise. The availability of markets among foreign firms, technology transfers and an emphasis on sectors that exploit indigenous strengths have meant considerable success in recent years.

Initially, foreign firms were attracted by a generous grant and taxation package. Taxation remains an important factor, but the availability of a skilled, competitively priced labour force has been the key factor for most firms in recent years. The US is by far the most important source of FDI, accounting for about 75 per cent of the total in recent years, making Ireland the fourth most important location for US FDI in the EU. Most has been concentrated in the electronics and pharmaceuticals sectors with services becoming increasingly important in recent years. These firms have had important knock-on effects on the Irish economy. For example, they all require new and high quality delivery mechanisms to get their outputs to the marketplace quickly. Some achieve this through in-house expertise, but the growth of Irish-based third-party logistics and transport providers in recent years is evidence of the widespread influence of the foreign sector on the economy.

FDI inflows to Ireland remain heavily sourced in the US and are concentrated in a small number of sectors. This concentration, and the high export content of the output of the multinational sector, has meant that the foreign sector has remained distinct from the indigenous sector for most of the period of industrialisation. However, this has been changing recently as firms become more embedded in the economy and as more successful high-tech indigenous firms have appeared. In addition, a downturn in the US economy, particularly one concentrated in the high-tech leading sectors, could have a serious impact on the Irish economy. Furthermore, the impact of EMU on flows of FDI remains to be seen. However, Ireland has created the industrial base required to exploit world markets, and the ability to do so will depend ultimately on the implementation of the appropriate policies to maintain competitiveness.

3.5 INTERNATIONAL TRADE

The opening up of the Irish economy over the past 35 years or so has had profound effects. It has resulted in enormous changes in the relative importance of various sectors of the economy and in the factors which determine economic performance. The economy is extremely open with international trade forming a large and increasing portion of economic activity. Furthermore, the sectors that have been driving economic growth are also those most engaged in international trade. The strong export performance means that Ireland can also afford to import a lot more. Irish consumers can access goods on world markets without causing any problems in regard to our ability to pay for these goods. This has vital implications for the external stability of the economy and Ireland's ability to pursue economic goals, such as participation in EMU.

The data show that the rapid growth in exports over the past decade preceded economic growth in other parts of the economy, such as the output of non-traded industry, domestic services and employment. Exports amounted to about 92 per cent and imports to 78 per cent of GDP in 1998 making the Irish economy very open. In other words, the markets of importance for both producers and consumers in Ireland are largely outside the Irish economy. With a ratio of international trade to output of 1.7:1, Irish economic performance is influenced significantly by international developments, particularly trends in our trading partners. The magnitude of the growth in international trade that has taken place is indicated by Figure 3.2.

Figure 3.2: Irish trade at constant 1990 prices

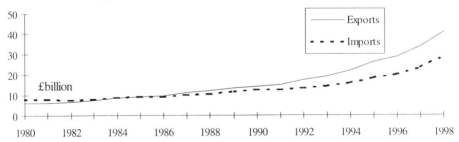

Source: Calculated from CSO *Trade Statistics*

Exports in 1998 were almost seven times the value of exports in 1980, when
allowance for inflation is made. Over this same period, imports grew to about
three times their 1980 value. This has meant that the value of exports has
exceeded imports since the mid-1980s, a reversal of the trend that had been
evident for most of the previous 40 years. The immediate result of this is a
major surplus on the balance of trade, which is estimated to have exceeded 13
per cent of GNP in 1998. This surplus has been sufficient throughout the 1990s
to ensure a surplus exists on the current account of the balance of payments,
that is, on the external account of the economy after interest payments on the
national debt and profit repatriations by multinationals are deducted.

The surplus on the balance of trade has been the result of the strong performance of the manufacturing sector and Ireland continues to import a greater
value of services than it exports. A major exception to this is tourism, which
has been important in reducing the services sector deficit in recent years. Although exports continue to exceed imports by a considerable margin, it is possible that this gap could narrow in the future as domestic demand continues to
grow strongly. Imports are also growing strongly since most are used in the
further production of goods, many of which are then exported. In fact, the
proportion of imports accounted for by goods for direct consumption has declined since 1993 from 23.6 per cent to 21.3 per cent of imports in 1996.

A number of changes have taken place in both the sectoral origin and
market distribution of exports over this high growth period. Most noticeably,
manufactured exports have increased in importance as a proportion of total
exports. Excluding non-classified exports, manufacturing industry accounted
for 81.5 per cent of exports in 1985. This had grown to 85.4 per cent in 1993
and exceeded 90 per cent for the first time in 1996.

The changes that have occurred in the sectoral origin of exports since
1985 are shown in Figure 3.3. The general trend could be summarised as a
move away from basic and crude products, in particular the products of the
primary sector, towards more high-tech, processed and high value-added products. In 1985, the food, drink and tobacco sector accounted for 25 per cent of
our exports, by 1998, this had declined to just over 10 per cent. On the other

hand, the chemical sector, including pharmaceuticals, had increased from 14.4 per cent to 31.7 per cent. The other main growth sector, the machinery sector, includes the computer and precision engineering industries and had grown from just under 30 per cent to almost 37 per cent of exports. This increased concentration of exports in a few industries reflects the impact that the growth of the multinationals has had on the Irish economy. These changes also explain the reduced transport intensity of Irish output and exports referred to in Chapter 2.

Figure 3.3: Sectoral origin of exports (percentage, 1985 and 1998

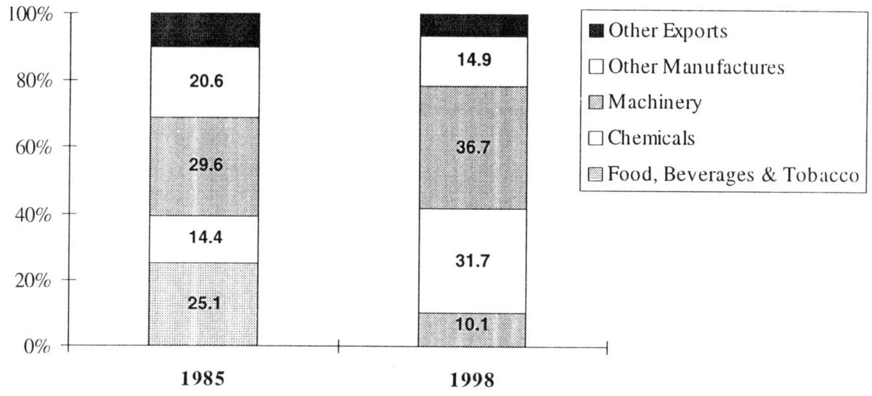

Source: CSO *Statistical Bulletin*

The other major change is in the geographical distribution of exports. This has seen a long-term decline in the importance of Britain and Northern Ireland as a market and an increase in importance of the EU other than Britain. This is likely to continue as the UK remains outside EMU for the first few years of its operation. As the integration of Europe proceeds, business cycles in the various economies will begin to move more in line with each other and, as a result, the EU region will behave more like a large national economy. This could leave Irish exports susceptible to a European economic downturn as could the increased concentration on a relatively small number of industries.

Taken together, these changes mean that four reinforcing factors have impacted on the role and scope of logistics in Irish industry:

1. Rapid growth means that inputs are being heavily utilised. As a result, resources and facilities such as transport infrastructure must be used as efficiently as possible.

2. The new industries and new products that are driving the Irish economy have greatly increased the need for highly efficient upstream and downstream supply structures.

3. New methods of delivery have appeared and must be utilised and developed to ensure that Irish products are competitive.

4. The move away from reliance on the UK market means that Ireland's relative peripherality in relation to major European markets must be overcome.

There is no reason to believe that the changes induced by these factors will be any less dramatic in future years than has been the case in Ireland in the recent past. In fact, all the indications are that the speed of change and the intensity of competition will increase. For example, the gradual integration of the countries of Central and Eastern Europe, many of which are much closer to the main markets of the EU and will retain cost advantages over Ireland for many years, will lead to a need for even greater efficiencies and changes in the way transport operates.

3.6 EXPLAINING THE BOOM

A wide range of factors has contributed to Irish economic success. Some of these are under our control, but many can be influenced only partially or indirectly. However, the impact which external changes will have on our economy is often open to our influence to a considerable degree. A key insight is that, in a world of integrated economies, international policy formulation and globalisation, the – mostly supply-side – policies that continue to reside at the national level have increased in importance. At the same time, many previously familiar areas of macroeconomic policymaking, which concentrate mostly on the management of demand, have become less useful.

The important external factors over which we have limited control include:

- the buoyancy of international economies;
- developments in Europe, including the continued development of the single European market and EU funding mechanisms over which we will only have a limited amount of influence;
- exchange rates and interest rates within EMU;
- technological developments and the way in which these influence our strategic position;
- factors which affect flows of foreign direct investment.

It is notable that this is a quite short list, and, in fact, we have some influence over some of these factors. There are, however, other factors which could be considered internal, but over which we have very little influence. These include:

- our English speaking skills and cultural qualities;
- the structural reform which has occurred in the Irish economy. This has been costly in the past and was a major cause of long-term unemployment as

traditional jobs disappeared. However, the benefits from the changes the economy has undergone are becoming clear;

• improved confidence in Ireland and the emergence of new social and cultural models.

Many of these factors are path dependent so, while we cannot influence the conditions which have developed, we can indirectly influence future developments and the impact which they have on our economic performance.

It is useful to separate the factors that we can influence into those that fall into the public domain and those that are subject to the actions of business. Naturally, there is considerable interaction between these two sectors of the economy with the actions of one affecting the decisions of the other. Among the most important factors that are the result of public sector decisions are:

• the fiscal balance and the rate of inflation;
• the structure of taxation and expenditure;
• the trade stance taken and the ability to avail of the single European market;
• the environment for foreign investment and industrial policy in general;
• investment in infrastructure;
• the educational and skills qualifications of the workforce;
• incomes policy and social partnership;
• developments in the commercialisation of public enterprise, the introduction of competition policy and new forms of regulation;
• institutional stability;
• measures to improve R&D and innovation.

While these factors are important, it must be recognised that it is the creation of an environment within which business can operate that is the greatest benefit that public policy can confer. Thus, the development of factors at the level of individual businesses has had an important role to play in improving economic performance. These have included:

• improvements in skills;
• improvements in the Irish business system and linkages between firms;
• improvements in efficiency leading to cost and quality advantages;
• engagement in social partnership;
• improved managerial abilities;
• new forms of work organisation;
• recognition of the need for a customer focus;
• improved R&D and innovation.

It is clear that the list of explanations for the boom in the Irish economy is long and that no single area of policy nor no single group can claim the credit. In fact, it is likely that it was a benign coincidence of a number of factors that produced the remarkable turnaround. This means that while some enlightened decisions were important, luck played a major role in the outcome.

3.7 CAPITAL INVESTMENT

An almost constant theme running through current commentaries on the Irish economy is that the rapid growth of recent years means that existing capacity is being stretched and that over-heating is a real danger. The prescription offered is usually along the lines that more investment in infrastructure is required. There is little doubt but that this is true, but it is not the whole solution. The fact is that labour is also becoming a constraint on growth. Thus, it is important that the available labour is used more productively. This means not just that more capital investment is required, but existing assets must be used more efficiently and investment must take place in capital and infrastructure that improves the productivity and value added output of the available workforce.

The impact of capital investment on the economy is poorly understood. It was generally believed that investment, whether by the public sector, by private business or by a combination of the two, would induce a higher level of economic growth. However, a look at the Irish economy shows that the relationship is not so simple. The rate of investment in Ireland peaked in the early-1980s and declined almost every year thereafter until the early-1990s. Despite this, Ireland then embarked on a sustained period of unprecedented economic growth. The ESRI (1997) went as far as to suggest that we were witnessing a period of *"investmentless growth"*. Investment has been growing rapidly in recent years, but this followed rather than led the upturn in overall performance. This implies that the level of growth may determine the level of investment rather than the reverse. In fact, this is in keeping with the conclusion reached in recent international studies such as Blomstrom *et al.* (1996). Alternatively, it may be the case, such has been the extent of the change in the sources of growth, that previous relationships between fixed assets and wealth creation are no longer meaningful.

Despite this uncertainty, it would be a mistake to conclude that there is not a problem in the existing level of the Irish capital stock. Foreign direct investment (FDI) has been one of the key factors behind Irish economic growth. FDI did not just increase the supply of capital. It brought new technology and new forms of working that have allowed Ireland to grow into new industries. The lesson from the Irish experience is not that capital investment does not have a role in promoting growth. Instead it is that appropriate investment can facilitate changes in the economy that allows it to operate much more efficiently and competitively with its available resources. A similar lesson can be applied to our infrastructural needs. Capital investment is required, but it will only be successful if it promotes new high value outputs and ways of undertaking business. This inevitably means that investment in human capital and areas such as logistics must go hand in hand with more infrastructural development. Growth that relies simply on utilising more resources is not sustainable and is seldom compatible, in a modern economy, with a rising standard of living. However, growth that comes from improved value-added as a result of using resources better indicates improved competitiveness. Logistics provides an important means through which this can be achieved.

3.8 NEW CHALLENGES

The 1990s have been a period of unparalleled progress in the Irish economy. The World Economic Forum (WEF), an international body that ranks countries according to a wide range of factors that determine international competitiveness, places Ireland tenth out of 59 developed economies. Only a few years ago, it was placed in the mid-20s. Clearly there has been considerable progress. However, the WEF point out that this progress does not indicate that all problems are solved. In fact, closer examination indicates that when macroeconomic factors (i.e. those indicators relating to the overall performance of the economy, such as inflation, unemployment and the government balance) are removed, Ireland's performance looks a lot less impressive. On transport related issues, such as railway infrastructure, Ireland is close to the bottom of the ranking. Averaged across all microeconomic measures (i.e. variables relating to the performance of markets within the economy) Ireland is ranked seventeenth. This divergence indicates that concentrated areas of problems still exist. This is particularly important since macroeconomic performance indicators, such as GDP growth, are indicative of past performance whereas microeconomic measures are a better indicator of the competitiveness of inputs. It is clear from the work of the WEF that there is considerable room for improvement on these factors and on transport related factors in particular.

Ireland has outperformed its trading partners, but the performances of other economies have important implications for Irish economic performance. These arise primarily through influencing the level of demand for the output of firms operating in Ireland and through the effect which economic growth will have on the profitability of foreign firms considering an investment in Ireland. The performance of the American economy is particularly vital in this latter respect. While Ireland has been a net capital exporter during the 1990s, FDI inflows have brought much more than capital and have revolutionised the Irish industrial base creating new sectors and introducing new technologies and management techniques. These have had profound effects on the structure and performance of the Irish economy.

The challenges that currently face Ireland are partly the product of success and emphasise the need to move on to the next stage of development if success is to be consolidated. They include:

• the much tighter labour market and the non-existence of an under-utilised pool of skilled labour;

- the need to develop higher value-added activities to ensure a more efficient use of ever scarcer resources, in particular, labour and transport infrastructure;
- rapid monetary growth which has funded rising property prices and a housing shortage;
- continuing financial outflows whilst Ireland's infrastructure remains underdeveloped and is becoming a constraint on growth;
- the need for a step change in telecommunications infrastructure;
- the difficulties of maintaining consensus economic policymaking in an era of rising expectations;
- the need to open up lagging regions through investment in transport infrastructure to relieve constraints by bringing under-utilised resources into play;
- a lack of overall experience in managing success.

The general problem is one of emerging imbalances: between output growth and input constraints; between expectations and the ability of the economy to meet those expectations while remaining competitive; between the needs of leading and lagging regions; between the demands of a successful dynamic economy and structures created in a period of limited success.

Ireland continues to lag Europe in its infrastructure and bottlenecks have emerged. However, for most of the past decade, capital has, effectively, been available in unlimited quantities. This is certainly the case today, and is likely to remain so into the foreseeable future. The problem in the past was to devise the means to combine this capital with a plentiful supply of labour. The success of recent years was that it became economical to do so in Ireland. The problem now is that the supply of labour is no longer plentiful. The challenge for the future is to discover how growth can continue to be achieved given this constraint. This is a major challenge for the whole economy and for specialist functional areas. It means that, to a large extent, the solutions of the past will not be enough. The answers lie in increasing the value-added and intellectual content of output. Logistics has a major role to play to ensure that delivery and supply mechanisms contribute to overall quality and competitiveness and to ensure that growth can continue given existing constraints on infrastructure.

New problems are also facing logistics practitioners. Recent growth has meant that the volume of goods has increased substantially. The associated requirements have been met successfully. Increasingly, however, it is not the volume, but the, ever greater, need for higher quality service that means new ideas and new solutions are required. This need cannot be met simply by infrastructural improvements, although these are important. The solution to this challenge lies in the enhanced skills and resources of the logistics specialist.

References and Further Reading

Barry, F (ed.), *Understanding Ireland's Economic Growth* (Basingstoke and London: Macmillan Press) 1999.

Blomstrom, M, R Lipsey & M Zejan, "Is Fixed Investment the Key to Economic Growth?" *Quarterly Economic Journal* (1996) Vol. 111 (1), pp. 267-276.

CSO *National Income and Expenditure 1998* (Dublin: Central Statistics Office).

CSO *Statistical Bulletin* (Dublin: Central Statistics Office).

CSO *Trade Statistics* (Dublin: Central Statistics Office).

Department of Finance, *Budget 1999* (Dublin: Government Publications) 1999.

ESRI, *Quarterly Economic Commentary* (Dublin: Economic and Social Research Institute) September 1999.

ESRI, *Medium Term Review 1999-2005* edited by D Duffy, J Fitzgerald, I Kearney and D Smyth (Dublin: Economic and Social Research Institute) 1999.

ESRI, *Medium Term Review 1997-2003* edited by D Duffy, J Fitzgerald, I Kearney & F Shortall (Dublin: Economic and Social Research Institute) 1997.

Fitzgerald, J, I Kearney, E Morgenroth & D Smyth, *National Investment Priorities for the Period 2000-2006* Policy Research Series, No. 33 (Dublin: ESRI) 1999.

Government of Ireland, *National Development Plan 2000-2006* (Dublin: Stationery Office) 1999.

Gray, A, *International Perspectives on the Irish Economy* (Dublin: Indecon) 1997.

Sweeney, P, *The Celtic Tiger* (Dublin: Oak Tree Press) 1998.

Chapter 4
The Economics of Transport

Harry McGeehan
Iarnród Éireann

4.1 THE SCOPE OF TRANSPORT ECONOMICS

Transport economics utilises the general principles of the theory of the firm and the consumer and applies them to the specific issues of personal mobility and the shipment of goods and services. As with any other branch of applied economics, the transport sector has its own special characteristics that make its analysis important.

All countries are dependent on trade and travel for their prosperity, but the problems of transport can create friction within the economic system and have adverse effects on efficiency and competitiveness. Congestion, urban sprawl, pollution, land-take, etc. are all subjects that have to be addressed within the transport economics discipline when the pursuit of sustainable economic development is weighed against wider societal impacts.

Transport is the lubricating mechanism in the logistics chain, from the movement of raw materials to production facilities, to distribution centres and onward to the customer. As such the provision and costs of transport are important for a small country, such as Ireland, particularly because of our peripheral location and the negative impact of distance on supplying geographically dispersed markets.

Transport is a derived demand that has no intrinsic value in itself, but facilitates other activities, such as work and leisure. A complicating factor in analysing transport demand is that each journey is unique, both spatially and temporally, and as such it cannot be stored or transferred. This means, for example, that capacity and resources have to be provided to service high demand peak periods which are then under-utilised in the off-peak. For example the size of the Dublin Bus fleet is dictated by the number of buses required to service the morning and evening peaks during the working week. The temporal element of transport is significant for many aspects of transport economics. When choosing which mode to use, individuals not only weigh up the money cost of the journey, but also the journey time. The implications for pricing policy between modes are obvious once the element of time is entered into the decision-making equation. Modes with a time advantage can charge higher fares than slower substitute modes.

Of more significance, however, are the time constraints imposed due to congestion and bottlenecks in transport systems. These can be alleviated by increasing the supply of infrastructure, but as will be seen, economists would favour a market-based solution based on rationing demand via the price mechanism. However, market-based solutions are not always appropriate in the transport sector. For example, where economies of scale exist, service provision by one operator leads to lower unit costs than if several operators produced the output. This has generally been the case for monopoly provision of railway infrastructure, and has led to its regulation by government.

State involvement has been prevalent in transport for most of this century, although the orthodoxy of government involvement in the market has been challenged in recent years. Increasingly, transport economics has been used to analyse the potential effects of introducing competition and replacing monopoly provision of public transport in particular. Although a potent tool for analytical purposes, transport economics must be applied within the framework of national and international policy. Latterly, the policy context in Ireland has been widened with the involvement of various European Commissions.

In the context of the above, the scope of transport economics is quite wide-ranging. In order to illustrate the characteristics of the subject, however, only the more important aspects are highlighted in the following discussion.

4.2 DEMAND FOR TRANSPORT

The demand for transport dictates to a large extent the level of investment required to satisfy travel needs. Obviously, both the analysis of demand and forecasts of future trends are required not only for transport planning, but also for housing and retail developments as well as the provision of public amenities. In recent years, industrial, commercial, and housing developments have given rise to urban sprawl, so that journeys to work/school and shopping/leisure trips have become longer. As cities spread, the need for transport access intensifies and improved links from outer suburban areas to central business districts are demanded. When analysing demand, economists are generally interested in isolating the major explanatory variables which dictate modal choice. From microeconomic theory, transport consumers are assumed to be influenced in their choices by the price of a mode, the prices of alternative or substitute modes, and their incomes.

For the transport economist, the price of a mode is called its generalised cost or user cost. When choosing which mode of transport to use individuals weigh up not only the money cost of the journey, but also the journey time (which includes in-vehicle time, and walking and waiting time). Hence, in urban areas in particular, a train journey may be quicker than a bus journey, but the latter may have a cheaper fares regime in place. The potential transport user has to trade-off the lower bus fares with the probability of a longer journey time. For the operator of transport services, an analysis of demand can give insights into the responsiveness of users to changes in operational characteristics. Responsiveness to changes in service variables can be measured by the derivation of elasticities, with the most important relating to price. The price elasticity of demand measures the change in ridership of a mode given a change in fares.

To estimate price elasticities, economists normally use the econometric technique of regression analysis which relates the demand for a mode to several explanatory variables, and 'sifts out' the relative importance of these variables. The method is based on analysis of observations of consumer behaviour over a period of time, so that consistent patterns can be detected. In the short run the demand model can be used to predict future trends given that the historical pattern of behaviour will be replicated in the future. For public transport in Ireland, several time series econometric models have been produced which have isolated the impact of price on bus and rail travel. For example, the price elasticity of demand for bus travel in Dublin has been estimated to be − 0.3, which suggests that if fares (in real terms) are increased by 1 per cent then passenger journeys will decrease by 0.3 per cent (McGeehan, 1998a). When the price elasticity of demand is determined, it can be utilised to measure the change in the operators revenue. Generally if the price elasticity of demand has an absolute value less than 1, then any increase in fare will increase revenue. For the Dublin Bus example, after the 1 per cent fare increase, even though passenger journeys fall, revenue will increase by approximately 0.7 per cent.

In passing it should be pointed out that price elasticities are contingent upon our generalised cost concept. The low estimate for the urban bus price elasticity is probably a product of the geographical spread of bus services. Rail services in urban areas are more geographically fixed, and so competition between the two modes may be limited to a small number of corridors. Within these corridors the price elasticity for the bus mode may be higher given that the 'expenditure of time' may be greater than by the rail mode. In the DART corridor, for example, the price elasticity for rail has been shown to be –0.4, and this low resistance to fare changes reflects the journey time premium which attaches to travelling by rail (McGeehan, 1992).

Attempts to measure the demand for car travel have usually been based on the assumption that there will be continuous growth in ownership per head until, in the long run, an upper limit is reached and there is saturation in demand. In the short run, the core of the demand modelling process is concerned with predicting the age and size distribution of the car fleet. Some simple assumptions are then used to further subdivide the fleet by fuel type and finally to determine the vehicle kilometres travelled by vehicles of each age, size and fuel type (Feeney, 1994).

Demand models for the air and shipping modes are less sophisticated, and are more or less related to the growth in international traffic. For example, in 1999, the percentage of international passengers at the three main airports (Dublin, Cork, and Shannon) totalled 93 per cent of traffic throughput. Therefore, in order to make projections cognisance is taken of developments in the relevant foreign economies (e.g. the U.S.A. for transatlantic flights) and tourism policy, together with future changes in operational characteristics such as aircraft size (Oscar Faber *et al.*, 1999). For shipping, the growth in cargo demand is highly correlated with growth in gross national product. Passenger traffic demand is less clear given the recent withdrawal of duty free concessions, as this could lead to a reduction in revenues to ship operators which may have to be recouped through higher fares.

4.3 SUPPLY OF INFRASTRUCTURE

Rising standards of living necessarily lead to higher demands for freight and passenger travel and hence to an increased supply of infrastructure. Transportation, particularly in economically advanced countries, has given rise to the commercialisation of agriculture, the specialisation of industry and ready access to raw materials. In developed countries, transport demand and usage are highly correlated with economic growth and incomes. As a consequence, investment in transport at the national and international level is crucial to continued economic development. In recent years, the emergence of the 'Celtic Tiger' has led to growth in Ireland's gross national product which has averaged about three times that of other European Union countries. Ireland is one of the most open economies in Europe with exports and imports representing 176 per cent of gross national product. It relies heavily on foreign trade for sustainable economic growth and employment creation and, because of its island status, is heavily dependent on shipping for trade and tourism. In fact, 80 per cent of trade by volume, and 40 per cent of visitors to Ireland, travel by sea.

In recent years, there have been dramatic changes in the European political map, as the drive towards economic, monetary and political union within the European Community has been intensified. Central to this closer union has been the advent of the single European market, and the freedom of movement of people, goods, services and capital. The European market now represents the largest economic entity in the world, with a population of over 350 million people, with no internal barriers to trade and with a combined purchasing power of over £3,000 billion. For the transport sector, the single market has acted as a catalyst for a number of major infrastructural proposals designed to facilitate and exploit the market expansion and economic growth contingent upon the removal of trading barriers. The Channel Tunnel and the Paris-London/Brussels-Low Countries/German elements of the European High Speed Rail System are notable examples of this.

Transportation developments in Ireland in recent years have benefited greatly from EU financing through various funds, including the Cohesion Fund and the European Development Fund (ERDF). ERDF finance has been allocated through the Operational Programmes on Peripherality (OPP) and Transport (OPT).

Given that transport infrastructure is expensive to construct and has a long life span, the need for State involvement in the provision of infrastructure has not diminished even though the idea of private/public partnerships (PPPs) is gathering momentum. The ESRI has recently assumed that there will be a substantial increase in the volume of publicly funded infrastructural investment over the next few years to meet the needs of a rapidly growing economy, because the rate of growth is putting severe pressure on the country's physical infrastructure, such as roads and urban transport systems (ESRI, 1997). The need for ongoing investment in transport infrastructure has also been emphasised by Forfás in its review of transport and logistics in Ireland (Forfás, 1996). One of its primary conclusions was that a minimum fifteen-year period should be used in planning transport infrastructure so that investment is maintained in the long-term at the levels necessary for Ireland to achieve best international practice in logistics management.

4.4 INVESTMENT

The essence of investment analysis in the private sector is the comparison of a future stream of revenues from a project with the future pattern of costs so that a decision can be made on which of several projects gives the highest financial return. On the other hand, the rationale of public sector investment is the improvement in the welfare of society as a whole. To that extent, cost benefit analysis is employed to secure the optimum allocation of capital, so as to maximise the social welfare function of the whole community.

From the transport viewpoint in Ireland, cost benefit analysis has been particularly utilised in all government-sponsored road projects. The basic approach to cost benefit analysis is the calculation of those 'user benefits' which accrue when an investment is undertaken. User benefits are calculated by the measurement of changes in consumer surplus. In simple terms, consumer surplus is defined as the difference between the maximum amount a consumer is willing to pay for a given amount of travel and the amount he/she actually pays. Any journey incurs for the traveller the cost of the 'fare', the time spent travelling, and the disutility of having to travel. As noted earlier, together these form the generalised or user cost of making a particular journey. A transport investment which reduces the user cost of travel will lead to an increase in consumer surplus. In transport economics the main benefits of an investment relate primarily to time savings, reductions in modal operating costs, reductions in accidents, and environmental improvements.

Time savings in transport investments bulk large in any appraisal, and accrue to users of the facility in which the investment is made, and to those who transfer from other modes. An example would be a bypass which reduces traffic in a town or village (e.g. the Naas bypass) or a railway improvement which reduces travel times for present rail users and those who switch to rail (e.g. the DART rail system). Time savings generally represent about 60 per cent to 80 per cent of the benefits of road and rail projects, but the problem with estimating time benefits is that they are not valued in the marketplace. As a consequence, a 'shadow price' has to be utilised to put a price on people's time. It is customary to distinguish between two types of time savings – savings in working time and savings in non-working time – and to value the two types differently. Loss of time during working or business hours is important because it may lead to a reduction in the amount of goods produced. Economic theory suggests that the level of the wage rate is a reasonable indicator of the productivity of labour and that one hour's loss of working time will result in a loss of production valued at the average earnings per hour of the person who incurs the time loss. Non-working time is valued as a proportion of the value derived for working time. Whilst time savings are significant in transport appraisals, in recent years more attention has been given to other external costs generated by transport.

4.5 EXTERNALITIES AND TRANSPORT

A necessary prerequisite for the efficient working of the free market is that all costs and benefits arising from the production and consumption of a good or service should be accounted for by the decision-maker. However, there are costs associated with transport that are not borne by those generating them, i.e. so-called externalities. Formally, externalities exist when the activities of one group affect the welfare of another group, without any payment or compensation being made.

In a recent study of the environmental impact of traffic on society, the costs associated with accidents, noise, air pollution and climatic change were examined (IWW/INFRAS, 1995). The estimates are shown in Table 4.1 below for Ireland in the reference year of 1991.

Table 4.1: External costs of transport 1991 (by type of effect and mode)

	Road	Rail	Aviation	Shipping
Type of Effect	IR£ million	IR£ million	IR£ million	IR£ million
Accidents	668	4.6	—	—
Noise	199	13.1	14.6	—
Air Pollution	179	4.6	13.1	0
Climate	163	4.6	40.8	0
Total	**1209**	**26.9**	**68.5**	**0**

Source: *IWW/INFRAS: 'External Effects of Transport', UIC, 1995.*

From Table 4.1 it can be seen that inland transport creates the largest external costs, with road accidents costing the economy an estimated £668 million in 1991. With the rapid growth in traffic since 1991, these costs have undoubtedly risen. Certainly, at the EU level, accidents are estimated to cost the Union 1.5 per cent of gross domestic product per annum and air pollution and noise at least another 0.6 per cent. Congestion costs are also of significance and cost 2 per cent of GDP, so that the sum of external costs is equivalent to some 250 BECU per year (European Commission, 1995).

From an economic point of view, the primary problem with these costs is that they are not borne directly by those who cause them. The available evidence suggests that existing charges and taxation are inadequate and fall short of covering these externalities. As a possible solution the EU Commission has recently examined the possibility of introducing the 'polluter pays' principle to transport activities. In the past, transport policies have largely focused on direct regulation (e.g. setting minimum emission standards, speed limits, etc.), and although useful, do not impact on specific groups but are applied in a general fashion.

4.6 COSTING AND TRANSPORT

A fundamental problem in transport operations is the identification of costs with individual traffics. If the cost of carrying individual passengers or individual freight consignments is indeterminate then the price charged will tend to be arbitrary. At a higher level, a loss-making rail service (or bus route) may be justified depending on the definition of costs. There are four main costing concepts that can be identified in transport operations (Ogden, 1985). These are:

- **Avoidable costs.** These costs are uniquely associated with a particular output. If that output was not produced (or withdrawn) the costs would not be incurred (or saved).

- **Joint costs.** These costs exist when the provision of a specific service necessarily entails the output of some other service. For example, return trips, where the supply of transport services in one direction automatically implies the provision of a return service, is a classic example of jointness. Joint costs do not vary with the quantity or proportions of the relevant outputs. Thus the costs of signal maintenance along a section of rail do not vary if the proportions of traffic in different groups vary. Hence joint costs are not avoidable between outputs, but can only be avoided jointly, i.e. if all outputs are withdrawn altogether.

- **Common costs.** These are similar to joint costs, in that they are incurred as a result of providing services to a range of users, but differ in that the use of resources to provide one service does not unavoidably result in the production of a different one (e.g. train crew costs are common to freight and passenger services). Because these costs are allocatable they can be included in the avoidable costs for the relevant output.

- **Allocated costs.** These are costs that are attributed to various outputs, with the joint costs being apportioned across output in an arbitrary fashion.

In general, it is impossible to identify the costs of one type of traffic separately from the costs of other traffic, particularly in the provision of a multiplicity of services, where joint costs are prevalent. It is only by averaging joint costs among passengers that a public transport undertaking can operate effectively. The importance of defining costs is particularly relevant in the case of service closures or withdrawals. If, for example, a passenger service is to be withdrawn from a railway and at the same time freight services continue on the route, then most track, signalling and infrastructure costs will not be avoided because they will still have to be incurred for the remaining services. At the same time, if avoidable costs are below the revenue generated by the passenger service then retention of the service could be justified on the grounds that it is making a contribution to the fixed costs of the rail route.

In essence therefore, it is important to distinguish the cost concepts carefully in order for correct policy judgements to be made. In 1980, the McKinsey Report posited the idea that closure of the entire rail system in Ireland should be considered. However, at no stage in their deliberations did McKinsey analyse the avoidable costs of withdrawal, and based their calculations on allocated costs only (McKinsey International, 1980).

For the road sector, costs tend to be delineated into four main categories, namely capital costs, maintenance costs, lighting and policing. Capital costs relate to investment in new roads, bridges, etc., and are not avoidable once the structure is built. However when planning new road infrastructure cognisance has to be taken of larger vehicles, specifically heavy goods vehicles (HGVs), which require higher standards of building than smaller vehicles. Maintenance costs relate to the costs of maintaining the road network and are dependent upon vehicle mileage, the weight of vehicles, and the axle weight. The latter is important for HGVs as road damage effects are related to the weight carried on each axle rather than by overall weight. Lighting and police costs are difficult to allocate on a cost responsibility basis, and there is a degree of arbitrariness in their apportionment.

What is significant in the road sector is that there is no direct link between pricing and costs. Road users pay taxes that could be considered as part of the general revenue fund of government. Certainly governments have been reluctant to adopt the process of hypothecation – where tax revenues from a specific group (road users) are earmarked to benefit that group (road investment). In the absence of hypothecation, the rates of tax paid by road users are not set with any pricing principle in mind, nor is there a relationship between the income derived from road users and expenditure on roads. Road taxes can be classified into three main categories – fuel taxes, vehicle taxes and VAT. If a system of road pricing were introduced only fuel taxes and vehicle taxes would be relevant, given that they are related to road usage.

4.7 COMPETITION AND TRANSPORT

In any discussion of competition in the transport market, it is necessary to distinguish between the different, although related, concepts of privatisation, deregulation and liberalisation. Privatisation is essentially concerned with the ownership of enterprises, namely changing ownership from the state to private firms. Deregulation generally means the relaxation of state controls on the provision of services or of entry into certain markets. Liberalisation usually means the opening up of a market to more competition.

Until recently, rail and bus operations in European countries were provided by publicly owned monopolies. There were two main reasons for government intervention. Firstly, public transport operations were seen to be natural monopolies, in the sense that the introduction of competition among many firms would be unstable and would quickly give way to oligopoly or monopoly. Secondly, the road transport sector creates significant externalities in terms of congestion and environmental impact, which can be relieved by a 'second best' solution of subsidising public transport operations.

In a market economy it is generally assumed that if a good or service is valued sufficiently highly to be worth producing then consumers should be charged the full cost of its production. Consequently, if the maximum revenue that can be obtained from its consumers does not cover production cost, the good should not be produced at all. However the assumptions upon which the free market paradigm is based are sometimes invalidated by so-called 'market failure'. One major source of market failure occurs when a particular industry experiences economies of scale. Scale economies exist where one firm has the lowest feasible average costs and operates in an interval of production where average costs are decreasing. As output increases unit costs decrease. Any revenue support that has the effect of increasing the demand for the product will also have the effect of reducing its unit costs of production. Traditionally, rail transport, because of its high proportion of fixed system costs, has been regarded as a decreasing cost industry. Even in the longer run, when capacity and signalling can be adjusted, infrastructure is subject to major indivisibilities and economies of scale (Nash and Preston, 1993).

Whilst the empirical evidence regarding the presence of economies of scale in railroad (and bus) operations is not conclusive, there is general agreement that significant economies can be realised from economies of density. If the network configuration is held fixed, then economies of density result from increased traffic volumes, and this measures the relationship between unit costs and the intensity of utilisation of capacity. In a study of the operations of Iarnród Éireann for the period 1973 to 1983 (McGeehan, 1993b), it was found that the economies of density were substantial, i.e. as output in terms of ton miles and passenger miles expanded, unit costs (short run) of production increased less than proportionately.

Much of the recent interest in the deregulation/privatisation of markets can be traced to developments in economic theory and in particular to the idea of contestability in markets (Baumol, 1982). The basic argument of contestability theory is that so long as there are no sunk costs involved in entering the market, and there are no constraints on the freedom of entry or exit, then only internally efficient firms of optimum size and structure, with an optimum product mix, and no cross subsidy, will survive. However, empirical research in the US airline market (Shepherd, 1988) and the UK local bus market (Mackie *et al.*, 1995), suggests that even when markets are deregulated, contestability is not perfect. Rather, it would seem with increased concentration of firms due to agglomeration, the theory of oligopoly may be more appropriate to our understanding of the functioning of some transport markets.

4.8 NATIONAL AND EU TRANSPORT POLICY

As noted earlier, State involvement in the transport sector has been prevalent throughout this century. Most of that involvement can be classified as financial or regulatory. In the former, government commits capital expenditure for the *provision* of infrastructure and subsidies for the *use* of that infrastructure. In the latter, government regulates the transport industry via licences (e.g. the bus industry) or by restrictions (e.g. speed limits, safety standards) which are in the public interest. Since Ireland's accession to the EEC in 1973, national transport policies have been influenced by legislation emanating from the European Parliament. In particular, since the formation of the single European market, the impetus of EU legislation has accelerated. From the transport viewpoint, the most relevant EU interest has centred on ensuring equitable competition between modes, and the introduction of fair and efficient pricing. These ideas had their genesis in the EU Green Paper of 1995 (European Commission, 1995) and were later refined in the EU White Paper of 1998 (European Commission, 1998).

The EU Green Paper basically envisaged that reform of travel costs was a crucial element of a broader EU strategy to achieve a more efficient transport system. The basic premise of the paper is that present transport pricing sends out the wrong signals to users. This has led to significant problems, particularly with regard to external costs. Individual externalities have usually been dealt with through regulations but this approach, argues the Green Paper, has failed to encourage users and manufacturers to examine further ways of reducing externalities. The paper sets out basic principles that should be adopted in charging for particular costs. On infrastructure, the onus should be on users to pay for infrastructure costs. Though road users pay on balance more in taxes than is spent on infrastructure, the Commission suggests that the system is distorted with HGVs paying significantly less, given the damage they cause to roads, whilst being subsidised by cars which pay proportionately more. Overall, the Commission favours the allocation of revenue from any charging system to the funding of roads, and possibly other transport infrastructure – in other words hypothecation. Furthermore, it claims that charging would enhance the viability of public-private investment partnerships (PPPs) – a form of investment that the EU is keen to promote.

The EU White Paper advocates a model of infrastructure cost recovery that they argue is consistent with the principle of efficient pricing, i.e. *marginal social cost pricing of all transport modes*. Under this regime, the welfare of society as a whole is maximised when all goods and services are made available to the consumer at this price. Marginal social costs are defined as those variable costs that reflect the cost of an extra vehicle using the infrastructure, including 'external' costs such as congestion, pollution and accidents. These vary with time, place, and condition, e.g. the cost of putting an extra lorry on an already crowded motorway may in practice be very high, while the cost of an extra carriage on a train may be almost zero.

According to current EU thinking, it is no longer sustainable to let costs incurred by the transport operator alone drive the market, since in some places, notably the highly congested urban road corridors, use of some forms of transport is now so close to saturation point that the system can no longer cope. Instead, the Commission's approach would work to minimise these distortions by setting common ground rules for charging in all sectors. If pricing at marginal social costs is introduced, then road transport costs could rise significantly, leading to modal transfers. However, EU policy has also concentrated on promoting combined transport and the integration of the various modes of transport. As noted by Forfás, this integration can only be achieved by the improved monitoring and tracking of goods, facilitated by modern information technology, and increased sophistication in the evaluation of route options made possible by well developed systems logistics (Forfás, 1996).

4.9 OVERVIEW

The discussion in the previous section illustrates the 'real world' policy topics involved in the transport sector. As this chapter has illustrated, the problems regarding the demand for transport, the need for investment, the allocation of costs, externalities, and competition/liberalisation, are all 'live' issues which need to be resolved. All of them can be analysed in an economic context so that guidance can be given as to their resolution. However, whilst economic principles can be enunciated, their practical implementation requires careful consideration. For example, whilst it is reasonable to assume that the prices paid by individual transport users will more accurately reflect the full costs of transport, the introduction of road pricing in Ireland could be problematic given our peripheral status. For road operators engaged in international haulage, any increase in charges would set them at a competitive disadvantage. A trade-off therefore exists between the economic principle of road pricing and the economic development of peripheral and economically less developed regions. But then, any derogation from road charges because of peripherality would need to be balanced with its impact on other indigenous modes such as railways.

Similarly, the implementation of the principle of charging for external costs would suggest that taxes in the general economy would rise. However, reducing congestion, air pollution, and accidents means that the associated costs would be reduced. For example, curbing congestion would reduce the time losses incurred by businesses and consumers, and a reduction in accidents would lead to lower health costs. Once again there is a trade-off between principle and practical implementation. Of course, trade-offs mean that choices have to be made. Transport economics is essentially concerned with the problems of choice in the transport sector and the impacts these choices have on the individual and society at large. In the world of transport, there are many conflicting objectives and policies. Economics can be used as an aid to understanding and clarifying the choices that confront society with regard to transport policy.

References and Further Reading

Baumol, W J and R Willig, "Contestability: Developments since the Book" *Oxford Economic Papers* (November 1986).

Baumol, W J, "Contestable Markets: An Uprising in the Theory of Industry Structure" *American Economic Review* (March 1982).

ESRI, "Medium Term Review 1997-2003" *Economic and Social Research Institute* (April 1997).

European Commission, "Fair payment for Infrastructure Use: A Phased Approach to a Common Transport Infrastructure Charging Framework in the EU" EU White Paper 1998.

European Commission, "Towards Fair and Efficient Pricing in Transport" EU Green Paper 1995, COM (95), 691 Final.

Feeney, B, "Car Ownership Forecasts 1995-2005" (An Foras Forbartha) 1994.

Forfás, "World Class to Serve the World" Report of the Forfás Transport and Logistics Group (1996).

IWW/INFRAS, "External Effects of Transport" (Paris: International Union of Railways) 1995.

Mackie, P, J Preston and C Nash, "Bus Deregulation: Ten Years On" *Transport Reviews* (July-August 1995).

McGeehan, H, "A Cost Benefit Analysis of the Howth/Bray (DART) Rail Electrification Project" Irish Universities Transport Studies Group, Occasional Paper No. 1, (June 1992).

McGeehan, H, "The Demand for Urban Bus Travel in Dublin" Paper presented to Irish Statistics Group, Trinity College Dublin (November 1993a).

McGeehan, H, "Railway Costs and Productivity Growth: the Case of the Republic of Ireland, 1973-1983" *Journal of Transport Economics and Policy* (1993b) 27.

McKinsey International, "The Transport Challenge" A Report for the Minister of Transport (December 1980).

Nash, C and J Preston, "Privatisation of Railways" ECMT 90th Round Table, Paris (1993).

Nash, C A, *Economics of Public Transport* (London: Longman) 1982.

Ogden, K W, "The Consistent Treatment of Rail and Road Freight Costs in Australia" in K Button & D Pitfield (eds), *International Railway Economics* (Aldershot: Gower) 1985.

Oscar Faber *et al.*, "Study of the Environmental Implications of Irish Transport Growth and of Related Sustainable Policies and Measures" Oscar Faber Consultants (1999).

Shepherd, W, "Competition, Contestability and Transport Mergers" *International Journal of Economics* (June 1988).

Chapter 5
The Role of Government

Tom Ferris
Department of Public Enterprise [1]

5.1 BACKGROUND TO GOVERNMENT INTERVENTION

There is a long tradition of intervention by national governments in the transport sector. The motivations for intervention are numerous and not all of them are mutually compatible. Interventions include investment in infrastructure, co-ordination of services, enforcement of operating and employment conditions and the implementation of environmental, safety and energy policies. The degree of intervention varies considerably, from slight intervention when market forces are allowed to dominate, to considerable intervention when government actions integrate the different transport modes to embrace physical planning, environmental impact and the transport responses of consumers, workers and society generally. This chapter examines the role that government plays in the transport market in Ireland, a role that usually lies between these extremes.

People need transport to move for both business and for pleasure. Food, goods and materials need to be transported to and from markets. Behind such movements lies the fact that the demand for transport is, in the main, derived. One transport economist – Denys Munby – although exaggerating the extent to which transport is a derived demand, stated that *"only the psychologically disturbed or inadequate want transport for its own sake"* (Munby, 1968, p.11). The Irish economy has quite an appetite for transport, which is not surprising given its needs as an island economy, which trades from the edge of Europe. Because of Ireland's peripheral location – an island off an island – sea and air routes fulfil the same role for Ireland as cross-frontier land transport links serve the central EU Member States; and that imposes extra costs on our exporters and importers. For example, the ESRI in a 1992 survey concluded that transport costs relative to turnover were over 20 per cent higher in Ireland than in the United Kingdom (ESRI, 1992).

Over 12 per cent of Irish national personal consumption is devoted to transport, nearly 20 per cent of fixed investment is earmarked for roads and transport equipment and the Irish transport sector accounts for over 35 per cent of final energy consumption. The commitment to transport in terms of human resources is equally significant. The Irish transport sector (including storage and communication) is estimated to account for nearly 6 per cent (or over 91,000) of the total number at work in the economy, according to the

---

[1] The views expressed in this chapter are those of the author and may not necessarily reflect the views of the Department of Public Enterprise.

latest Quarterly National Household Survey (Department of Finance, 1999).

Internally, roads are the dominant mode of transport, accounting for 92 per cent of freight traffic and 97 per cent of passenger traffic. Rail accounts for virtually all of the balance. It has a higher relative share on the main road/rail corridors, accounting on average for nearly a quarter of end-to-end journeys in the passenger markets in which it competes. In addition, rail carries significant volumes of bulk and other freight traffic, much of which is unsuited to transport by road. Air transport accounts for only a very small share of the internal transport freight and passenger markets. In 1998 there were nearly 18½ million passenger movements into and out of Irish airports and ports. Nearly 74 per cent of those journeys were by air, with just over 26 per cent by sea. By contrast,the shares for air and sea had been 50/50 in the mid-1980s.

In 1998, Irish merchandise exports reached nearly £45 billion. In tonnage terms, the dominant access mode is sea, accounting for over three-quarters of total merchandise trade. Tonnage crossing the land frontier with Northern Ireland accounts for nearly a quarter of trade and traffic. Tonnage by air represents less than 1 per cent of total merchandise trade. As shown in Table 5.1 the total number of freight units (both roll-on/roll-off and lift-on/lift-off units) to and from Ireland' sea ports was over 1½ million units in 1997 with 47 per cent going through Northern Ireland. This market share enjoyed by Northern Ireland is over two-thirds greater than would be expected on the basis of the relative scale of GDP in Northern Ireland *vis-à-vis* the Republic.

Table 5.1: Freight Movements for Ireland, 1997

	Gross Domestic Product IR£ billion	Freight Units (million)
Northern Ireland	£17.982	0.754
Republic of Ireland	£46.437	0.859
Total	**£64.419**	**1.613**
Northern Ireland as percentage of the total	27.9%	46.8%

Source: GDP data from NI Department of Finance and Personnel, Belfast and CSO, Dublin.
Freight Unit data are from Department of Economic Development, Belfast and CSO, Dublin.

Transport is not just one homogenous market, but a host of separate markets, built around distinct transport modes. These markets are all interrelated, either by virtue of sharing a common source of supply or by similarities in demand which may be served by different modes of transport or by a combination of modes. Such is the case in combined transport where freight travels partly by road, partly by rail and partly by sea or air.

5.2 THE NATURE OF GOVERNMENT INTERVENTION

There is no universally accepted economic law that lays down the extent to which governments should intervene in their transport markets. Markets for transport evolve historically and the structures that emerge display different characteristics – a mix of public, private, monopolistic and competitive characteristics. Government intervention in such transport markets takes place in both the production of transport services and the provision of infrastructure. When governments intervene they usually do so deliberately to influence both suppliers and users in order to achieve market operational results that differ from those which would be achieved through the free-reign of competition or to provide transport services where gaps exist in the market. In investing in transport infrastructure, governments largely determine the overall supply of infrastructure capacity and the conditions they lay down for its use influence the resultant markets for transport services.

Governments' interventions generally have agendas wider than mere transport objectives. Their policies often include economic, social, environmental and land-use objectives. In achieving their objectives, governments use a range of regulatory, investment and financial policy instruments. The regulatory role of governments is the primary intervention tool for managing the transport market. As Vito Tanzi puts it (Tanzi, 1999, p.20):

> *To function well, market economies need Governments that can establish and enforce the 'rules of the game' [and] they also need a pared-down set of regulations that are clear and leave little margin for interpretation and discretion.*

However, some governments place the transport sector almost exclusively under public control; others control transport companies, e.g. railways and airlines, so that the manner in which markets develop can be influenced by the activities of such publicly owned companies.

As regards infrastructure provision, governments are concerned with the question of how much to invest in infrastructure, having regard to overall budget constraints, and what additional steps are required to ensure that such infrastructure is used in the most efficient and effective manner. Governments can and do influence market developments depending on the scale and quality of the infrastructure provided and the conditions laid down for the use of such infrastructure. Taxes and subsidies are also used by governments to intervene and influence the market results for transport. Social intervention is another tool used by governments – conditions are imposed on transport undertakings, including route configurations, safety standards, working conditions, social provisions, control of atmospheric emissions and general monitoring regulations. These conditions obviously influence the costs of transport undertakings and, in turn, affect the degree of their competitiveness.

5.3 THE INTERNATIONAL DIMENSION OF TRANSPORT INTERVENTION

Many areas of transport intervention by governments at the national level also have an international dimension. Indeed, the international dimension of transport regulation continues to grow in line with the growing globalisation of economic activity. There are numerous examples of such regulation both at government level and at the commercial level. At government level, many of the agreements are made under the auspices of the United Nations, for example, the International Maritime Organisation (IMO), the primary source of international regulations on maritime safety issues. In the case of air transport, the International Civil Aviation Organisation (ICAO) and the European Civil Aviation Conference (ECAC) were established to develop the principles and techniques of international air navigation and to foster the planning and development of international and European air transport. As regards air traffic control, Eurocontrol provides the institutional framework to manage air traffic flows in Europe.

There is also the European Conference of Ministers of Transport (ECMT), an inter-governmental organisation which provides ministers responsible for transport (especially the inland transport sector) with a forum to discuss policy and to agree on joint approaches aimed at improving transport utilisation. It also aims to ensure the rational development of internationally important European transport systems. There are also a number of commercial organisations at international level. For example, the International Air Transport Association (IATA) provides a forum for collaboration among airlines while promoting safe, reliable and secure air services throughout the world; the International Road Transport Union (IRU) promotes the development of road transport in the interests of road carriers and the economy as a whole, and the International Railway Union (UIC) promotes co-operation between railway companies at international level and executes activities which focus on the development of the railway mode of transport.

The ultimate step in international regulation is the transfer of powers from member governments to an international organisation. A case in point is the European Union, where there is increasing evidence that the regulation of Europe's transport is ceasing to be a matter reserved to national governments. As in other sectors, the balance of power is shifting and, transport is being increasingly regulated by legislation adopted at an overall EU level (Ferris, 1990).In the single market now being promoted by the EU, it is clear that weaknesses and gaps in the transport sector are being remedied and filled by the introduction of market conditions, coupled with deregulation, privatisation and competition. In the view of the European Commission, the challenge for the Community's transport system is how to provide, in the most efficient manner, the services that are necessary for the continued success of the single market and the mobility of the individual traveller, while continuing to reduce the inefficiencies and imbalances of the system and safeguard against the harmful effects that increased transport activities generate (European Commission, 1992).

5.4 INSTITUTIONAL FRAMEWORK FOR IRISH TRANSPORT

Government in Ireland, in common with other EU Member States' governments, intervenes in the transport sector for a number of reasons. In particular, the government has responsibility to create the regulatory and operational framework which facilitates the development of efficient and environmentally acceptable transport systems that are not only safe, but also cater for the needs of industry and commerce and of the general public. It is the specific task of the government departments with responsibility for transport to develop a co-ordinated approach to national transport requirements. Within central government in Ireland, three departments have a direct responsibility for transport: the Department of the Environment and Local Government, the Department of Public Enterprise and the Department of the Marine and Natural Resources. Other departments have significant, albeit somewhat indirect, interests in transport. For example, there are taxation and investment issues relating to transport which are the responsibility of the Department of Finance; health, safety and research and development issues which are the responsibility of the Department of Enterprise, Trade and Employment and the enforcement of traffic and certain road safety standards for which the Garda Síochána have responsibility under the ambit of the Department of Justice, Equality and Law Reform.

The main functions of the three lead departments are as follows.

- **The Department of the Environment and Local Government**, through local authorities and the *National Roads Authority*, is responsible for public roads. It is also responsible for the Road Traffic Acts, motor taxation and vehicle and driver standards and control. The promotion of programme-based improvements and the maintenance of national, regional and local roads is the primary strategy being implemented by the department to remedy deficiencies in Ireland's basic infrastructure (Department of the Environment and Local Government, 1999). At a broader level, the department aims to ensure, in partnership with local authorities and its specialised agencies, that Ireland has a high quality environment, where infrastructure and amenities meet economic, social and environmental needs and where development is properly planned and sustainable.

- **The Department of Public Enterprise** is responsible for the formulation of national transport policies in relation to railways, road freight, public road passenger services and air services. The transport, State-sponsored bodies are charged with the implementation of these policies. There are four such State bodies: *Aer Lingus*, the State-owned airline; *Aer Rianta*, responsible for the State airports at Dublin, Cork and Shannon; *Córas Iompair Éireann*, the statutory body providing public transport services, through its three main subsidiaries – Iarnród Éireann (Irish Rail), Bus Átha Cliath (Dublin Bus) and Bus Éireann (Provincial Bus) – and *the Irish Aviation Authority* which carries out a range of operational and regulatory functions and services relating to the safety and technical aspects of civil aviation.

- **The Department of the Marine and Natural Resources** is responsible for transport policy as it affects ports, shipping and maritime transport. The department oversees the work of a number of agencies in the context of its responsibilities – the eight port companies and fourteen harbour authorities (which are responsible for the actual management of ports and harbours)[2] and the *Marine Institute* (which is responsible for marine research and development). The department also has a close relationship with the *Commissioners of Irish Lights* (who are responsible for maintaining aids to navigation around the coast of Ireland) and *the Royal National Lifeboat Institute (Ireland)*. The RNLI's function is to save lives at sea and it maintains lifeboat stations around the coast of Ireland. In the case of the latter two organisations, the provision of their services around the whole island of Ireland provides clear evidence of close co-operation between Ireland and Northern Ireland.

In overall terms, the three key transport departments have a responsibility to develop internal transport systems throughout the country, that are integrated with our access transport services. Since 1989, co-ordination of transport investment has been fostered under a single programme approach; with the Department of the Environment and Local Government as the lead authority, working in co-operation with the Department of Public Enterprise and the Department of the Marine and Natural Resources. Because of Dublin's particular transport problems, a separate Dublin Transportation Office (DTO) was set-up in 1995 under the aegis of the Department of the Environment and Local Government. The establishment of the DTO on a statutory basis has given a renewed and focused impetus to the various implementing agencies to press ahead with the infrastructural and management measures approved by the government under the strategy laid-out in the Dublin Transportation Initiative.

The fact that the transport portfolio is spread over three government departments has been questioned on occasions by transport commentators. It is argued that it would be more effective to have a single Department for Transport, as in Great Britain where there is the single Department of Environment, Transport and the Regions. This issue was debated in Dáil Éireann in 1992, when the then Taoiseach Albert Reynolds argued that he believed that the assignment of full responsibility for all transport functions to a single department or organisation was not the only, or necessarily the best, way of achieving the best integration of policy and programmes (Dáil Debates, 1992). In Mr Reynolds' view, the key to the coherent implementation of government policy – including transport policy – across departmental lines is proper co-ordination. Moreover, it should be noted that the two Operational Programmes on Transport that have covered the past decade represent a major advance towards an integrated transport policy. While the Minister for the Environment

---

2 The management and development role of the eight commercial ports is set out in the Harbours Act, 1996, while the eighteen harbour authorities operate under the Harbour Acts 1946 to 1996.

and his Department have been assigned the lead role in the preparation of these Programmes, the Ministers for Public Enterprise and the Marine together with their subsidiary agencies, have also been fully involved. The result has been an integrated set of measures relating to all elements of the transport system, including finance, planning, roads, railways, ports and airports. To that extent, the question is less how departmental responsibilities for transport should be allocated and more a question of whether truly integrated decisions are being made across the spectrum of transport policy (regardless of whether there is a single Department of Transport or two or three departments).

5.5 GOVERNMENT AND TRANSPORT INFRASTRUCTURE

The government has ultimate responsibility for virtually all existing transport infrastructure in Ireland. There are some exceptions, such as a number of privately owned ports and roads infrastructure that have been developed by National Toll Roads. The government also has responsibility for ensuring that there is sufficient investment in new transport infrastructure to meet market demand, as well as making sure that new and existing infrastructure is used in the most efficient and effective manner. The investment needs of transport infrastructure in Ireland for the coming years have been identified in some recent studies. NRA (1998) shows that the national road network remains seriously underdeveloped and that investment of over £6 billion is required over the period to 2019. In the case of public transport, CIE's reviews have indicated the need for aggregate investment of over £1 billion in the period 2000-2006. Seaport and airport infrastructure also needs considerable investment having regard to increased demands of passengers and freight.

The National Development Plan (NDP) for the period 2000-2006 includes the allocation of resources to meet transport investment needs. The Plan was prepared against the background of decisions taken at the EU Summit in Berlin in April 1999 which will see a much lower allocation of EU Structural Funds for Ireland than in the period 1994-1999. In this regard, the Economic and Social Research Institute was engaged, as an independent research institute, by the Irish government, with support from the European Commission, to identify priorities for investment over the period 2000-2006. The report produced by the ESRI places top priority on public physical infrastructure – including roads and public transport (ESRI, 1999). While the ESRI has specified its priorities for transport, that is only one ingredient in the process of decision-making for transport investment for the coming years. Much discussion and debate at government level and with the European Commission will have to take place before final decisions emerge towards the end of 1999. Accordingly, the best that can be done at the time of writing is to reproduce the ESRI's priority list for transport, recognising that this could change on foot of the negotiations between the government and the European Commission. Table 5.2 sets out the ESRI projections.

Table 5.2: ESRI's indicative annual spending on transport, 2000-2006, £ million, 1999 prices, by comparison with 1998 and 1999 data

	1998	1999	2000-2006*
Roads – National	263	312	500
Roads – Other	166	191	200
Urban Public Transport	15	64	150
Mainline Rail	26	54	25
Ports and Airports	16	24	5
Total	**488**	**646**	**880**

*Average Annual Spending
Source: ESRI (1999), Table 4.10

While the government has responsibility to ensure planned and co-ordinated investment across the transport sector, there is a fairly widespread recognition that funding should not come exclusively from the public sector. In this context, DKM Economic Consultants in their review of transport infrastructure investment needs, while recognising the need for a high level of investment in transport infrastructure during the years 2000-2006, pointed out that any commitment of public funds to subsidise investment in commercial, user-financed sea and air ports in future should be strictly limited (DKM, 1999, p.127). As regards roads investment, the consultants conclude that should it transpire that conventional tolls on inter-urban roads are not feasible, the authorities might consider the option of *shadow tolls*, which may be a more practical method of deploying private finance in the Irish situation. This would mean that motorists and truckers using these roads would not actually pay tolls, but their trips would be recorded and an agreed amount would be paid per trip by government to the private developer. In essence, the private developer, having designed, built, financed and operated the roads, would receive payments over the lifetime of the concession contracts linked to the volume of traffic using the roads. Traffic volume would be metered but the road users would not be charged for using such roads. The theory is that the private sector can be more cost effective than government in providing shadow-tolled roads and that, taking account of the value of time, it will cost the government less to pay tolls to the developer over the life of the concession than to build and operate the roads itself.

The government has been examining new mechanisms for the financing of infrastructure through co-operation with the private sector. In particular, the potential of Public Private Partnerships (PPP) for certain key investment projects was examined for the government in 1998. It has now decided to adopt a PPP approach to public capital projects on a pilot basis in a number of key departments, notably the Department of the Environment and Local Government and the Department of Public Enterprise. The initial concentration is to be on economic infrastructure projects, roads in particular. The parameters to be adopted in deciding on the merits of the PPP approach for projects will depend on the economic case for the project; the impact, if any, on the general government balance; cost effectiveness of private funding under PPP as compared with normal public funding; efficiency gains which private sector involvement could secure; and other criteria including the potential to generate revenue; legal and regulatory aspects; and possible supply constraints in the construction sector. The conceptually most straightforward form of PPP is the consortium based DBFOM (design, build, finance, operate and maintain). This has been adopted in the United Kingdom at Manchester, Wolverhampton-Birmingham, Croydon and Nottingham (Arthur Andersen, 1999). It must be recognised, however, that PPP is but one form of alternative financing that is being considered in Ireland at present. There are others, ranging from strategic alliances to employee shareholding arrangements, being examined in different areas of public-backed transport operations. Clearly, regardless of the form of funding, it is important that alternative sources of funding are brought to bear and new procurement methods developed to deliver projects more speedily and more efficiently while achieving the optimum value for money.

Transport Policy and Competitiveness

The investment gap that needs to be tackled in the coming years is only one side of the coin; the other side is the efficiency with which those facilities are used. It is particularly important to ensure that new and enhanced infrastructure, and indeed existing infrastructure, is used and managed efficiently; and that is where the competitiveness of the operators that use the transport infrastructure comes into focus. The acid test is the level of charges for transport services that have to be absorbed by Irish exporters and importers. That, in turn, puts an onus on Irish transport operators to adapt and adjust to new and improved operating techniques and infrastructures and modern communications systems if they are to raise their level of competitiveness, particularly as their foreign competitors are likely to respond quickly to new and changed circumstances. This is especially true as far as logistics systems are concerned. It is quite clear that such systems are facing a transformation as long-established supply chain conventions are revolutionised by technological change. Ireland must, therefore, now aim specifically for a leadership position in skills and expertise across the broad logistical area. This, according the National Competitiveness Council (1999), can be best achieved through partnership drawing on the complementary expertise possessed by business and third level research interests.

In short, new transport infrastructure, enhanced logistics systems and modern communications systems (including e-commerce) may benefit foreign transport operators as much as they benefit domestic operators. Underlying this point is the fact that Ireland has to live with the reality of its peripheral location, and that particular reality now includes the Channel Tunnel. In this regard, the National Competitiveness Council has pointed out that Ireland has particular requirements in terms of its transport infrastructure, including the need to ensure efficient access to seaports and airports, in order to minimise the economic disadvantages of peripherality. There are, of course, initiatives being taken at an EU level to ensure closer cohesion of the Union. An example is the development of the Trans-European Networks (TENs). In the case of transport TENs, the Christophersen Group, which reported to the European Summit in Essen in December 1994, included two priority projects, out of a total of fourteen, which relate directly to Ireland – the Cork/Dublin/Belfast/Larne Rail Link, and the Ireland/UK/Benelux Road Link.

These networks are important not only from a transport perspective, but also from the perspective of ensuring closer co-operation between Northern Ireland and Ireland from the political and commercial perspectives. Of course, the extent of the benefits from individual TENs projects can only be relative, given that our trading partners will also benefit from such enhancement of transport linkages. Therefore, the real challenge for Ireland, recognising the infrastructures that will be in place in Europe in the future, is how to minimise the disadvantages of extra distance and the additional transport costs associated with accessing central markets.

5.6 INCREASING COMPETITION IN TRANSPORT

As the trading environment becomes increasingly competitive, the implications of such cost impositions on the economic performance of the periphery become ever more serious as European and national legislation impacting on competition increases. For example, the 1991 Competition Act, in extending the principles of EU competition law to Ireland's economic activities, provided the legislative basis for the removal of many of the restraints which impact on the allocation of resources in the service sectors of the economy. The Competition (Amendment) Act 1996, has gone even further, insofar as it has introduced criminalisation of breaches of competition law. The OECD has commented recently (OECD, 1999, p.115) on the evidence of more competition in the Irish marketplace. Indeed, it has stated that corporate behaviour may have improved in recent years thanks to the more aggressive enforcement of the code by the Competition Authority. At an overall level, the OECD has concluded that the nation has a generally high degree of product market competition, thanks to its open trading system and a relatively low level of government regulation.

In tandem with the enhanced work of the Competition Authority, deregulation of different strands of transport has also been taking place. In particular, air and road freight transport markets have been opened-up as part of an intra-European trend, with the consequence of increased market pressures and demands. As regards Irish airlines, if they are to continue to prosper they will have to ensure that their operations are sufficiently flexible in responding to the structural adjustments that are likely in the European airline industry. In this regard, it should be noted that the Irish government decided in July 1999 to give the go-ahead for Aer Lingus, the State-owned airline, to enter into a strategic alliance with American Airlines/British Airways, the major partners in the Oneworld global alliance. This decision was driven mainly by the need for Aer Lingus to increase its profit potential, while recognising that strategic alliances are likely to continue to drive developments in this global, and very competitive, aviation industry.

The road haulage industry is also facing much sharper competition. A recent consultancy report, commissioned by the government, put forward a range of recommendations designed to enable the road haulage industry to realise its potential (Department of Public Enterprise, 1999a). The recommendations were directed towards ensuring an improved regulatory/policy environment, enhanced support services for the industry, improvements to operational performance, as well as measures to address time and delivery challenges and the development of more accurate pricing of services. Many of the recommendations have implications for government, State agencies, employers, the haulage industry itself and individual haulage operators. The pace at which these recommendations are implemented will determine how quickly the road haulage industry will be in a position to improve its competitiveness.

For ports and airports, increased competition, as between the different facilities throughout the island of Ireland, is producing more efficient and cost effective services which benefit users in particular and the economy in general. As regards sea ports, the Strategy Statement of the Department of the Marine and Natural Resources has highlighted the importance of ensuring competitive port services (Department of the Marine and Natural Resources, 1998, p.27). Accordingly, the department, in facilitating the co-ordination and integration of maritime transport within the total transport chain, is setting challenging efficiency and charges targets for ports. This should help to further enhance Irish Sea transport services have had a long history of competitive open-market operations. In the same vein, there is increasing pressure on Irish airports to provide even more competitive services for their customers and airlines. At present the position of Aer Rianta, the State company which operates the airports at Dublin, Cork and Shannon, is being examined to ensure that it is strategically placed for future competitive operations.

As regards the domestic bus market in Ireland, the evolution of European policy in relation to cabotage (i.e. foreign operators being allowed to operate over purely domestic routes) will be among the key factors influencing the development of a more liberal and market sensitive approach to licensing and competition. It should also be noted that the current Strategy Statement from the Department of Public Enterprise (Department of Public Enterprise, 1998) has announced plans to carry out a review of options for the effective regulation of the bus market, with a view to introducing legislation to replace the 1932 legislation, which still governs operations in the Irish bus sector. The review is to focus on improving customer service, effective enforcement, fair competition and appropriate integration of services.

The EU also continues to develop policies aimed at achieving more commercially oriented railways, with a particular focus on improving accessibility between national networks. However, this is of limited relevance to Ireland, given the isolation of Ireland's railway system. The main national objective, as regards Ireland's railways, is to support and encourage a safe, competitive, commercial ethos and to improve the competitive position of Irish Rail's operations *vis-à-vis* the roads – a policy objective supported by the investment programme co-funded by the EU.

In the case of the State transport companies in general, Ireland has not been immune from the trend towards deregulation and having to compete in much more open markets. At the same time, it is clear that the European Commission favours greater transparency in the provision of state funding for non-commercial public transport services. It also is in favour of further liberalisation of the public transport market, including greater third party access to the railways and increased bus cabotage. All in all, regulatory developments associated with the single European market and technological advances, which reduce market entry costs or provide new means of entry, will make for a much more open and competitive environment.

5.7 TRANSPORT CHALLENGES FOR THE 21st CENTURY

It is evident that all national governments have multiple objectives in pursuing their transport policies. It is equally clear that the ranking and range of such multiple objectives continue to change in the light of significant technological developments, sharper market forces, continuing globalisation of trade, and growing environmental concerns. At a European level, the objectives for transport continue to be adapted and changed in the light of new demands. For example, the European Commission believes that the continued development of the TENs will serve to enhance both sustainable development and the internal cohesion of the Union by tying regions closer together. They also recognise that this will need to be accompanied, by a move towards sounder transport systems, drawing fully on new technology, to address the problems of congestion, pollution and climate change (European Commission, 1997).

The Irish government, in turn, is being challenged to create an environment which facilitates a more competitive transport sector in the context of growing globalisation and more sophisticated communications systems. In this context, Paul Krugman, the American economist, is quite optimistic about Ireland's prospects – he argues (Krugman, 1997) that since crude transport cost considerations have been replaced with more subtle issues of communication and personal contact, Ireland's insular location and distance from continental markets matter much less than they used to. However, this should not lead to any complacency. The world does not stand still. The government's policy for transport has to be enhanced and amended in the light of economic, technological, social and environmental developments. There are also developments in other economic sectors that impact on the transport sector. A case in point is the communications sector: modern telecommunications systems have a very important role to play in helping to reduce Ireland's peripherality. As part of the government's campaign to open fully the telecommunications markets, the derogation from full liberalisation, which was to apply until 1 January, 2000, was ended from the close of December 1998. This decision brought forward by over a year the benefits of competition in the voice telephony market to the Irish public. As regards e-commerce, the government is at present engaged in a number of initiatives to ensure that Ireland has an e-commerce friendly environment. This is very important if Ireland is to retain existing overseas investment, build on the successes achieved in areas such as software, electronics, and financial services, as well as having the capability to compete for and attract the new digital industries and opportunities that are emerging.

The environment is another area that will continue to be affected by transport. Already Ireland is committed to the control of atmospheric emissions which arise from transport and other economic and social activities. This commitment derives both from international accords and from domestic policy as articulated by successive governments. DKM Consultants have pointed out (DKM, 1999) that environmental concerns extend widely to the impact of transport on noise, low-level air pollution, physical separation, accidents and other external effects. They argue that future policy needs to address, in addition to the questions of provision of adequate physical capacity, overall demand management, through a careful assessment of taxes and charges. In this regard, the Department of Public Enterprise has recently prepared a Green Paper on Sustainable Energy to assist in the formulating of policy for these matters of environmental concern.

Regulation is another area of change that will continue to impact on transport. Traditionally, government departments responsible for economic sectors have had three main functions – regulation, shareholding in State companies and policy development. With many more private companies entering the market, it is now necessary to separate the shareholding role from the regulatory role. While policy development will remain with ministers, it is possible for them to relinquish either their regulatory roles or their shareholder roles, or indeed both roles. Already in the telecommunications and energy sectors, government has appointed independent regulators to cater for more open operating conditions, including the advent of new market entrants. In the area of transport, the government recently gave approval for the appointment of a Regulator for Irish Airports. The Regulator's functions will include airport charges, ground handling services, airport-slot allocations, licensing Irish airlines under EU licensing regulations, and related matters. As regards the regulation of other modes of transport, it is clear from the Department of Public Enterprise's 1998 Statement of Strategy that consideration is being given to this matter. On a wider front, the OECD has recently commented (OECD, 1999, p.117) on the wisdom of having the Competition Authority as the sole enforcer of competition in the deregulated sectors. This is an important debate according to the OECD because effective enforcement could be critical to ensuring that hoped-for benefits from liberalisation are not delayed or denied by anti-competitive conduct, especially by strong incumbent firms.

5.8 CONCLUSION

It is clear that much change and considerable developments have been taking place in recent years, in terms of investment, organisation, operation and the regulation of transport in Ireland. The evidence that is available suggests that the pace of change will accelerate further in the coming years. In tandem with market changes of recent years, transport in Ireland has been fortunate to benefit from considerable investment, much of it funded by the EU. The funds which have flowed under the EU-backed Operational Programmes produced benefits particularly in terms of the upgrading of national primary and secondary roads in Ireland. In addition, Irish public transport has been given an increased emphasis in the Operational Programmes. Accordingly, there is no reason to suspect that the substantial progress that was made in improving Ireland's transport in the late 1990's will not be continued under future Operational Programmes for Transport.

Government will continue to have an important role in ensuring that transport services in Ireland operate at internationally competitive and cost effective rates. Transport operators, in turn, have their role to play by ensuring that new management systems, especially logistics (in all its aspects) are given a much higher priority. In the final analysis, the real challenge for Irish business in the new millennium will be to exploit the market opportunities that new transport services, by air and sea, will provide in trading with Europe. The enlargement of the European Union will create great challenges for Ireland's transport in the coming years. In short, Irish transport must ensure that the improvements that will take place in infrastructure, regulation and systems are used to the best advantage, raising the efficiency and competitiveness of the Irish economy to even higher levels.

References and Further Reading

Arthur Andersen, *Report on a Private Public Partnership Approach to the Dublin Light Rail Project* (Dublin: Department of Public Enterprise) April 1999.

Dáil Debates, *Parliamentary Questions*, 25 February, Columns 225-226 (Dublin: Stationery Office) 1992.

Department of the Environment and Local Government, *Annual Report 1998* (Dublin) 1999.

Department of Finance, *Economic Review and Outlook* (Dublin: Stationery Office) 1999.

Department of Public Enterprise *Statement of Strategy*. (Dublin: Stationery Office) 1998.

Department of Public Enterprise, *A Strategy for the Successful Development of the Irish Road Haulage Industry* Report by Indecon International Economic Consultants and PricewaterhouseCoopers Management Consultants in association with NEA Transport Research and Training, Dublin 1999a.

Department of Public Enterprise, Green Paper on Sustainable Energy (Dublin: Stationery Office) 1999b.

Department of the Marine and Natural Resources, *Making the Most of Ireland's Marine and Natural Resources,* Strategy Statement 1999-2000 (Dublin: Stationery Office) 1998.

DKM, *Review of Transport Infrastructure Investment Needs* EE Report 34 DKM Economic Consultants (February 1999).

ESRI, *The Role of the Structural Funds: Analysis of Consequences for Ireland in the Context of 1992,* Policy Research Paper No. 13 (Dublin: Economic and Social Research Institute) 1992.

ESRI, *National Investment Priorities for the Period 2000-2006,* Policy Research Paper No. 33 (Dublin: Economic and Social Research Institute) 1999.

European Commission, *The Future Development of the Common Transport Policy,* Com (92) 494 Final. Luxembourg: Office for Official Publications of the European Communities (1992).

European Commission, *Agenda 2000: For a Stronger and Wider Union* Bulletin of the European Union, Supplement 5/97 (Luxembourg: Office for Official Publications of the European Communities) 1997.

European Conference of Ministers of Transport (ECMT), *Which Changes for Transport in the Next Century?* 14th International Symposium, Innsbruck, 1997 (published by ECMT, Paris, 1999).

Ferris, Tom, "Transport" in Anthony Foley & Michael Mulreany (eds), *The Single European Market and the Irish Economy* (Dublin: Institute of Public Administration) 1990.

Krugman, Paul R, "Good News from Ireland: A Geographical Perspective" in Alan W Gray (ed.), *International Perspectives on the Irish Economy* (Dublin: Indecon Economic Consultants) 1997 pp. 38-53.

Munby, Denys, *Transport* (London: Penguin Books) 1968.

National Competitiveness Council, *Annual Competitiveness Report 1999* (Dublin: Forfás) 1999.

NRA, *Road Needs Study* Report prepared by Scetaroute and O'Sullivan Consultants for the National Roads Authority (1998).

OECD, *Economic Surveys: Ireland* (Paris: Organisation for Economic Cooperation and Development) 1999.

Tanzi, Vito, "Transition and the Changing Role of Government" in *Finance and Development* (Washington: International Monetary Fund) 1999.

Chapter 6
Regulation and Deregulation

Sean Barrett
Trinity College Dublin

6.1 ECONOMISTS AND REGULATION

> *The monopolists by keeping the market constantly under-stocked,*
> *by never fully supplying the effectual demand, sell their commodi-*
> *ties much above their natural price, and raise their emoluments,*
> *whether they consist in wages or profit, greatly above the natural*
> *rate* (Smith, 1776).

Throughout the 19th and well into the 20th century, the views of Adam Smith on competition prevailed. From the late-1920s to the late-1970s, the efficiency gains of competition were ignored by policy makers in most countries and neglected by many economists. Much recent economic and legal thought has gone into dismantling the anti-competition policies dating from the protectionist era.

The election of William Baumol as president of the American Economics Association in 1982 recognised that his theory of contestable markets reinstated the importance of markets in economics. Contestability theory insights have generated many papers in economic journals. A contestable market is one where the efficiency of incumbents is ensured by potential new entrants. Inefficient incumbents attract new entrants and the economic rents earned are eliminated. Price tends towards long run marginal cost and the industry will always have the optimal number of firms. The assumptions of the model are that the new entrant has access to the same technology as the incumbents, is able to woo the incumbents' customers and that sunk costs are low. The implications for policy are that the state should not establish barriers to entry to a sector. It should not obstruct market exit. Few firms in an industry may be a sign of virtue rather than vice. The incumbents may be operating so efficiently that new firms do not wish to enter. The role of the state, therefore, is to end barriers to entry, many of them set up by the state itself, and to devise policy measures to counter post-deregulation barriers to contestability, such as the abuse of dominance in a market by predatory pricing (Baumol, 1983). Where high sunk costs are a barrier to entry the Demsetz (Demsetz, 1968) proposal is to have competition for the market if it is not possible to have competition in the market.

Transport has a tradition of persuading governments to allow the sector to opt out of normal market competition. The tradition embraces countries that otherwise have a strong market emphasis. In the United States competition in the internal aviation market was restricted from 1928 until 1978. The deregulation of US internal aviation in 1978 began a marked change in attitude to transport markets by policy makers. The protectionist tradition also includes countries with a strong history of interventionism in economic affairs, such as Ireland, where competition in transport was severely restricted from the 1930s until the mid-1980s. Part of that legacy persists to the present day.

The examination of transport interventionism is a case study of how policy can be diverted from serving the economy as a whole to the service of producers in the transport sector. Successful influencing of government policy to secure from the state benefits, such as protection from competition, fiscal privileges, or subsides, for a sector is called rent-seeking or unproductive entrepreneurship. The successful sector gains, at least in the short run. The burden is borne by customers, taxpayers and by the unsheltered sector of the economy. Output in the economy is reduced by the transfer of resources from their area of comparative advantage to the rent-seeking sector. Investment decisions are distorted by the protection enjoyed by the rent-seeking sector and the overall efficiency of investment is reduced. Labour markets are distorted by the rents earned in the rent-seeking sector at the expense of employees in the unsheltered sector.

6.2 PROTECTIONISM IN PRACTICE

In Ireland in 1932 and 1933 legislation was passed to restrict competition in the bus and road freight sectors. The object of the legislation was to protect the railways. New entrant operators in both the bus and road freight sectors were restricted by a licensing system and railway companies were permitted to engage in either voluntary or compulsory acquisition of road transport services. Table 6.1 shows the reductions in independent road transport under this legislation.

Table 6.1: Independent bus and road freight services eliminated under the Road Transport Acts 1932 and 1933, during the years 1933-1941

(a) Bus Services

Eliminating Company	Eliminations		
	Voluntary	**Compulsory**	**Total**
Great Southern Railway	634	275	909
Great Northern Railway	11	91	102
Dublin United	18	52	70
Other railways*			10
Total Bus Services affected			1091

(b) **Road Freight**

Licenses Acquired	470
Total road transport services eliminated	1561

*Small cross border railways not included in the Great Southern System
Source: Transport Tribunal, 1939

Why did governments pursue policies that, in hindsight, seem bizarre? The first explanation is successful rent seeking by the railways. The legislation was a response to intensive lobbying by the railways. At the annual general meetings of the Great Southern Railways in 1931 and 1932 the chairman, Sir Walter Nugent, called for regulation of road transport in order to protect the railways. In 1931 he stated that:

> ... *it is obvious, moreover, that unless legislation is passed regulating transport and removing the disabilities at present imposed on the railways the companies cannot continue to adequately operate and maintain them.*

The following year Sir Walter claimed that *"nowhere in the world was the whole matter of road and rail competition allowed to drift as it has been, until quite recently, in Great Britain or the Irish Free State"*. The lobbying worked, and the ministers introducing the anti-competitive legislation echoed the railway statements. Abolishing bus competition in 1932, Minister McGilligan stated that the tendency in the Act was:

> ... *to divert traffic into the hands of the three companies operating on a big scale at present...we do allow for the existence side by side with these three agencies of the independent bus proprietor or bus company. Personally, I look forward to seeing these people disappearing by degrees either by process of amalgamation with other companies or by the main companies deciding that their future lay in certain areas in the country and leaving other areas for exploitation by independent bus owners.*

Abolishing road freight competition, Minister Lemass in 1933 hoped:

> ... *to make it possible for the Great Southern Railway in its area and other railway companies in their areas to establish themselves in what is described as a monopoly position.*

Railway managers, shareholders and employees represented a powerful interest group at the time. The small bus and road freight companies did not. The Great Southern Railway carried 11.9 million passengers in 1931 before the changes in legislation or only 34 per cent of the 34.5 million carried by the independent bus companies. The railways succeeded in lobbying, if not in the market.

The second explanation for the transport legislation of the early 1930s lies in the interventionist traditions of Irish nationalism. According to Daly (1982, p.4):

> *... one major legacy of the thirties was the institutionalisation on an Irish dependence on the state, and on politicians, for economic benefits.*

Irish economic policy in the 1930s was highly interventionist. A successful lobbyist for protection against competing imports could expect the most detailed intervention on his behalf in the form of tariffs from the Department of Industry and Commerce which intervened even in matters such as industry ownership and location. This department also prepared the legislation banning bus and road freight competition in 1932 and 1933. The Dairy Disposal Company was established in 1927 to acquire bankrupt creameries. An electricity industry had existed in Ireland for over 40 years before the State established the Electricity Supply Board in 1927. In the early-1920s there were 160 electricity undertakings in the State. These operations were compulsorily acquired and typically shut down; for example, in 1930-1931, 24 generating stations were closed down. The State chose the public sector Shannon scheme in preference to a private sector proposal to install hydro stations on the Liffey (Manning and McDowell, 1985). Policy interventions to help bankrupt operations in dairying and to compulsorily eliminate competing electricity services were thus being replicated in transport policy.

The third factor behind the Irish transport legislation of the 1930s was the reaction to the world recession. The Irish antipathy to the market was more pronounced than in most countries, but was not unique. Governments responded to the crash of 1929 by a variety of public works programmes. While in prosperous times economists see bankruptcies as a transfer of resources from inefficient to efficient entrepreneurs, in the depressed economic circumstances of the 1930s, policy makers did not wish to see railway companies either go bankrupt or even reform or downsize their operations in order to avert bankruptcy.

The fourth factor in explaining the success of lobbying for protectionism in the 1930s in Ireland was the weak position of the study and practice of economics at the time. University departments of economics were small and had little influence on government departments (Fanning, 1985). It was not until 1950 that economists were employed in the civil service and in the initial stages they were confined to the Department of Finance.

6.3 AIR TRANSPORT REGULATION AND THE RESTRICTION OF COMPETITION

The Air Navigation (International Lines) Order of 1935 extended protectionism to the aviation sector. The Order required ministerial authorisation for air services *"with a view to the limitation or regulation of competition as may be considered necessary in the public interest"* (Share, 1988, p.3). A long tradition of protectionism in Irish aviation policy was thus begun. In 1935 Crilly Airways, seeking to operate air services between Ireland and Britain was told that:

> ... *the Minister was unable to entertain his proposals. The reason given was the government's intention to set up a national airline at the earliest possible date (ibid., p.3).*

In 1949, the government turned down a proposal for an air service from Cork to Britain *"on the grounds that air transport policy did not contemplate that airlines other than Aer Lingus would operate scheduled services between the two countries" (ibid.,* p.69). Share also recounts a refusal of a Dublin-Liverpool service licence in 1950:

> *In October 1950 the Minister for Industry and Commerce informed the Independent Air Transport Association of Britain that in his view Aer Lingus was providing adequate services between Ireland and that country and that where additional services were justified the company would provide them in due course. One of the independents, Silver City, was proposing to start a car ferry from Liverpool, and Aer Lingus asked the Minister to protect the company's position as they were considering the opening of a similar service on the route (ibid., p.69).*

Right up to 1986, Aer Lingus achieved regulatory capture so successfully that its company interest was identified as the national interest and the Department of Transport was referred to informally as *"the downtown office of Aer Lingus"*. Share recounts the launch of a New York service in 1960:

> *You saw for the first time an Irish plane with a shamrock. There was a great deal of emotional pride in the thing (ibid., p.95).*

Aer Lingus held out for protectionism because Irish routes and not the airline were inherently uneconomic. The chief executive wrote in 1988 that:

> ... *the traditional Aer Lingus view was that the short-haul and seasonal nature of our European network was inherently not economic, or at least only marginally so, and would have to be supported by a profitable Atlantic operation* (Kennedy, 1988).

It was also government policy that the airline should build up ancillary activities to cross-subsidise the airline. Irish aviation policy was among the most protectionist in Europe. Other countries with conservative aviation policies, such as the southern European states, were liberal in their licensing of charter airlines in order to develop their tourism sectors while protecting the scheduled services of their national airlines. Ireland restricted both scheduled and charter airline competition.

6.4 FURTHER PROTECTIONIST INLAND TRANSPORT POLICIES, 1944-1956

In the internal transport sector it became apparent within a few years that protection was not assisting the railways. In 1938 the Chairman of the Great Southern Railways complained of *"widespread and ingenious evasion"* of the 1933 Act. He added that:

> ... *some restriction in the use of privately owned commercial vehicles is imperative if efficient public transport services are to be maintained* (Barrett, 1982, p.12).

In 1944, the Great Southern Railways absorbed the Dublin bus services into CIE with the goal of cross subsidising the railways from the city bus service. Further *"wasteful competition"* was eliminated in 1950 by the takeover of the Grand Canal Company whose barge traffic was transferred to rail. Further successful lobbying in 1956 brought the inclusion of vehicle leasing within the Road Transport Act 1933 as the equivalent of carrying on a hired haulage business. CIE proposed to the Beddy Committee in 1956 that all commercial vehicles would be restricted in their area of operation. The initial limit was to be 50 miles but this would be steadily reduced until the full traffic capacity of the railways was achieved. Beddy rejected this but CIE returned to the issue in the Pacemaker Report of 1963:

> *It is not a function of CIE to say whether or not long-distance road trunk haulage should be restricted but it has a duty to say that ultimately the community may have to choose between having railways and additional restrictions or no additional restrictions and no railways.*

In the 1960s, the Irish economy began slowly to move away from regulation towards freer trade both externally and internally.

6.5 DISCONTENT WITH REGULATION AND THE DEREGULATION MOVEMENT

The Road Freight Sample Survey of 1964 found that 83 per cent of road freight moved in own account vehicles, that is fleets owned by the industrialists themselves. The share of the remaining licensed hauliers was 11 per cent and CIE's share was 6 per cent. Road freight licensing was, therefore, distorting the market in a way which the legislators did not intend because industry preferred the extra costs of setting up its own transport rather than avail of the limited choice of hired haulage permitted or avail to the extent envisaged of the rail and road services of CIE, the company which the legislation was intended to assist. The National Prices Commission in 1972 stated that the restrictions on competition in road freight had four negative consequences for the economy:

- diversion of traffic from least cost modes;
- curtailment of traffic because of the high cost of rail and own account transport relative to commercial transport;
- heavy reliance on own account transport;
- since haulage licences command a £5,000 premium there is an income transfer from society to licence holders.

By 1980 the scarcity value of a road freight licence was £12,000 or £31,000 at 1999 prices. The deregulation of road freight in the United Kingdom in 1968 while licensing was retained in the Republic for a further twenty years saw cross border haulage change from equal shares for both northern and southern hauliers in 1967 to a 75 per cent share for northern hauliers in 1977.

Liberalisation began in 1970 with the deregulation of the carriage of cattle, sheep, and pigs, and the removal of weight, area and commodity restrictions. Extra licences were awarded to national licence holders. In 1978, each licence holder was allowed to operate six vehicles per licence. The legislation to deregulate was passed in 1986 with a two-year phasing-in period. By 1998 the hired haulage sector held over 50 per cent of the market and in 1994, just under 65 per cent. CIE availed of the free market in road haulage to contract out some 47 per cent of its road freight in 1992 (Oireachtas Joint Committee on State-Sponsored Bodies, 1995, p.42).

Consumer dissatisfaction with the regulation of airfares grew throughout the 1970s and 1980s, in particular with the London fares of £208 from Dublin and £240 from Cork and Shannon up to 1986. Before deregulation, air travel between Britain and Ireland was stagnant for eight years. A study by the Civil Aviation Authority of eleven major routes from London to points in Western Europe over the years 1980 to 1985 showed that the passenger growth to Dublin, at only 2.8 per cent between 1980 and 1985, was less than one-tenth of the average for the eleven routes. The fare increase on London-Dublin was 72.6 per cent over the period, compared with an average of 43.7 per cent for the eleven routes and a retail price index increase of 41.5 per cent. The volume increase between London and Belfast over the years 1980 to 1985 was 31 per cent and the fare rise was 41 per cent. The Air Transport Users Committee of the Chambers of Commerce of Ireland advocated flying via Belfast as a response to high airfares from the Republic.

In June 1984, a measure to make the regulation of airfares more restrictive proved to be the regulators' downfall and within two years the sector was deregulated. The Air Transport Bill 1984 was introduced on 27 June 1984 and proposed fines of £100,000, the loss of the travel agents' licence and two years in prison for discounting airline tickets. The Bill was proposed by the government to deal with a court judgment after an unsuccessful prosecution of a travel agent for selling tickets on TransAmerica airlines to the United States and between Shannon and Amsterdam below official approved fares. Many deputies saw the Bill as further evidence of the control of air transport policy by Aer Lingus and the Bill encountered difficulties in the Dáil. Ten economists issued an immediate statement claiming that the Bill was designed to protect the monopoly position of Aer Lingus at the expense of the consumer (*Irish Press*, 28 June 1984).

Deregulation occurred on 23 May 1986. Fares fell on that day from £208 on Dublin-London to £94.99, a fall of 54 per cent. In the first full year of deregulation, 1987, the number of passengers on the Dublin-London route in August was 92 per cent higher than in August 1985, the last full year of the old regulation policy. Dublin-London passenger numbers increased to over 4 million in 1998, making it the busiest international route in the world. As deregulation was gradually extended to Irish and British provincial routes the gains multiplied. By 1998, over 8 million people flew between Britain and Ireland, and it was the leading scheduled market from Britain to Western Europe with more passengers than large country markets such as Britain to France, Germany and Italy. In August 1999, Aer Lingus advertised a £39 return fare to London. Before 1985, the comparable fares charged were £95 for a 28 day Apex, £119 for a 14 day Apex and £159 for a Saturday night away fare.

In the deregulated market, Aer Lingus has chosen to position itself as a full service airline, as have British Midland and Cityjet. Ryanair has positioned itself in the budget end of the market and is now the longest surviving discount airline in Europe, the second most profitable airline in the world in 1998, and the first new European airline to rival a national airline in terms of passenger numbers. Low fare tickets are more freely available from all the airlines. Airport competition also applies with four alternatives to the former Heathrow monopoly in the London area and airport competition also in the north of England and Scotland. The productivity gains from aviation deregulation have been substantial and unprecedented at the budget end of the market. In 1998, Ryanair had 48 staff per aircraft and 4,800 passengers per staff member compared to the Association of European Airlines average of 116 and 752 respectively. Southwest Airlines in the US had 91 staff per aircraft and 1,893 passengers per staff per year and are frequently cited as the best example of a US deregulated airline. The passenger thus has the choice between very low fares or retaining a high level of passenger service. Mainland Europe's airfares are frequently found to be the highest in the world in the annual ICAO surveys and are thus likely to fall in a more competitive market. Airline deregulation has also led to competition among service providers at airports such as passenger and baggage handling, which were previously controlled by host airlines or airport authorities. It has also led to competition between travel agents and telemarketing bodies such as Ryanair Direct.

The policy choice to deregulate aviation in 1986 was innovative and was made eleven years before EU deregulation on 1 April 1997. While EU competition law will help to sustain the benefits of airline deregulation the initiative for deregulation came from within Ireland.

The gains for the Irish economy in terms of reduced access costs have been large. Airline deregulation started the revival of Irish tourism, which stagnated from 1966 to 1986 and then became the fastest growing in the OECD. The savings from deregulation on the London route were repeated even more emphatically with the arrival of competition on routes to Manchester, Glasgow and Birmingham in 1994. Since air fares from Ireland to mainland Europe were traditionally much higher per mile than to Britain the gains from competition on the Dublin services to Brussels and Paris in 1997 were correspondingly greater. Airline deregulation also undermined the shipping cartel between Britain and Ireland. The shipping companies are now privatised and profitable and fares have fallen to compete with the lower airfares.

Further steps to efficient competition in aviation concern control of predatory pricing by incumbent large airlines to drive out new entrants. Cases of predatory pricing are difficult to prove since airlines have always operated schemes of discounted fares to fill empty seats. Nonetheless, the prospect of an EU dawn raid to inspect airline documents on fares policy on contested routes is a useful deterrent. A further serious problem is the 'grandfather rights' system which allocates slots at busy airports to airlines in order of seniority. This is an obvious barrier to contestability which EU States have been unwilling to address. Where airline alliances are formed the EU has however made approval conditional on the surrender of some of the slots held by the alliance airlines in order to counterbalance the potential anti-competitive aspects of airline collusion. Ireland has also to address the issue of airport competition since cheap airport access is the key to continuing enjoyment of the benefits of airline deregulation. The airport authority, Aer Rianta, is scheduled for privatisation. Congestion at Dublin Airport is a major problem and the airport has a monopoly in the province of Leinster. Options for competitive privatisation include competitive terminals at Dublin or the development of competing airports at sites such as the Air Corps facility at Baldonnel on the west of the city.

6.6 THE REMAINING DEREGULATION CHALLENGES

Bus deregulation was examined in the Green Paper on Transport Policy in 1985. The arguments for deregulation included fare and service competition, greater efficiency, innovation and the challenge to CIE road and rail. The arguments against deregulation were reduced safety, gaps in the network, loss of cross subsidisation, and adverse impacts on CIE and its staff. The National Development Plan (1989-1993) promised to replace the outdated Road Transport Act 1932. The planned changes would bring in the liberalisation of the bus transport industry to provide greater competition and increased flexibility in the range of services. No legislation resulted either from the 1985 Green Paper or the National Development Plan. The dynamism that enthused the political and administrative system to deregulate air services is notably absent in the bus case. The underlying fear appears to be that bus deregulation would undermine further the finances of the railways whose defence was the reason for road transport regulation in the first place.

An informal bus deregulation has evolved in the absence of a willingness to formally deregulate. In some cases it has been a spectacular success. On the Dublin-Galway route a high frequency service by three operators, Bus Éireann, Citylink (Burkes) and Nestors, offers an £8 return fare for the 270 mile round trip, a fare of 3p per mile. The independent operators are not subsidised and have purchased replacement vehicles several times during intense competition on the Dublin-Galway route. The 3p per mile fare thus covers the fixed and variable costs of the service. By contrast, the fare on the uncontested route from Dublin city to the airport is £6 return for a twelve mile round trip, or 50p per mile. Governments have known since the Prices Commission reported in 1972 that private bus operators charged lower fares than CIE, in some cases significantly lower. Barrett (1982, pp.130–133) estimated that savings of 40 to 50 per cent would result from bus deregulation. Independent bus competition also operates on routes serving the south midlands, and the Ulster counties in the Republic. Despite the savings they offer passengers, independent bus operators risk prosecution should the State decide to suspend the informal system which allows them to operate. The independent operators also risk antagonising CIE, which has a public subsidy of over £100m per year and the sheer market size to force any independent operator to withdraw from a route.

CIE's policy of using its bus services as the first line of defence of the railways is flawed. Since many of its train services are both overcrowded and loss-making, train fares are too low. The comparative advantage of railways lies in their greater speed and comfort than the bus. Their consequent ability to charge higher train fares should reflect these benefits and recoup their higher costs.

It is especially strange that the government wishes to reduce car traffic in Dublin but refuses to deregulate either the bus or taxi sector. Measures such as car clamping, higher parking charges, bus corridors and road pricing will, without deregulation, enhance rent-seeking in the protected public transport sectors. A taxi licence in Dublin had a scarcity value of £3,500 in 1980. The value currently is over £80,000. The scarcity value arose from a street-blocking protest in 1977 by the licence holders. The only beneficiaries of the ban on new entrants are the existing licence holders. The longer the government has postponed dealing with the problem the higher has become the value of a taxi licence. This in turn provokes complaints that deregulation would destroy the licence "investment" of the incumbents. There is no economic case for compensating the licence holders for deregulation. Those who gamble that governments will not adopt sensible economic policies take a greater risk in the

Ireland of the 1990s than in the 1930s. Policy change might be introduced gradually to allow for a controlled reallocation of resources within the sector but the incumbents' veto on new entrants cannot be sustained.[1]

6.7 CONCLUSION

The UK experience of bus deregulation indicates that it has generated large increases in productivity, large reductions in fares and in subsidies required, greater availability of service, and 85 per cent of routes being operated commercially. A red herring in bus deregulation debates is that monopolists are safer than competing bus companies. Between 1980 and 1988 the accident rates for buses in Britain fell by two-thirds.

The British model of competition within the rail sector in 1995 was based on the separation of fixed costs (such as track, signalling and stations) from operating companies. The data for 1994/1995, when British Rail was a nationalised railway monopoly, and 19971998, when it was privatised, show that privatisation reduced the subsidies required, increased traffic productivity, punctuality and reliability. The increase in fares was minimal. Passenger receipts in 1997/1998 were 21 per cent greater in real terms than in 1994/1995. Passenger kilometres rose by 19 per cent and freight by 30 per cent.

Inducing competition on Ireland's railways might be more difficult than in Britain given the smaller size of the Irish market and the unique Irish track gauge. New Zealand Railways were privatised as a single entity and their protections were withdrawn. It changed from a loss making government department with 22,000 staff to a profitable company with a staff of 4,000 but carrying more freight (Milne, 1996). Tackling rent-seeking by Irish railways offers both the benefits of increased productivity within the sector itself and ending the rail veto over the development of a competing independent bus sector in Ireland.

Railway shareholders and management in the early-1930s successfully lobbied government against the development of competitive road transport for both passengers and freight. The power of railway management and employees continues almost 70 years later to prevent the growth of independent bus services. The exercise of that power in the 1930s in eliminating over 1,500 road transport rival services is remarkable. That power persists 70 years later in the subsidisation of railways for over half their costs and the preference of governments for heavily subsidised railway investments over bus deregulation. The success of taxi licence holders in resisting new entrants is also an example of regulatory capture. On the other hand, Ireland has had outstanding success in airline and road freight deregulation. These experiences underline the wisdom of Baumol in his American Economics Association presidential address. Barriers to entry, such as regulators are long inclined to impose, should start with a heavy presumption against their adoption.

---

[1] For proposals to deregulate the sector see Fingleton (1997).

References and Further Reading

Barrett, Sean D, "Peripheral Market Entry, Product Differentiation, Supplier Rents and Sustainability in the Deregulated European Aviation Market: a Case Study" *Journal of Air Transport Management* (1999) Vol. 5 (1).

Barrett, Sean D, *Airports for Sale: the Case for Competition* (London: Adam Smith Institute) 1984.

Barrett, Sean D, *Transport Policy in Ireland* (Dublin: Irish Management Institute) 1982.

Baumol, W J, "Contestable Markets: An Uprising in the Theory of Industrial Structure" *American Economic Review* (March 1983) Vol. 73 (1).

Civil Aviation Authority, *Competition on the Main Domestic Trunk Routes* Paper 510 (Cheltenham: CAA) 1987.

Daly, M, *Industrial Development and Irish National Identity, 1922-1939* (Dublin: Gill and Macmillan) 1982.

Demsetz, H, "Why Regulate Utilities?" *Journal of Law and Economics* (April 1968).

Fanning, R, "Economists and Governments: Ireland 1922-52" in A E Murphy (ed.), *Economists and the Irish Economy* (Dublin: Irish Academic Press) 1985.

Fingleton, J, "The Dublin Taxi Market: Regulate or Stay Queuing?" *Mimeo* Department of Economics, Trinity College Dublin (1997).

Government of Ireland, *Green Paper on Transport Policy* (Dublin: Stationery Office) 1985.

Kennedy, D, "Aer Lingus" in R Nelson & D Clutterbuck (eds), *Turnaround: How Twenty Well-known Companies Came Back from the Brink* (place of publication: Mercury Business Books) 1988.

Manning, M & M McDowell, *Electricity Supply in Ireland: the History of the ESB* (Dublin: Gill and Macmillan) 1985.

Milne, S, *New Zealand Transport Reforms* Chartered Institute of Transport International Paper (April 1996).

National Prices Commission, *CIE Rates and Fares* Occasional Paper 4 (Dublin: Stationery Office) 1972.

Oireachtas Joint Committee on State-Sponsored Bodies, *Report on Iarnród Eireann.* (Dublin: Stationery Office) 1995.

Share, B, *The Flight of the Iolar: the Aer Lingus Experience 1936-8* (Dublin: Gill and Macmillan) 1988.

Smith, A, *The Wealth of Nations*, Book 1, Chapter 7 (Oxford: Clarendon Press) 1776.

Chapter 7
Transport, Logistics and the Environment

Kevin Hannigan and John Mangan
Irish Management Institute

and
James Cunningham
National University of Ireland, Galway

7.1 INTRODUCTION: THE ENVIRONMENTAL CHALLENGE

> *When the history of the twentieth century is finally written, the single most important social movement of the period will be judged to be environmentalism.*[1]

The quality of the environment we inhabit has been deteriorating rapidly. At a global level, the greenhouse effect and the depletion of the ozone layer represent major threats to the continued viability of the earth's ecosystem. At national and local level, issues such as the quality of air, noise, water pollution and waste disposal are increasingly important. A series of catastrophic environmental events during the 1980s – Bhopal, Sandoz, Chernobyl and Exxon Valdez – captured public attention and pushed governments to assuage popular anxiety through reassuring rhetoric and intergovernmental declarations. Eventually, by the beginning of the 1990s, governments began developing national responses for the protection of the environment.

The challenge facing everyone, and particularly business, is enormous. The natural environment supplies many of the raw materials required for modern living. However, the availability of these natural inputs is coming under threat, with a consequent undermining of the quality of life. Just as ensuring the free flow of goods throughout a country is an integral element of national competitiveness, minimising the environmental damage of the various modes of transport is vital to ensuring that the standard of living rises as a result of gains in competitiveness. The challenge for policy makers and business is to strike a balance between ensuring the short and medium-term competitiveness of the national economy and its firms on the one hand and the conservation of the natural environment on the other.

Sustainable development represents an important approach to resolving this dichotomy. Sustainable development is defined as meeting the needs of the present generation without compromising the ability of future generations

---

[1] Ramphal (1987).

to meet their own needs. Economic systems are challenged to meet the sustainability criterion as society continues to increase consumption. Transport policy makers include the sustainability issue in their decision-making processes, whilst attempting not to compromise economic competitiveness. The development of sustainable transport systems requires society to change its travel patterns. This requires a shift in mindset among transport users. The response from government takes many forms including support for research activity regarding transport, capital investment, taxation, restrictions on the use of some transport modes, and the subsidisation of environmentally friendly modes.

This chapter provides an overview of the interaction between the environment and both transport and logistics systems. It describes the ways in which various modes of transport impact on the environment and suggests ways in which the damage caused may be reduced. A brief review of policy initiatives in this area is provided. The efficient use of transport is one important way in which the impact can be reduced without impacting on competitiveness at either the level of the firm or the economy. Logistics has a major role to play in this respect. The chapter also discusses the development of reverse logistics, Total Quality Environmental Management (TQEM) and green supply chains in recent years. These practices involve the return of used containers for reuse and measures to ensure that the firm in question, and firms with which it has trading relationships, follow best practice in relation to the environment. Whilst this is often commercially unattractive in the short run, the likelihood of an increasingly restrictive regulatory regime means that achieving these objectives professionally is potentially one of the major growth areas for logistics professionals in the next century.

7.2 TRANSPORT TRENDS AND THE ENVIRONMENT

From the mid-1970s to the mid-1990s, within the OECD countries, the car fleet trebled, passenger car traffic doubled, road freight traffic doubled, passenger railway traffic increased by 20 per cent, railway freight traffic decreased by 10 per cent, and air traffic was multiplied by four.[2] These are staggering statistics and point to both dramatic growth and, in particular, a shift from the more environmentally friendly rail mode to the less environmentally friendly road mode. Transport is responsible for over 25 per cent of world energy consumption and forms the most rapidly growing sector of energy use – it is likely that these figures will double over the next 25 years. The industrialised countries will contribute the majority of this figure for the next two decades, but then it is likely that the newly emerging economies of the Asian Pacific region, Eastern Europe and the CIS will take over.

---

[2] Alexandre, A, "The Need to Reconcile Transport and the Environment" *Global Transport* (Spring 1995).

The negative external effects ('externalities'[3]) of transport include air pollution, noise, vibration effects (damaging roads, houses, etc.) accidents, congestion, use of scarce land and other resources, and social exclusion (new road developments, for example, dividing communities). In Japan, for example, expressways in the vicinity of Tokyo are so congested that Toyota uses coastal ships to deliver cars to its dealers!

Various forms of air pollution result from transport activity. Carbon monoxide (CO) results from the incomplete combustion of fuels, while nitrogen oxides (NO_x) are produced in internal combustion engines. Both CO and NO_x can affect the balance of the natural greenhouse gases which regulate the earth's temperature, thus leading to global warming (i.e. the greenhouse effect). Sulphur oxides SO_x are produced from the oxidation of fuels such as oil, and both NO_x and SO_x can lead to acid rain. Incomplete combustion of gasoline can result in emissions of various hydrocarbons including, for example, benzopyrene, a notorious carcinogen (cancer causing agent).

Road Transport

Road transport, in the form of cars, buses, heavy goods vehicles (HGVs) and light goods vehicles (LGVs), is the most popular mode of transport. A growing economy has resulted in more vehicular traffic, increased pollution levels and congestion on the Irish road network. However, while some general trends can be identified, the scale and diversity of road transport means that a range of solutions are required, depending on the type of road, the road user and the root cause of the increase in usage. For example, the increase in house prices in Dublin has given an impetus to the growth of commuter belts. Many commuters use car transport, as there is no other equally convenient mode of transport available locally.

Additional roads have been seen as the obvious solution to these problems. However, the notion of sustainable transport development must be at the core of any such plans. In essence this means justifying the need for road development, instead of some alternative development or reform, and outlining what impact such an expansion would have on the natural environment. It also means that a holistic view of the problem must be adopted. In other words, it is seldom adequate to deal with traffic pollution simply by attempting to reduce the amount of traffic without addressing the underlying factors that may be contributing to the problem. This often means reviewing economic incentives and reforming planning practices.

Governments can help to internalise the external costs of car usage by imposing congestion taxes on entering urban centres, taxing company car parking spaces, introducing tolls on primary roads, increasing the benefit in kind on company cars and by raising the road tax on cars over a certain cubic capac-

---

[3] Transport externalities are discussed by Harry McGeehan in Chapter 4; Table 4.1 in that chapter quantifies the externalities associated with each transport mode.

ity. However, probably the most important way to encourage car users to use other modes of transport would be through the planning and provision of other modes. Improvements in car technology can also contribute to a better environmental performance.

Road Freight and the Impact of Logistics

Road freight has grown in line with, if not ahead of, gross domestic product in most European countries, including Ireland. Part of this growth in road freight reflects the transfer of goods from the rail and water modes to road. Growth in road freight obviously also results from increased manufacturing and other economic activity. In addition increased adoption of various logistics practices, in particular just-in-time (JIT) inventory management, has resulted in smaller, but much more frequent loads travelling by road. Indeed some manufacturers actually use the road mode as a mobile production line for adding value to their products! For example some food producers delay goods labelling until product is in transit so as to extend product shelf life. It was shown in Chapter 2 that transport costs as a proportion of the value of goods being transported have fallen. Deregulation, technology improvements and efficiency gains have made transport much more cost effective from the perspective of the shipper. Another driver of increased road freight transportation is the increased trend towards reverse logistics, discussed further later in this chapter. All of these developments then have led to substantial increases in road freight transportation.

The extant manufacturing and retailing models could however be radically altered in the future if there is increased internalisation of the various externalities that result from road freight transportation. This is particularly pertinent in the Irish context given the focus of many Irish businesses and their practice of serving European customer's needs from an Irish base, with a heavy dependence on road freight transportation.

Interestingly, research has shown that it is quite difficult to quantify at a macro level the indirect costs of traffic congestion to the efficiency of logistical operations. The problem is twofold, firstly the difficulty associated with isolating pertinent costs at the micro scale, and then generalising them at the macro scale (McKinnon, 1999).

The introduction of environmental regulations can cause unintended problems. For example, the Swiss government imposed a limit of 28 tonnes for HGVs, compared to the normal European limits of 40 to 44 tonnes, to protect the environment of the Alpine region.[4] This limit has created serious problems for logistics providers and has resulted in increased transit traffic in Austria and France. This clearly shows that increased environmental awareness can impact logistics systems. The economic consequences of Swiss policy percolate across Europe because of the higher transport costs that result from diver-

---

[4] Linkline, Newsletter of the Chartered Institute of Transport in Ireland (March 1998).

sion or from having to drive across Switzerland with half empty trucks. A resolution to these issues is however being negotiated between the European Commission and the Swiss government.

Strict environmental emission controls in relation to NO_x and CO_2 have been introduced over the last number of years for heavy goods vehicles (HGVs). In order to improve the fuel consumption of HGVs advances have been made in aerodynamics, use of lighter construction material for body parts, improvements to thermal and mechanical efficiencies, improved air suspension and the use of electronics to assist vehicle operations.

Light goods vehicles (LGVs) are ubiquitous in urban areas; typically an LGV can have five or six stops per mile. In order to reduce air and noise pollution and the congestion experienced in urban areas, some cities and towns have reduced the access of LGVs to early in the morning and late at night. In addition, local authorities and corporations have provided special loading bays for LGVs in order to reduce traffic congestion. Some advances have also been made in relation to LGVs in areas such as combustion systems, electronic engine management, vehicle weight and payload flexibility.

Public Bus Transport

One of the main advantages of bus transport is its carrying capacity, particularly for urban use at peak times. The use of a single bus in an urban area has the capacity to carry the equivalent of 60 car passengers. However, the high frequency of stops requires the bus to consume more fuel, which in turn increases air and noise emissions. To improve the operational efficiency, environmental performance and energy efficiency of urban buses, improvements have been made in their operating conditions, such as the introduction of special bus lanes. A number of EU sponsored initiatives through the ENTRANCE project have also been undertaken to experiment with alternative fuels and silencer technology to improve the environmental performance of the bus. In Ireland, CIE operates the public bus transport service through two subsidiaries, namely Bus Éireann and Dublin Bus. Some of the urban bus fleet operated by the two subsidiaries are over fifteen years old. EU financial support has facilitated the purchase of new bus fleets for Cork, Galway, Limerick and Waterford. These new buses have a higher capacity for passengers (standing and sitting), reduced levels of noise and air pollution, and better fuel consumption due to the design of the bus and the provision of bus lanes, which improve their operational efficiency and consequently their environmental performance.

Railways

Rail transport is, comparatively speaking, the most environmentally friendly mode of transport. Its advantages stem from low land take, low levels of pollution and effectiveness on long distance routes between high-density population centres. Investment in railways has generally been concentrated on routes where the volume of traffic justifies the large capital outlay. Despite its benefits, there has been a decline in rail freight transportation in Ireland over the last twenty years. Road transport offers greater flexibility and is often less costly for the user.

Air Transport

Air transport has varying impacts upon the environment. It has been suggested that its most negative impacts result not from aircraft movements *per se*, but from the resulting road traffic that is attracted to airports! Reducing aircraft noise (by, for example, hushkitting aircraft, enforcing nighttime operating bans at certain airports, etc.) is an issue of current interest in the sector.

The International Air Transport Association (IATA) and the European Regional Airlines Association have argued that further environmental restraints on airline operators would shackle the development of air transport and curtail the movement of goods and people in the business and leisure sectors. In an effort to prevent further restrictions, individual airline companies have responded variously, sometimes in a somewhat esoteric fashion, by attempting to reduce the environmental damage of air transportation. For example, SAS has a separate annual report for its environmental activities.

Maritime Transport

Similar to air transport, maritime transport is comparatively environmentally friendly, in that it allows large volumes of goods (and people) to be transported over long distances without serious environmental effects. Issues which do arise in the sector include the risk of oil spillages if accidents occur, disposal of ships waste, noise pollution from vessel loading and unloading at ports, etc. As with airports, significant road traffic congestion and pollution can result from road traffic movements in the vicinity of ports.

7.3 STRATEGIES TO REDUCE THE ENVIRONMENTAL EFFECTS OF TRANSPORT

Demand for transport has grown rapidly but, as shown in Chapter 4, market solutions are unlikely to produce the optimum outcome. As a result, governments have intervened in transport operations for many reasons, one of the most important currently being to alleviate pollution. According to the sustainable development criterion, the main policy thrust of transport planners and users needs to focus on striking a balance between development of the earth's resources to improve living conditions and the conservation of the natural environment for future generations.

There are a number of strategies that policy makers can pursue to reduce the environmental damage caused by transport. The first falls under the heading of *regulation* of the industry. This means imposing rigorous air and noise emission standards on all modes of transport. In addition, with the growth of population in urban areas in particular, this may also require regulations that are designed to contain the demand for transport. Such regulations stimulate further technological innovations among transport industry participants and open up new competitive opportunities. Another element of regulation is the strict enforcement of transport legislation regarding the inspection, maintenance and safety levels of modes of transport. This should be co-ordinated across national and local authorities or, alternatively, the responsibility given to one single agency.

The second element of an effective environmentally sustainable transport strategy includes *incentives* for stakeholders to alter their travel patterns or to bring new viable products and services to the market. This means offering tax incentives for environmentally friendly modes and taxing the usage of transport in particular areas at certain times. In addition, it means government support for positive discrimination towards the promotion and usage of environmentally friendly fuels and vehicles. The promotion of public transport and the development of financial incentives for users should increase its usage, thereby making future investment more attractive for private and public transport providers.

The final element of an effective and environmentally sustainable transport policy is one of *sustainable planning*. This means better traffic management in certain areas with priority given to public transport services where possible. This requires better land use as a result of a rigorous planning process, resulting in the development of sustainable transport to meet the current and future needs of a community. New development in towns and cities should minimise the need for travel and the location of key travel generating land uses should be designed so as to improve their accessibility to clean and environmentally efficient modes of transport.

Green Transport Planning (GTP) is the initiative being used by governments, particularly in the EU, to encourage industry to improve their environmental performance regarding transport and is aimed at reducing car use for travel to work and for travel on business. Usually a green transport plan for a company includes a package of practical measures to encourage staff. This may include developing a plan specific to a firm's location and may include, for example, setting up a car pool scheme, providing cycle facilities, facilitating flexible working hours and tele-working, restricting car parking and negotiating discount deals with local transport providers. The aim of a green transport plan is to pass on real benefits to the firm, employees, local communities and other stakeholders. The UK government will have green transport plans in place for all key government department buildings by March 2000. This concept of a GTP was first introduced in the USA over a decade ago as part of industry's response to its environmental responsibilities.

Environmental impact statements for new industrial and office developments are now taking greater account of the road traffic impacts of these developments. A good example of this was the new ferry terminal and linkspan development at Dún Laoghaire Harbour in the mid 1990s for the HSS fast ferry. Perhaps the single greatest issue which had to be taken account of in this development was the road freight traffic impact of the development on the local hinterland.

Business Strategies

Usually firms react to environmental issues when more restrictive legislation is enacted by the national government – this is the traditional approach to environmental management. Compliance with the restrictive legislation is usually at the operational level of the firm and it takes some time before it becomes a strategic issue. The new legislative approach currently being favoured by international and national regulators is voluntary agreements. Voluntary agreements are commitments from industrial sectors and firms to improve their environmental performance and can cover a large variety of different arrangements. Voluntary agreements provide firms in an industry with discretionary powers in target setting and in monitoring and compliance. Responding to the environmental challenges facing the firm, management needs to take the long-term perspective and accept the necessary financial investment. This requires an understanding of the environmental issues facing the firm. In addition, the firm has to incorporate environmental issues into its corporate planning, thus making it an integral element of its strategic planning capability. By institutionalising these issues the firm can achieve environmental objectives that exceed the targets required by legislation, which then can be used to enhance the firm's public standing. Table 7.1 sets out some issues a firm should examine when developing a strategic response to the environmental challenge.

Table 7.1: Strategic issues in responding to the environmental challenge

- Product design focuses on the associated waste and other environmental problems.
- New product development attempts to minimise adverse environmental effects.
- Use alternative sources of raw material by minimising inputs and harmful contents.
- Completion of environmental audits.
- Ensure environmental considerations pervade the internal planning procedures.
- Examine methods of improving the environmental performance of suppliers and third parties.
- Develop employee training programmes to alter the culture of the firm regarding waste and the environment.
- Reduce the amount of primary and secondary packaging required for the products.
- Buy in technologies and change working methods to reduce pollution.

Source: Bennett (1999)

The barriers to adopting environmental initiatives however include:

- The belief that the costs incurred in developing environmentally friendly products and introducing new technologies could bankrupt the firm and return poor competitive success.
- The existing firm structure may be unsuitable for the new work practices and the incorporation of environmental issues into its operations.
- Some key decision-makers and section leaders don't have any interest in environmental issues.
- A belief may pervade the firm that incorporating environmental issues will reduce the productivity levels, increase operating costs and reduce the overall consumption of the firm's goods, and therefore, the size of the firm's market.
- Market forces may drive the firm to pursue profit at the expense of the environment.

Incorporating the environmental issues into the firm's corporate strategy yield a number of benefits:

- improved materials efficiency;
- better quality of outputs;
- enhanced employee commitment;
- more positive images;
- less risk of government interference;
- better relations with local communities.

The difficulty is getting environmental issues into the boardroom and onto the corporate strategy agenda. Once this is achieved the problem is keeping it on the corporate agenda on a continual basis.

7.4 REVERSE LOGISTICS – CLOSING THE LOOP

Previous sections of this chapter have dealt with the role of logistics in the context of the development of environmentally sustainable transport operations. However, it is clear that the issue of sustainability cannot be dealt with in isolation. As a result, other parts of the firm's activities will require reform if environmental requirements are to be met. The focus of environmental legislation is to place 'cradle to grave' responsibilities on businesses for products and processes. This means the business must evaluate the product life cycle from raw material sources to final disposal. The logistics discipline has a critical role in limiting environmental damage caused by waste and is an area where logistics operators can provide real added value for their clients, be innovative in the logistical solutions they provide, and ensure client compliance regarding packaging waste.

Reverse logistics refers to the logistics management skills and activities involved in reducing, managing, and disposing of hazardous or non-hazardous waste that results from packaging and products (Kroom and Vrijens, 1995). In essence this is reversing the flow of information and goods from the normal. This relatively new area in logistics is a response to pressures from society and government that business has to be proactive regarding recycling and reuse of products and materials.

Reverse logistics focuses on two main areas, namely returnable containers (Returnable Transit Packaging) and physical distribution. Primary packaging of products is essential for effective food and product safety. The concern of logistics is usually focused on secondary and tertiary packaging. Secondary packaging is the packaging material used for transporting the products and usually consists of one way packaging material, normally cardboard boxes. The advent of the returnable container means the packaging can be used more than once. Returnable containers consist of plastic containers, pallets, or slipsheets. These containers can be used in an industry setting and are also used for household waste collection systems. An example is Musgraves who operate a chilled distribution system for fresh, frozen and chilled products and who operate a reverse logistics operation. These chilled products are delivered daily to the grocery stores throughout Ireland in returnable containers. The containers are collected the day after and are washed and cleaned.

There are three types of return logistic systems, namely switch pool systems, systems with return logistics, and systems without return logistics. Switch pool systems consist of every participant having their own allotment of containers, for which they are responsible. Cleaning, controlling, maintenance and storage of containers are the responsibility of each pool participant, including both senders and receivers of goods using returnable containers. Systems with return logistics mean that an agency is responsible for the return of containers after the recipient has emptied them. They are then stored on site until a number have accumulated for cost effective collection. The system without return logistics is where the containers are owned by a central agency and the sender rents the containers from the agency. The sender is responsible for the associated maintenance of the system, including the return logistics. In essence the sender is decreasing its fixed costs by renting varying numbers of containers depending on demand.

The benefits to the environment are clear, but there are commercial implications for the business. The sender of returnable containers will have a higher service fee compared to cardboard boxes. However, this may change if more users are brought into the system, thereby allocating the costs among a number of participants. Another disadvantage is that the sender or other participants have to invest heavily in setting up the system in terms of purchasing the returnable containers and in the maintenance of the system. In addition some containers will leak out of the system through misuse, such as grocery stores using them to prop up display units. However, there are benefits such as back loads for delivery trucks, greater flexibility regarding delivery times, elimination of shrink wrapping and cardboard boxes, and better handling of the product.

A downside to reverse logistics however is the possibility of increased road traffic congestion as a result of increased volumes of freight (in this instance recycled packaging, etc.). Anderson *et al.* (1999), for example, calculated that the packaging waste regulations introduced by the UK government in 1997 will lead to a 14 per cent increase in freight vehicle kilometres attributable to packaging waste.

7.5 GREEN SUPPLY CHAINS

Developing an environmental management system is a constructive way to integrate corporate objectives into the operational activities of the firm. An effective environmental management system is one where its processes are integrated fully into all aspects of the supply chain. Hence the notion of the green supply chain is becoming popular among many multinational firms in order to meet their diverse environmental responsibilities in various countries. To this end, Total Quality Environmental Management (TQEM) has been developed as a response to the need to develop a green supply chain. Building on existing Total Quality Management (TQM) techniques, environmental considerations focus on environmentally friendly practices for purchasing and materials management. The objective of a TQEM is to ensure zero defects in products produced in addition to having zero impact on the environment. TQEM needs the whole firm to be involved and it must pervade into all of its operations. Before a firm attempts to 'green' its supply chain, the initial environmental focus begins with attempts to reduce waste and emissions. The development of this approach is an attempt to deal with the sustainability issue at an industry and firm level.

In developing a green supply chain the firm should work with suppliers who are willing to improve their environmental performance. The firm, through a partnership approach, attempts to influence suppliers' environmental performance. This may include encouraging suppliers to use less harmful components in their end products, deal with waste arising on site in a proper manner, and make alterations to its operations to reduce environment damage. In addition, the firm should examine its own environmental performance and co-ordinate any changes in operations with its suppliers to reduce environmental damage. The firm should carry out a life cycle analysis of all the material it uses to produce the product. This life cycle analysis encompasses a 'cradle to grave' assessment. This involves examining all the inflows and outflows of products used to make the product, the resultant byproducts from the production process, the potential for recycling byproducts, and the actual product once its has completed its life. The basis for supplier process improvements is trust between the firm and the suppliers. This may not be forthcoming among all suppliers and therefore some firms use the enacted government legislation as a trigger to encourage supplier process improvements. Enarsson (1998), who conducted research on environmental management within Swedish companies, noted that increasingly firms are insisting on higher environmental standards from their suppliers. One of the key issues is, of course, the public perception of the firm. A related scenario arises, for instance, in the increasing tendency among some investors to only invest in certain 'ethical' stocks.

7.6 CONCLUSION

The importance of considering the impact of the environment arises for two reasons. Firstly, the rapid growth of the economy and the importance of international trade and competitiveness have resulted in a rapid rise in the volume of traffic. In addition, for a variety of reasons, there has been a general move towards the less environmentally friendly modes of transport. Secondly, the growth and influence of environmental lobby groups and consumer pressure groups has provided an impetus to stricter regulation and opportunities for product differentiation on the basis of environmental issues.

Governmental initiatives to solve the problems of congestion and overcome environmental damage are becoming increasingly important. This chapter shows that the solution to many of the environmental problems associated with transport requires the provision of new infrastructure and new ways of operating to ensure that new and existing facilities are used efficiently while reducing pollution. The tendency has been for firms to act only when faced with restrictions with which they must comply. This is understandable since compliance often imposes costs. However, it is preferable if firms act proactively. This is the essence of sustainable growth in the transport system. The role for logistics is to provide solutions to the problems this may cause, most importantly through designing more efficient practices to alleviate any costs that may arise.

References and Further Reading

Alexandre, A, "The Need to Reconcile Transport and the Environment" *Global Transport* (Spring 1995).

Anderson, S, M Browne & J Allen, "Logistics Implications of the UK Packaging Waste Regulations" *International Journal of Logistics: Research and Applications* (1999) Vol. 2, 2, pp. 129-145.

Azzone, G & U Bertele, "Exploiting Green Strategies for Competitive Advantage" *Long Range Planning* (1994) Vol. 17, 6, pp. 69-81.

Bennett, R *Corporate Strategy* (London: Financial Times/Pitman Publishing) 2nd edition 1999 pp.280-293.

Department of Transport, *White Paper on Transport* (London: HMSO) 1998.

Enarsson, L, "Evaluation of Suppliers. How to Consider the Environment" *International Journal of Physical Distribution and Logistics Management* (1998) Vol. 28, 1, pp. 5-17.

Guss, L, *Packaging is Marketing* (New York: American Management Association) New York, 1967 p.12.

Jahre, M, "Household Waste Collection as a Reverse Channel: A theoretical Perspective" *International Journal of Physical Distribution and Logistics Management* (1995) Vol 25, 2, pp39-55.

Kimble, J, *Biology* (London: Addison Wesley) 5th edition, 1983.

Kroom, L & G Vrijens, "Returnable Containers: An Example of Reverse Logistics" *International Journal of Physical Distribution and Logistics Management* (1995) Vol. 25, 2, pp. 56-68.

Linkline, Newsletter of the Chartered Institute of Transport in Ireland (March 1998).

McKinnon, A, "The Effect of Traffic Congestion on the Efficiency of Logistical Operations" *International Journal of Logistics: Research and Applications* (1999) Vol 2, 2, pp. 111-128.

Murphy, P R, R F Poist & C D Braunschweig, "Role and Relevance of Logistics to Corporate Environmentalism: An empirical assessment" *International Journal of Physical Distribution and Logistics Management* (1995) Vol. 25, 2, 5-19.

Prendergast, G & P Leyland, "Packaging, Marketing. Logistics and the Environment: Are There Trade-Offs" *International Journal of Physical Distribution and Logistics Management* (1996) Vol 26, 6, pp. 60-72.

Ramphal, S S, "The Environment and Sustainable Development" *Journal of the Royal Society of Arts* (1987) 135 pp. 879-909.

Transport Policy Research Institute, University College Dublin "Energy Opportunities for Transport in Ireland" Report to the Irish Energy Centre (1996).

Walton, S V, R B Handfield & S A Melnyk, "The Green Supply Chain: Integrating Suppliers into Environmental Management Processes" *International Journal of Purchasing and Materials Management* (Spring 1998) pp. 2-11.

Chapter 8
Air Transport

Aisling Reynolds-Feighan
University College Dublin

8.1 INTRODUCTION

This chapter explores the structure and operation of the air transport industry
in Ireland, focusing heavily on the air freight sector. In the first section of the
chapter, a brief overview of Irish air transport is presented and the recent performance of the sector is linked to the economic performance of the national
economy. Passenger services are reviewed in the context of the changing nature and structure of European air transport regulations. The regulatory environment is also reviewed. The air freight sector is then examined and the Irish
performance is compared and contrasted with the European and global experience. Finally, the future prospects and problems for the sector are sketched.

8.2 OVERVIEW OF IRISH AIR TRANSPORT

The Republic of Ireland has experienced very high growth rates in air traffic in
the period from 1993 to 1999, reflecting the high levels of economic growth in
the economy generally. The Republic is served by three State-owned airports,
operated by Aer Rianta (Dublin, Cork and Shannon) and six privately owned
and operated regional airports (Knock, Kerry County Airport (Farranfore),
Waterford Regional Airport, Donegal Airport (Carrickfin), Sligo Regional
Airport and Galway Airport). Northern Ireland has a network of four airports
serving international scheduled traffic. These are Belfast Aldergrove Airport,
Belfast City Airport, Eglinton Airport in County Derry and Enniskillen, County
Fermanagh. The Republic currently has five registered carriers, the largest of
which, Aer Lingus, is currently 100 per cent owned by the State. In Table 8.1
the operations of Irish and UK carriers to, from and within their home states
are detailed. These data are taken from the UK Civil Aviation Authority and
pertain to December 1997.

Table 8.1: Details on the operations of Irish and UK airlines to/from and within their home state

Carrier & Code		International				Domestic				Total			
		Routes		*Flights*		*Routes*		*Flights*		*Routes*		*Flights*	
		Dec 92	Dec 97	Dec 92	Dec 97	Dec 92	Dec 97	Dec 92	Dec 97	Dec 92	Dec 97	Dec 92	Dec 97
Irish Republic													
Aer Lingus	EI	19	21	1464	1817	6	5	433	411	25	26	1897	2228
Ryanair	FR	6	15	446	1474					6	15	446	1474
Cityjet	WX		2		259					0	2	0	259
Ireland Airways	2E						1		31	0	1	0	31
Aer Arann	RE					4		182		4	0	182	0
Total		**25**	**38**	**1910**	**3550**	**10**	**6**	**615**	**442**	**35**	**44**	**2525**	**3992**
UK													
British Airways	BA	65	55	4480	5325	27	26	2649	3572	92	81	7129	8897
British Regional	JE		9		389		40		2053	0	49	0	2442
CityFlyer	FD	2	9	174	858	2	4	167	462	4	13	341	1320
Maersk Air	VB		6		290		2		169	0	8	0	459
GB Airways	GT		7		239	2		28		3	7	37	239
Brymon Airways	BC					16		628		25	0	1050	0
Dan-Air	DA					8		426		21	0	1187	0
Air UK	UK		22		2331	20	10	1179	1055	39	32	2175	3386
British Midland	BD		19		1628	11	14	1357	1412	21	33	2598	3040
Jersey European	JY		1		30	18	17	876	1364	20	18	957	1394
Gill Airways	9C		3		186	5	7	281	497	6	10	290	683
Aurigny Air Services	GR		2		61	4	4	626	600	6	6	694	661
EasyJet	U2		5		266		4		317	0	9	0	583
Manx Airlines	JE		2		79	13	9	660	460	19	11	847	539
Debonair	2G		7		332					0	7	0	332
Loganair	LC					30	16	1235	322	32	16	1279	322
Business Air	II		1		26	4	6	238	266	5	7	261	292
Suckling Airways	CB		3		141	1	2	46	70	2	5	92	211
AB Airlines	7L		2		120					0	2	0	120
Emerald Airways	G3						1		106	0	1	0	106
European Airways	L8						3		85	0	3	0	85
Isles of Scilly Skybus	5Y						1		77	0	1	0	77
Interline Aviation	5W						1		73	0	1	0	73
Monarch	ZB		6		69					4	6	30	69
British International	BS					1	1	51	59	1	1	51	59
Euroscot Express	MY						3		47	0	3	0	47
Love Air	4J		1		35					0	1	0	35
Virgin Atlantic	VS		1		34					0	1	0	34
Britannia	BY					1		56		1	0	56	0
Air Corbiere	NL					6		36		6	0	36	0
Total		138	161	8571	12439	169	171	10537	13066	307	332	19108	25505

Source: UK Civil Aviation Authority (1998)

As with most other European countries, a very high proportion of Irish air passenger and air freight traffic is international (94.32 per cent and 100 per cent respectively in 1997), reflecting the small size of the country and the cost advantages of air transport over longer distances.

8.3 AIR PASSENGER MARKETS

Irish air passenger traffic grew at an average annual rate of 13.9 per cent over the five years from 1993 to 1998. Table 8.2 gives passenger traffic statistics for the three Aer Rianta airports and for the regional airports collectively for the period 1991-1998. Traffic growth at Dublin and Cork has averaged 13.5 per cent and 13.1 per cent per annum over the 1993-1998 period. The average annual growth rate for Shannon over the same period was 4.8 per cent. This lower growth rate reflects a number of developments, including the revision in some transatlantic routings by Aer Lingus and the extension of the runway at Farranfore (Kerry County Airport) in 1994 to facilitate jet services and en-courage charter and other traffic directly into the Kerry region, the second biggest tourist destination in the Republic.

Table 8.2: Passenger traffic trends at Irish airports, 1991-1998

Direct Passenger Movements by Air from and to Ireland (Republic), ('000) (excluding transit passengers)					
Year	**Dublin**	**Cork**	**Shannon**	**Regional Airports**	**Overall Total**
1991	4,575	471	936	194	6,176
1992	5,072	511	1,106	140	6,829
1993	5,266	553	1,157	123	7,099
1994	6,395	627	1,090	165	8,277
1995	7,407	773	1,175	205	9,560
1996	8,437	915	1,291	222	10,865
1997	9,570	976	1,286	262	12,094
1998	10,787	1,066	1,447	315	13,615

Source: Central Statistics Office, *Statistical Bulletin* (June 1999) p. 398.

The Irish and UK governments decided to liberalise cross-channel air trans-port operations in 1986, by allowing new entrants on a limited number of cross-channel routes. This had a significant positive impact on air passenger traffic mainly because of lower fares. Irish air transport is now governed by Euro-pean regulations, which changed significantly in 1993. In the next sections these changes are set out in detail.

8.4 THE EUROPEAN REGULATORY ENVIRONMENT

The 'First Package' of air transport liberalisation measures of 1987 and 'Second Package' of 1989, represented modest moves to liberalisation and came in the wake of European Court of Justice rulings which applied for the first time, articles 85 and 86 of the Treaty of Rome (relating to antitrust-type restrictions) to air transport.[1] The first two packages were related only to scheduled passenger services. The Second Package contained limited liberalisation of passenger fares, full cargo pricing freedom, capacity restrictions (60/40) and some fifth freedom rights and public service obligations.

The EU took substantial steps towards liberalising the internal European air transport market in July 1992 with the adoption of Council Regulations No. L240, the so-called 'Third Package' relating to several key aspects of the industry's operation including access for community air carriers to intra-community air routes, licensing and fares. The adoption of the Third Package came at a time of crisis for the airline industry, with the sector in Europe and elsewhere coming to terms with the effects of the Gulf War and subsequent recession. The Third Package applied to the twelve Member States from 1 January 1993, and also to Norway and Sweden from mid-1993, because of the unusual situation of co-operation between the three Scandinavian countries in international aviation. The second package of air transport liberalisation measures was adopted in Austria, Finland and Iceland on 1 January 1994 with the Third Package adopted in 1995. Switzerland has also adopted the Third Package measures. The eighteen countries covered by these regulations account for 20 per cent of the global scheduled air transport passenger market in terms of revenue passenger kilometres (RPKs) (21 per cent in terms of passengers carried) and 32 per cent of global scheduled air freight RTKs.

The Third Package removed the distinction between scheduled and non-scheduled operations in air transport although it has to be noted that the distinctions were becoming more ill-defined over time as scheduled carriers had been offering increasing numbers of charter services or setting up subsidiary charter companies. The charter carriers for their part had been offering scheduled services on a limited number of North-South intra-European routes in the early-1990s. Europe's charter industry accounted for over half of all intra-European passengers and about two-thirds of total intra-European RPKs in the ten years to 1993.[2] In the Third Package (Council Regulations No 2407/92 through 2411/92) a wide range of issues in the scheduled and non-scheduled passenger *and* cargo markets are covered: the package thus removed any regulatory distinction between passenger and freight services.

The main changes introduced under the Third Package are as follows:

- Council Regulation 2407/92 of L240 deals with common licensing arrangements and the rights of community registered carriers to operate aircraft

---

[1] For a review of the legal and political progress towards the Third Package, see Button and Swann (1992) and McGowan (1994).
[2] See *Avmark Aviation Economist* (April 1994) and Doganis (1994).

owned anywhere in the Community. The licensing regulation requires that the principal place of business and registered office be located in the State in which the carrier is registered, that the carrier carries insurance and that air transport is the main concern of the licensee. Licensed carriers are not required to own their own aircraft, but they must have at least one at their disposal. These aircraft must be registered in the State's aircraft register, although it is left to the discretion of the Member State to issue a licence to the carrier if the aircraft at their disposal are registered elsewhere in the EU.

- Council Regulation 2408/92 of L240 covers access to intra-community air routes. This includes the abolition of capacity restrictions between Member States, and the removal of restrictions concerning fifth-freedom[3] and multiple designation[4] rights along with a gradual phasing-in of cabotage[5] rights. Full cabotage was not required before April 1997. In the interim, consecutive cabotage was permitted where a carrier used less than 50 per cent of its seasonal capacity on a service on which the cabotage segment was an extension or preliminary to an interstate route. This regulation also makes provision for the imposition of public service obligations (i.e. state designated routes, subsidised if necessary, which are deemed essential for the purposes of regional economic development or for social or political purposes) and permits entry to be restricted on new routes between regional airports (these aspects are discussed in detail in Reynolds-Feighan (1995). Provision is made for Member States to establish non-discriminatory rules for distributing air traffic between airports within an airport-system (e.g. the London or Paris airport systems).

- Council Regulation No 2409/92 grants freedom for Community carriers to set air fares and rates for services, except in specific limited circumstances. In Council Regulation 2410/92, the Community competition rules are formally extended to the air transport sector while amendments to certain categories of agreements and concerted practices in the air transport sector are made in Council Regulation No 2411/92. Several of the negative outcomes associated with deregulation in the US are now subject to safeguard provisions in the European liberalisation programme (e.g. computer reservation system ownership and bias, predatory pricing practices, slot allocation issues relating to hub airport dominance).

---

[3] A fifth freedom right is the right to carry passengers and/or freight between two foreign countries on a route originating or destined for the country of registration or ownership of the carrier.

[4] Multiple designation is where multiple carriers are permitted to offer air services on an international route.

[5] Cabotage is the right of a carrier of one state to carry traffic exclusively between two points within another state. Consecutive cabotage occurs when a carrier flies between two points within another state as a preliminary or continuation of a service to the home state.

These Regulations permit carriers to significantly extend their market areas and offer substantial opportunities for greater efficiency for airlines through scale and scope economies. On the demand side, greater product differentiation will have a significant effect on traffic volumes. These Regulations will impact on the pattern of consumer demand, on carrier profitability and airline industry structure. The Public Service Obligation Route regulation has been applied in Ireland to several routes between the regional airports and Dublin, in order to guarantee continuity of air services in cyclical economic and seasonal downturns.

8.5 AIR FREIGHT MARKETS

For the past decade the volume of air freight has grown faster than air passenger volumes and this trend is expected to continue according to the major industry forecasts (e.g. International Civil Aviation Organisation, Boeing, Airbus, forecasting 6-7 per cent annual growth rates globally). The correlation between world GDP and world air freight traffic forms the basis for forecasts. Accordingly, the growth is expected to be greatest in Asian markets (i.e. intra-Asia, North America-Asia and Europe-Asia and Australasia) with international air cargo traffic continuing to expand faster than domestic air cargo traffic. Irish air freight volume has grown at an average annual rate of 12 per cent per annum since 1990, with the total volume increasing by 144 per cent in the 1990-1998 period. Because of the cyclical nature of GDP growth, air freight traffic growth is also subject to cyclical effects.

The process of physical distribution of freight has become a highly sophisticated operation with increasingly greater reliance being placed on the use of new technology to assist in the movement, storage and tracking of consignments. Transport is but one component in this logistics chain. It is most likely that the future development of air freight transport will continue to be integrated to an increasing degree with developments in logistics.

8.6 AIR FREIGHT INDUSTRY ORGANISATION

Air freight markets are difficult to delimit and analyse for a number of reasons. The air freight providers are a heterogeneous group of operators, offering different types of services and different levels of logistical expertise. There are three main categories of air freight operators.

1. **Line Haul operators** move cargo from airport to airport and rely on freight forwarders or consolidators to deal directly with customers. Line haul operators can be:

   (i) *all-cargo operators* (scheduled and non-scheduled), moving only freight in dedicated freighter/cargo aircraft (for example, Cargolux (EU) and Arrow Air (USA)). All-cargo operators offer relatively high reliability and have the capability to move large volumes over long distances.

(ii) *combination passenger and cargo operators* who use both dedicated freighter aircraft and the belly-holds in passenger aircraft to move freight (for example, Lufthansa (EU) and Air France (EU)). For the combination carriers, the cargo operations are mainly long haul, with a large amount of freight being interlined on to shorter haul feeder services. The high utilisation of long haul aircraft justifies the purchase of new aircraft for these services.

(iii) *passenger operators* who use the belly-holds in passenger aircraft. Passenger carriers have tended to view cargo as a by-product of passenger operations. They are seen to offer the lowest prices and the least reliable service. Passenger carriers move cargo in the belly-holds of passenger aircraft where it has traditionally taken second place to passenger services. Unlike passenger services, shippers do not have access to price information analogous to passenger Computer Reservation Systems (CRSs). Freight forwarders play an important role in consolidating shipments for line hauliers.

2. *Integrated/Courier/Express operators* move consignments from door-to-door, with time-definite delivery services (examples: UPS, Federal Express, TNT, DHL). Courier operators operate multi-modal networks, combining air services with extensive surface transport to meet customer demands. These courier operators offer a variety of products to shippers and supplement air services with extensive ground transport to provide time-definite delivery with continuous shipment tracking and, if necessary, logistical expertise to support '*just in time*' (JIT) inventory control strategies. In order for courier operators to be able to offer door to door next day deliveries, they require nighttime operations. In terms of aircraft requirements, they need to operate quiet, reliable aircraft with low utilisation levels (as few as two hours flying time per day in some cases). Courier operators seek to purchase a combination of new aircraft, with high capital costs and better utilisation on long haul segments, with less expensive renovated second-hand aircraft for the medium-haul operations with lower utilisations.

3. *Niche operators* operate or leverage specialised equipment or indeed expertise in order to fill extraordinary requirements (for example Heavylift (Netherlands) and Challenge Air Cargo (USA)). These operators attract business through their capabilities for handling outsize freight or special consignments, including line haul to locations with poor infrastructural facilities. For chartered freight and niche operators, the discontinuous use of aircraft makes it financially preferable to acquire freighter aircraft on a second-hand basis

8.7 AIR FREIGHT PRICING

Air freight services are sold and marketed in a number of different ways. The line haul operators sell a relatively small proportion of their cargo space directly to their customers. The greater proportion of their space is sold through general sales agents (GSAs) or freight forwarders, who negotiate with the airlines for fixed amounts of space. The agents or forwarders then sell on the freight space to customers. The line haul airlines publish their cargo tariffs as agreed at International Air Transport Association (IATA) tariff conferences. In practice, only a small percentage of customers pay these published tariffs, which can be considered as an upper-band on air cargo rates. As with passenger fares, discounting is widely applied and in the case of cargo, rates will be determined on the basis of a number of characteristics and circumstances, including the following:

- commodity type;
- volume, density and weight;
- routing;
- season;
- regularity of shipments;
- imports or exports;
- priority or speed of delivery.

Consolidated shipments, aggregated by forwarders and carried by the line-haul operators, typically travel under a single air waybill. Integrated operators offer a variety of products or services depending on (a) the weight of the consignment and (b) the speed of delivery required by the customer. Discounting is applied to these services on the basis of the volume and regularity of custom. However, because each consignment is treated as a separate piece of freight, with an individual air waybill and customs declaration, the integrated carriers provide and practice electronic tracking of individual shipments.

8.8 RECENT TRENDS IN AIR FREIGHT

In global terms, the dominant air cargo flows are in three main markets: (1) the North Atlantic (i.e. North America-Europe) (2) Europe-Far East and (3) Pacific rim. The Europe-Asia market is expected to have one of the top growth rates over the period 1996-2015. Boeing estimate that air freight on this sector will grow by 7.4 per cent per annum. Intra-Europe freight has the lowest forecast growth rate of 4.3 per cent. The international air express market is expected to grow at a tremendous rate over this period. Boeing forecasts an annual growth rate of 18 per cent which they claim will result in express services accounting for c.40 per cent of the total international cargo business by 2015; it currently accounts for 5 per cent of the total market. This mirrors the US experience, where express services accounted for 4 per cent of the US market in 1977 and with an average annual growth rate of c.25 per cent, express operators now claim close to 60 per cent of the US domestic market in 1996. It is believed that this experience in the US raised customer expectations for air freight services worldwide.

Air freight markets are shifting as the economic growth pattern of developing countries accelerates past that of already industrialised economies. The main influences or drivers behind these trends are as follows:

1. Primary influence of world economic activity (world GDP is the best single measure of global economic activity with a high correlation between changes in world GDP and changes in world air cargo RTKs).

2. Impact of the range of services in the express and small package market.

3. Inventory management techniques.

4. Deregulation and liberalisation.

5. National development programmes.

6. Stream of new air-eligible commodities.

The EU and EFTA air freight markets are dominated by the flag carriers of the Member States as are the passenger markets. Europe's air freight is carried by passenger carriers and by combination passenger-cargo carriers (such as Lufthansa and Air France). The integrated carriers have increased the size of their European operations in recent years and it has been suggested that they now perform most of the total Intra-European RTKs. Comprehensive data on the integrated carrier services and volumes at the European level are not available however.

Air trucking in European markets: Within Europe, competition from surface modes has had and will continue to have a downward impact on air freight growth rates (4-5 per cent per annum for 1997-2017). This factor along with a relatively low overall economic growth rate explain the below-average long term growth rate for air freight. 'Air trucking'[6] has been expanding at a rate of 15 per cent per annum since 1975, according to Boeing, with an estimated 7,340 frequencies per week in Europe in 1997. They suggest that the number of routes served within Europe has expanded from 38 in 1975 to 386 in 1995, including four domestic and five international Irish routes.

In 1971, international airlines through IATA introduced and adopted IATA Resolution 507b, which clearly defined the circumstances under which trucking could be undertaken. The main circumstances involved:

• the lack of available space on aircraft;

• where consignments could not be handled on aircraft operated by an airline due to the size, weight or nature of the consignments (certain commodities

---

[6] Air trucking involves the movement of air cargo by road under air waybill.

may only be shipped in freighter or all-cargo aircraft) or because the carrier refuses carriage on some other grounds;

• where the carriage by air will result in delayed transit times or in carriage not being accomplished within twelve hours of acceptance;

• where carriage by air will result in missed connections.

Today the practice of air trucking is predominantly oriented towards moving intercontinental freight traffic to gateway airports. This process is described diagrammatically in Figure 8.1.

Figure 8.1: Air trucking in the freight logistics chain

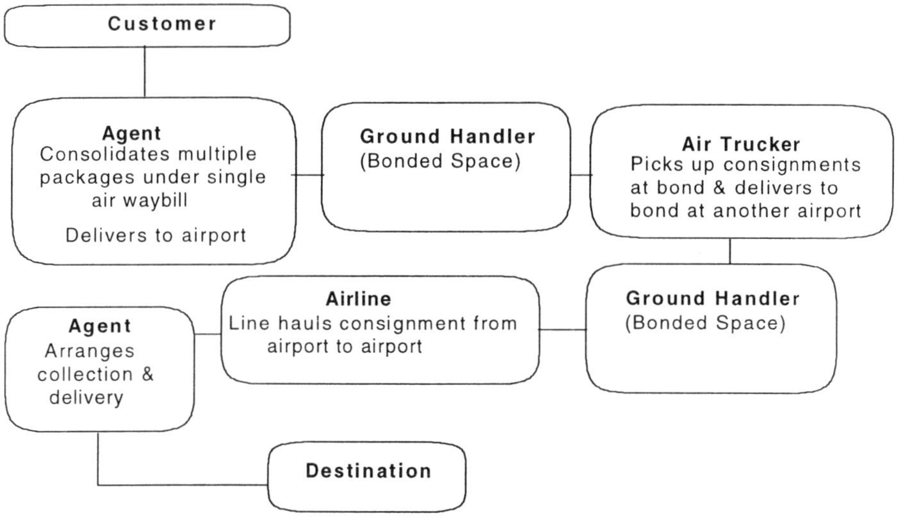

Integrated/express carrier services in Europe: As was pointed out earlier, Europe's internal air freight market has seen significant growth and development in the express sector, with many of the line haul carriers reducing or discontinuing their intra-European freight operations. Data on Europe's express market is piecemeal, of variable quality and not published or available for all of the EU states. Because this sector has experienced such rapid growth in a relatively short period of time, the lack of data makes it difficult to identify trends and key characteristics of the European sector.

In Figure 8.2, the express operator's service chain is presented in schematic form. This facilitates a comparison with the air trucking process illustrated earlier. The key advantages of the express operators service over traditional air freight services are: (i) the relatively small lapsed time between pickup and delivery, and (ii) the fact that a single company handles the package or

Figure 8.2: Freight logistics chain of express operators

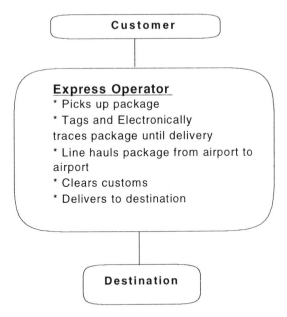

freight from pickup to delivery. Customers can purchase different services based on speed and delivery requirement.[7]

The express operator will typically provide electronic tracking of packages, with customers having access to this tracking facility. Each package/consignment is separately tagged and tracked and will be cleared through customs. Customs services in most European countries now operate electronically, so that consignments receive clearance en route to their destination airport. The customs authority can notify the operator of consignments which will be required to be cleared on the ground and this information can be forwarded to the customer via the tracking system. Because each consignment requires separate documentation and custom clearance, charges are levied individually.

8.9 THE IRISH AIR FREIGHT MARKET
In 1998, 191,505 tonnes of air freight were carried through Irish airports. This represented a 30.5 per cent increase on the 1996 volume, and a 143 per cent

---

[7] For example, TNT Express Worldwide offer next-day parcels and freight services, 2/3 day services or 4 day parcels and freight within Europe. With their worldwide services, customers can also choose different pickup and delivery options (e.g. door to door or door to airport).

increase since 1990. These rates are similar to the growth rates of total trade in the same period. Irish air freight volumes for the period 1984-1998 are illustrated in Figures 8.3 and 8.4, where trends at the three main Aer Rianta airports are given. Typically, 70 per cent of the air freight volume passes through Dublin, with 27 per cent handled at Shannon and 3 per cent at Cork. The Irish air freight market is served by the three main types of operators described earlier in this chapter. In 1997, there were thirteen cargo airlines operating to/from Ireland of which three were express carrier specialists. In addition, some 24 scheduled passenger or combination carriers served Ireland. There are two ground handling agents operating at Dublin and Cork airports, Aer Lingus and Servisair (since 1991).

Figure 8.3: Irish air freight volumes, 1986-1998

Total Volume of Air Freight through Aer Rianta Airports and through Dublin Airport

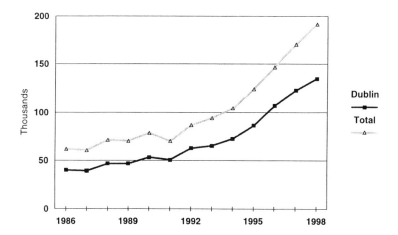

Source: Aer Rianta

Freight Forwarders: There are roughly 30 freight forwarders operating in the Irish market who use air transport services,[8] although 80-90 per cent of air freight turnover is performed by the top eight firms. The distinction between freight forwarders, line hauliers and some integrators is becoming increasingly blurred as liberalisation/deregulation in the various transport modes allows firms to operate a wider range of logistics services. The freight forwarders process a high proportion of cargo business for the scheduled passenger and cargo airlines, typically in excess of 80 per cent of available capacity.

---

[8] A full listing of freight forwarders in the Irish market can be found at website http://www.itco.ie/freight/freight.html

Figure 8.4: Irish air freight volumes, 1986-1998

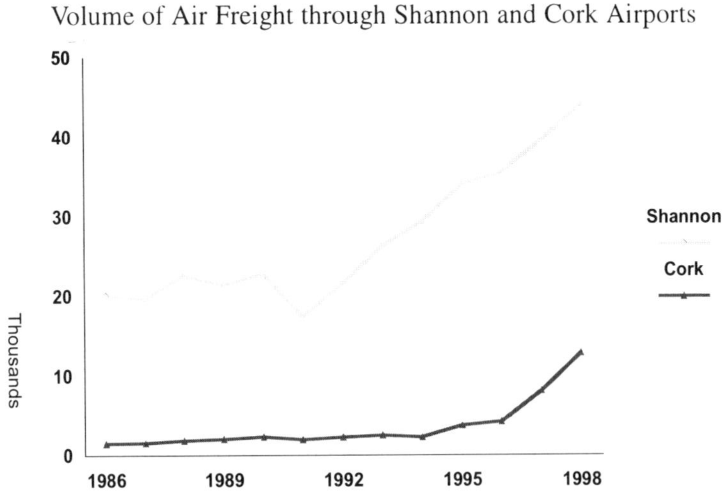

Volume of Air Freight through Shannon and Cork Airports

Source: Aer Rianta

As in the US, European airlines have been losing market share to express operators because these operators offer an integrated service with what is accepted to be a higher quality of service. This is because shipments are handled in-house and responsibilities lie within a single management structure. In order for the line-haul carriers to compete with the integrators, there is a need for closer co-operation between airlines and freight forwarders. This realisation is apparent to the airlines and forwarders. Internationally, there were significant moves towards this kind of co-operation in September 1996 when IATA's Air Cargo Committee organised a working session exploring how the two groups might work more closely. The US experience shows the rapid growth and dominance of the integrators in the US domestic market in a relatively short period of time. The emergence of the integrators raised customer expectations of service standards and quality.

Airlines operating in the Irish market generally use short-haul aircraft reflecting the short stage length and the fact that cargo services are hubbed through European airports. The economic viability of short haul air freight services is precarious. Aer Lingus, for example, withdrew their short-haul European freighter service in 1996 because of lowering yields. Surface modes can compete effectively with air when distances are less than 500 miles and total travel time is 24-48 hours. The rise in air trucking in Europe and in Ireland highlights the potential for erosion of air freight's share of trade tonnage.

Air trucking: Air trucking of freight has grown in the last five years from an estimated 13 per cent of total cargo throughput in 1992 to 21 per cent in 1996, according to Aer Rianta. There are three main reasons why Ireland has significant volumes of air freight trucked by road.

- Most of the air routes from Ireland, and particularly from Dublin are short-haul intra-European routes: the cargo space available in the aircraft serving these routes is limited and cannot facilitate large pallets/loads, unless large combination or all-cargo aircraft are utilised.

- Ireland is located at a relatively short distance from the world's busiest international airport (London-Heathrow), where there are a wide range of direct long-haul services available and a choice of operator on most of the long-haul routes.

- For security purposes, air freight consignments that cannot be x-rayed or scanned must be held for twelve hours prior to being loaded onboard aircraft. Until the mid-1990s, most of the air freight being trucked from Ireland was boarded directly onto aircraft in the UK once it had been accepted at the Irish airport bonded space twelve hours earlier. Thus the trucking journey time made use of the twelve hour wait to relocate the consignment. The Irish Department of Public Enterprise has introduced new air cargo security measures, as part of the European Conference of Civil Aviation (ECAC) policy on air cargo security. Under this regime, which comes into force on 1 January 2000,[9] freight forwarders may apply to become 'Final Forwarders' and air cargo will only be accepted by airlines from such freight forwarders.

8.10 CONSTRAINTS AND FUTURE PROSPECTS

Several factors can be identified as significant constraints on the growth of air freight transport to and from Ireland. These include:

- The significant growth of air trucking, which was discussed earlier.

- The reduction in freight carrying capacity of the passenger airlines. In the longer term, the express operators and all-cargo airlines can be expected to increase their share of the air freight market, as passenger carriers are forced to charge more realistic cargo rates which are in line with the costs of producing the services. Passenger carriers have been facing declining passenger and freight yields (revenue per seat km and per tonne km) as competition has forced efficiencies on many aspects of their operations.

- Environmental regulations which have reduced the fleets of older, noisier aircraft available and have delayed or altered the infrastructure planning process and contributed to the capacity constraints at many European airports. The noise and pollution requirements now in place at many of the large airports raise operating costs for many carriers.

- The congestion of air transport infrastructure in Europe has been identified in several studies as a major bottleneck to the development of competitive air passenger and freight transport markets.

- Security problems are a key factor constraining the growth and development

---

[9] For further details, see http://www.irlgov.ie/tec/transport/aircargo.htm

of both express operations and air trucking. More flexible ferry sailing schedules will have a positive influence on Irish air trucking growth in the short to medium-term.

The liberalisation of European air transport has had a very significant positive impact on Irish air passenger transport, with rapid growth in traffic volumes driven by the entry and network growth of Ryanair. The prospects for similar trends in Europe will depend on the availability of slots at the main airports, although there are many routes with scope for significant growth and competition. Smaller carriers will play an important role in this process, once they are free to enter and compete in Europe's air transport markets. Europe's external aviation policy remains substantially regulated by individual state governments. For both passenger and freight markets, the evolving regulatory regime for external policy will play an important role in the competitiveness and structure of the industry in Europe.

References and Further Readings

Avmark Aviation Economist (Various issues, 1989-1999).

Boeing Commercial Airplane Group, "1998/99 World Air Cargo Forecast" (Seattle, WA) 1998.

Button, K J, K Haynes and R Stough, *Flying into the Future: Air Transport Policy in the European Union* (Cheltenham, UK: Edward Elgar) 1998.

Button, K J and D Swann, "Transatlantic Lessons in Aviation Deregulation: EEC and US Experiences" *Antitrust Bulletin* (1992) Vol. XXXVII (1), pp.207-255.

Doganis, R, "The Impact of Liberalization on European Airline Strategies and Operations" *Journal of Air Transport Management* (1994) 1(1), pp. 15-26.

McGowan, F, "The EEA Air Transport Industry and a Single European Air Transport Market" Occasional Paper No. 47, European Free Trade Association, Economic Affairs Department, Geneva (July 1994).

Reynolds-Feighan, A J and J Durkan, *The Impact of Air Transport on Ireland's Export Performance* (Dublin: Institute of International Trade of Ireland) 1997.

Reynolds-Feighan, A J and K J Button, "An Assessment of the Capacity and Congestion Levels at European Airports" *Journal of Air Transport Management* (July 1999) Vol. 5, Issue: 3, pp. 113-134.

Reynolds-Feighan, A J and K J Feighan, "Airport Services and Airport Charging Systems: A Critical Review of the EU Common Framework" *Transportation Research E: Logistics and Transport Review* (1997) 33(4), pp. 311-320.

Reynolds-Feighan, A J, "European and American Approaches to Air Transport Liberalisation: Some Implications for Small Communities" *Transportation Research A* (1995) 29A(6), pp. 467-483.

Reynolds-Feighan, A J, "EC and US Air Freight Markets: Network Organisation in a Deregulated Environment" *Transport Reviews* (1994) 14(3) pp.193-217.

UK Civil Aviation Authority, *The Single European Aviation Market: The First Five Years* CAP 685, (London: Civil Aviation Authority) June 1998.

Chapter 9
Maritime Transport

Mary Gallagher
Stena Line

9.1 INTRODUCTION

Because it is an island, Ireland has a necessary interest in maritime transport. As an island nation with an open economy situated on the edge of Europe, its principal trading partner, Ireland is strongly dependent on maritime transport. This chapter defines the importance of maritime transport to the Irish economy and describes the flows of traffic through the principal ports. It also discusses recent developments in relation to the management of ports and looks at the dynamics of competition within the unitised and ferry sectors. While the primary focus of this chapter is the Republic of Ireland, it is impossible to exclude reference to the ports of Northern Ireland which handle a significant share of the island's unitised trade.

9.2 PROFILE OF PORT TRAFFIC

Almost all of Ireland's trade by volume is estimated to pass through the country's seaports (no data on the split by sea, air and land frontier have been available since 1992 because of a change in reporting requirements brought about by the creation of the single European market). There are five categories of goods moving through Irish ports. Table 9.1 defines the relative importance of each in terms of volume. Between 1988 and 1997, the overall volume of goods handled by ports grew by 51 per cent. Each category of traffic experienced growth, with the RoRo sector being by far the most dynamic.

Table 9.1: Tonnage Through Irish Ports by Type of Traffic, 1988-1997

(000's tonnes)

	1988	1989	1990	1991	1992	1993	1994	1995	1996	1997	1988-97
TOTAL TONNES	24057	24896	26073	26240	27079	28360	30930	32380	33918	36330	51%
RoRo	2092	2344	2564	2746	2801	2677	3180	3894	5587	6354	204%
LoLo	2854	3099	3045	2962	2973	3371	3899	4175	4404	4423	55%
Bulk liquid	6525	7151	7797	8048	8540	8553	9418	9384	9828	11117	70%
Dry bulk	11353	10895	11059	11026	11053	11744	13009	13538	12266	12739	12%
Break bulk	1243	1407	1606	1458	1711	1424	1424	1389	1564	1697	37%

Source: CSO Statistics of Port Traffic 1988-97

Officially the island of Ireland has about 30 ports. However over 80 per cent of the trade is handled by just four ports: Dublin, Shannon, Cork and Rosslare. Table 9.2 shows the distribution of trade by port in terms of volume (tonnes) for 1997. Only the ports of Dublin and Cork handle all types of traffic. The other ports tend to concentrate on one or two traffic flows. Ports on the east and south coasts generally dominate Ireland's sea trade. The only significant port outside this area is the Shannon estuary which has a somewhat specialised role by virtue of the industry in its hinterland and the availability of very deep water in the estuary. It is the largest handler of bulk traffic because of its role as the port serving the needs of the Aughinish Alumina Plant (principally the import of bauxite and export of alumina) and of the ESB generating station at Moneypoint (import of coal).

Table 9.2: Tonnage by Port by Category of Traffic, 1997

	RoRo	LoLo	Bulk Liquid	Bulk Solid	Break Bulk	TOTAL
Arklow			1	167	51	219
Cork	116	746	5475	1315	564	8216
Drogheda			188	262	341	791
Dublin	5012	3089	2555	1236	243	12135
Dundalk			23	194	1	218
Dun Laoghaire	448					448
Foynes			268	841	91	1200
Galway			445	89	1	535
Greenore			48	273	23	344
Shannon Estuary			1540	6744	48	8332
New Ross			391	717		1108
Rosslare	1227					1227
Sligo			2	28	9	39
Waterford		589	157	306	129	1181
Wicklow				55	116	171
Others			24	512	81	617
TOTAL	6803	4424	11117	12739	1698	36781

Source: CSO Statistics of Port Traffic

9.3 The Unitised Sector

Table 9.1 shows that although volumes of all bulk traffics have grown, growth in the unitised sector has been relatively stable. An assessment of the pattern of bulk shipments (see CSO Statistics of Port Traffic) shows that the flow is mostly westbound, reflecting Ireland's continuing dependence on imported raw materials. The most dynamic sector of maritime transport in terms of growth and competitive activity however is the unitised sector, i.e. LoLo (Lift on Lift off) and RoRo (Roll on Roll off). Because the goods carried by the unitised sector tend to be finished goods, the performance of this mode is linked closely with that of the Irish economy. Thus, the economic growth of the 1990s is mirrored very closely by the growth in unitised traffic, in particular RoRo traffic.

In 1988, unitised traffic (i.e. RoRo and LoLo), when measured in tonnes, accounted for 20 per cent of the total. Its share had grown by 1997 to 30 per cent (see Table 9.1 above). However, measuring unitised traffic in tonnes is rather misleading as the weight of containers or trucks is irrelevant to the charging systems used by the ports and the shipping operators which is a unit-based charge. If it were possible, an assessment of the unitised sector's share of the value of Irish trade would be of more interest. Though the lack of the relevant raw data makes this impossible, common sense indicates that its share of the country's maritime trade by value would be much greater (this statistical gap is also the result of the changes in reporting arrangements to which reference was made above.) Table 9.3 shows the volume of unitised traffic (in units) as opposed to tonnes through the relevant ports. The Table includes ports in Northern Ireland as these handle a significant volume of the unitised traffic originating in or destined for the Republic of Ireland.

Table 9.3 Unitised Traffic through Irish Ports, 1993-98

(000's units)

	1993	1994	1995	1996	1997	1998
Larne	364	376	374	280	273	299
Belfast	240	247	272	389	418	447
Warrenpoint	85	97	76	36	61	66
Drogheda	3	2	4	4	2	3
Dublin	264	299	387	407	609	655
Dun Laoghaire	35	41	41	15	32	42
Rosslare	62	72	74	70	75	91
Waterford	84	85	85	75	34	47
Cork	39	40	44	47	59	67
Total	1176	1259	1357	1323	1563	1717

Source: Dept of Economic Development, Northern Ireland & CSO Statistics of Port Traffic

Prior to the advent of unitisation, ports tended to handle all types of traffic and to serve their immediate hinterland. However, the existence of economies of scale in unitised terminals has forced operators to seek traffic nationally rather than locally. Thus the traffic is concentrated in eight ports: Larne, Belfast, Warrenpoint, Dublin, Dún Laoghaire, Rosslare, Waterford and Cork. Of those, Dún Laoghaire and Rosslare handle only RoRo traffic while Waterford only handles LoLo traffic. Unitised freight services are provided by a variety of operators on routes linking Ireland with Great Britain and with the continent. RoRo dominates the former and LoLo the latter (see Table 9.4).

The LoLo and RoRo sectors are quite different in terms of their traffic patterns, economics and service network and it is worth looking at them separately.

Table 9.4: Unitised Traffic through Irish Ports by Mode and Sector, 1997

(000's tonnes)

	GB	Other EU	Non EU
TOTAL	13502	9169	12182
RoRo	5966	339	49
LoLo	1242	3111	60

Source: CSO Statistics of Port Traffic

9.3.1: RoRo Traffic

The RoRo service network comprises twenty routes operated by nine carriers (see Figure 9.1). The routes vary in length from 30 miles (Larne to the Lochryan ports of Cairnryan and Stranraer) to 300 miles (Rosslare-Cherbourg) and in their accessibility to centres of economic activity. Ferry operators tend to gravitate towards short sea crossings where they exploit the advantages of efficient ship utilisation and the customers enjoy high frequency of service. These advantages are sufficient to attract operators and hauliers to ports such as Cairnryan, Holyhead and Fishguard which are remote from major centres of population but which offer access to short sea crossings. However, while short sea routes tended to dominate in the past, longer sea routes are now prospering. The terminals of the longer routes such as Belfast-Liverpool or Dublin-Liverpool tend to be more advantageously positioned in terms of access to markets and motorway networks. Table 9.5 shows RoRo traffic volumes by port for 1993-1998.

Figure 9.1: Ireland to Britain/Continent ferry routes

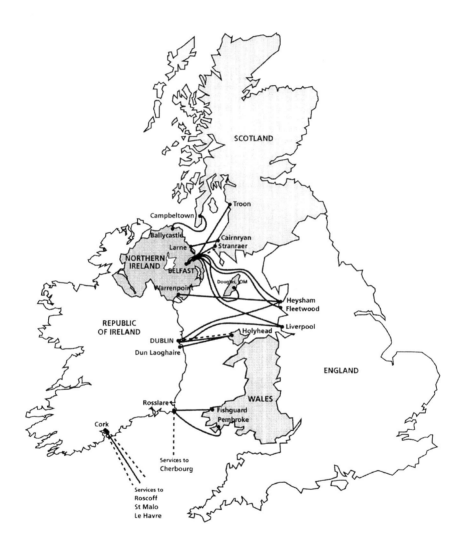

Table 9.5: RoRo Traffic by Port, 1993-98

(000's units)

	1993	1994	1995	1996	1997	1998
Larne	364	376	374	280	273	299
Belfast	130	149	166	282	309	330
Warrenpoint	67	80	60	22	45	49
Dublin	122	133	205	341	378	399
Dun Laoghaire	35	41	41	15	32	42
Rosslare	62	72	74	70	75	91
Cork	4	5	6	6	5	6
Total	784	856	926	1016	1117	1216

Source: Dept of Economic Development, Northern Ireland and the port companies in Cork, Dublin and Dun Laoghaire and CIE in Rosslare

RoRo traffic is carried on two types of service: multi-purpose ferry services, which also carry passengers and cars, and dedicated freight services. The latter tend to be licensed to carry between 150 and 500 passengers, this being sufficient to accommodate freight drivers. But more recently operators of these ships (commonly termed Ro-Pax ships) have branched into the carriage of passengers and their cars in order to make more use of the available space, especially on daytime sailings.

All operators handle both accompanied (trailer with cab unit and driver) and unaccompanied (trailer only) traffic, the only exception being the fast craft, Stena Explorer, which operates the Dún Laoghaire-Holyhead service and which, in order to maintain a very fast turnaround in port, carries accompanied traffic only.

RoRo services are provided by three different types of operator:

- **Multi-purpose ferry operators,** such as Stena Line and Irish Ferries, whose vessels carry passengers, cars and coaches as well as freight units.
- **RoRo operators,** such as Merchant Ferries and Norse Irish Ferries, whose ships are essentially designed to carry freight, but which usually have passenger capacity for about 250 (Ro-Pax vessels.) The recent introduction of new, large Ro-Pax ships by both of these operators has prompted them to carry passenger and car traffic in order to take advantage of their increased passenger capacity.
- **Trailer operators** such as Belfast Freight Ferries who specialise in carrying unaccompanied trailers on ships with capacity for twelve passengers.

Multi-purpose ships are expensive (approximately £60 million for a ship of 2,000 lane metres with a passenger capacity of 1,800) and there is pressure on operators to take full advantage of the flexibility of the deck space by carrying all types of traffic. The patterns of the principal traffic types tend to be complementary with passenger traffic moving by day and freight by night. This gives the multi-purpose operator an opportunity to meet the needs of both markets without undue compromise.

RoRo traffic moves to and from Ireland along four corridors:

- **Northern**: The short sea routes linking Larne and Belfast with Stranraer, Cairnryan and Ardrossan.
- **Diagonal**: The longer sea routes linking Belfast and Larne with Fleetwood, Heysham and Liverpool
- **Central**: The routes linking Dublin Port and Dún Laoghaire with Holyhead, Liverpool and Heysham
- **Southern**: The routes linking Rosslare and Cork with Fishguard, Pembroke and Swansea. It also includes the direct routes between Ireland and France.

In the 1980's, concern was regularly expressed about the movement through Northern Ireland ports of RoRo traffic generated in or destined for the Republic of Ireland. It was felt that the 'diversion' of this traffic, generally estimated to be about 120,000 units annually, represented a loss to the Irish economy and in particular to Irish ports. Sufficient capacity, frequency of service and low freight rates combined to make the Northern ports attractive even to hauliers from the midlands of Ireland. Apart from the loss of revenue to the Republic of Ireland ports, it is difficult to see what other loss was experienced by the Irish economy as a result of the extensive use of the Northern Ireland ports. Mangan and Furlong (1998) note that if the Northern ports are better able to handle Republic of Ireland traffic, then perhaps, from an EU-wide perspective, the EU assisted investment in Irish ports may be partially misguided. Table 9.6 showing RoRo market shares by corridor confirms that the northern and diagonal corridors, though still strong, have lost market share since 1995. The table also highlights the dramatic growth of traffic through the central corridor since 1995. That growth, most of which happened in Dublin, is the result of the provision of capacity to a market that needed it. However, perhaps the current distribution of RoRo traffic to and from Ireland demonstrates that the most appropriate perspective on the development of ports is an all-island one.

RoRo traffic between Ireland and Continental Europe uses either direct services from Rosslare and Cork to France or the landbridge system, i.e. ferry services, between Ireland and the UK and between England and Continental Europe. The volume of traffic on the direct services is small as the length of the journey and the lack of frequency (at best three times a week by any operator) makes it less attractive than the landbridge option. A number of the RoRo operators run services on the Irish Sea as well as the English Channel and are able to offer freight customers a 'through' booking service. Others have formed

Table 9.6: RoRo Traffic – Market Share By Corridor, 1993-98

(%)

	1993	1994	1995	1996	1997	1998
Northern	35	33	32	30	28	28
Diagonal	36	37	32	28	29	28
Central	21	21	27	34	36	36
Southern	8	9	9	8	7	8

Source: Ferry Companies

alliances with Channel operators, including Eurotunnel, and are able to offer similar 'through' services.

The pattern of the distribution of RoRo traffic by port is the result of decisions made by various participants in the transport chain, such as consignors, hauliers and drivers. The decision-making process is a complex one involving various players and the assessment of many factors. From empirical research conducted in Ireland, Mangan (1998) concluded that the factors which actually determined choice of route were the availability of space, cost of service, facilities for drivers, proximity of ports to origin/ destination of traffic, and opportunity for driver's rest break. The research also indicated that the role of the port itself was a small one and that drivers have a critical role to play in the decision-making process because of their experience of ferry services and the regulations which govern their working hours. The research also confirmed the commonly held view that consignors had little involvement in the choice of route.

The ferry operator's key relationship is naturally with the direct customer, the haulier. At a time when the benefits of managing the entire supply chain efficiently are being highlighted, it is notable that there is almost no direct contact between the ferry operator and the consignor. Hauliers tend to spread their business among a number of ferry operators in order to preserve flexibility in planning their itineraries. But usually they will negotiate a discounted rate with at least one operator to whom they will give a significant portion of their business. In return for their loyalty, they will be allocated space (known as block bookings) on particular sailings each day. This arrangement strengthens the control of the haulier and to date has also suited the ferry operator. However, as it is the consignor/manufacturer who tends to be at the leading edge of logistical developments, some benefit could accrue to the ferry operators through the establishment of closer links with consignors/manufacturers as they would gain a clearer insight into emerging trends which might have an influence on future service developments.

In 1993 the first fast craft were introduced to regular service on the Irish

Sea by Stena Line and Sea Containers on the Dún Laoghaire-Holyhead and Belfast-Stranraer routes respectively. These catamarans were capable of twice the speed of conventional ferries (35 knots compared with 18 knots) and carried passengers and cars only. In 1996, the world's largest fast ferry, capable of carrying freight as well as passengers and cars, was introduced to the Dún Laoghaire-Holyhead route by Stena Line. The success of the service provided by the HSS (high-speed sea service), which is more expensive than that of conventional ferries, confirms that here is a segment of the market for whom speed really matters. The service also attracts a significant flow of freight traffic on its daylight sailings. Much of this consists of UK originating vehicles servicing Dublin branches of UK retail chains and for whom the speed and frequency of sailings allows much better utilisation of road vehicles.

Fast ferries, especially the smaller craft, have proved successful in the passenger and car markets. However, they are unlikely to replace conventional ferries, whose sea-keeping qualities they cannot match in an area such as the Irish Sea. Therefore, large conventional ferries will continue to constitute the core capacity in the marketplace and because it is available year-round, freight traffic will continue to be the core traffic, supplemented by large volumes of cars during the peak tourism periods.

Passenger and Car Traffic

The issue of adequate and attractively priced access transport services is an important one to a country like Ireland with a small population and heavily dependent on foreign visitors to support its significant tourism industry. Until the middle of the 20th century, most passenger traffic moved to and from Ireland by sea; it was cheap and available when compared with air transport. In the late-1960s, the advent of car ferries spawned a new trade as passengers travelled with their cars. Today, air is the dominant passenger mode (See Figure 9.2). However while the ferries may have lost large volumes of foot passengers, the carriage of passenger vehicles continues to grow (See Table 9.7). In the past, the pattern of passenger traffic on ferries was highly peaked. However, that profile has begun to soften as short holiday breaks become more popular and as car ownership increases.

The emergence of RoRo technology had a dramatic impact on shipping services, on the ports industry and on patterns of inland transport. There are economies of scale in the operation of ships and terminals which are enhanced by the system's ability to cope with a wide range of traffic types. The commercial interest in exploiting these scale economies has helped determine the current shape of the network of ports and services.

9.3.2: LoLo Traffic

Within the unitised sector, LoLo dominates the market between Ireland and the rest of the EU excluding Great Britain. There are regular services from

Figure 9.2: Irish Air/Sea Market 1993–1998

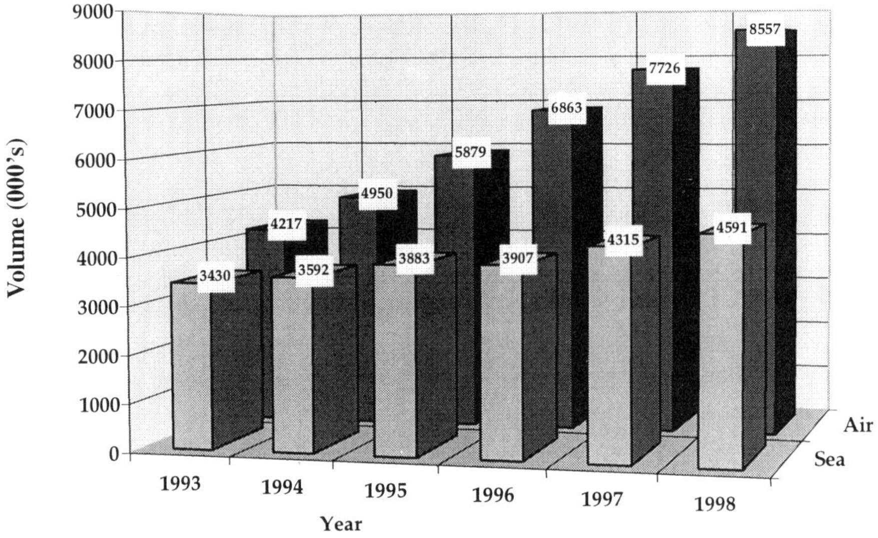

Table 9.7: Car and Coach Traffic by Port, 1993-98

(000's)

	1993	1994	1995	1996	1997	1998
Larne	398	424	446	193	171	189
Belfast	120	115	149	395	417	403
Dublin	118	120	133	139	186	249
Dun Laoghaire	247	254	284	288	271	305
Rosslare	274	248	307	283	342	357
Cork	77	90	87	87	67	65

Source: Department of Economic Development, Northern Ireland and CSO Statistics of Port Traffic

Ireland to UK ports, such as Liverpool, Felixstowe, Southampton and Cardiff, and to the principal continental ports of Rotterdam, Antwerp, Hamburg and Le Harve. This traffic includes feeder traffic for services to/from North and South America and the Far East. When compared with RoRo, the LoLo service network is more extensive but offers a much lower frequency. Most of the services are represented in Ireland by agents rather than the principals themselves. The somewhat erratic patterns of past growth in some ports reflect both discrete events and the greater flexibility of a LoLo service to move to another port (see Table 9.8). For example, the dramatic decrease in Waterford's traffic in 1997 reflects the collapse of Bell Lines, one of the dominant competitors in the market between Ireland and Western Europe. While a number of operators moved to fill the gap, a large portion of the traffic leaked away to other ports. The fall in LoLo traffic through Dublin in 1992 was the result of labour problems which caused the closure of the deep-sea section of the port for eleven months. The dispute arose as a result of efforts being made by Dublin Cargo Handling (Dublin Port's wholly owned stevedore) to reform dock labour practices. By the end of 1992, many of the reforms sought had been achieved and DCH had gone into liquidation. Table 9.2 illustrates that the traffic returned to Dublin in 1993, once the labour dispute was resolved.

Table 9.8: LoLo Traffic Through Irish Ports, 1993-98

(000's units)

	1993	1994	1995	1996	1997	1998	Growth 1993-98
Belfast	109463	97964	105019	107091	108979	117456	7%
Warrenpoint	16994	17143	16549	14336	15310	17357	2%
Drogheda	2860	2069	4585	4232	2199		#VALUE!
Dublin	142149	166171	182125	202468	231028	256000	80%
Waterford	84052	85685	85371	75117	33956	−100%	
Cork	34749	35393	38159	41678	54462	61541	77%

Source: Dept of Economic Development, Northern Ireland and the port companies in Cork, Dublin and Waterford and the port authority in Drogheda

Though the RoRo and LoLo modes compete for some business, traditionally certain traffics have been perceived to be captive to each mode. RoRo is more expensive and is seen to be suited to high-value and perishable goods which require an accompanied service, door to door. LoLo on the other hand seems to be suited to low value, high volume goods which are less time sensitive.

9.3.3 Cruise Ship Traffic

A number of the major ports, principally Dublin, Waterford and Cork, also handle cruise ships. The ports on the island of Ireland have adopted an innovative marketing approach to this business. Rather than the ports competing with each other in a large international market place, they came together to form a marketing company with Bord Fáilte (the Irish Tourist Board) called 'Cruise Ireland'. This sector is the fastest growing travel sector and the Irish ports currently handle over 100 cruise ship calls per annum.

9.4 THE ROLE OF PORTS

The role of ports in the transport network is central as they provide access, berthage and terminal facilities. Ports compete to attract service operators who in turn attract customers. The ability of a port to attract services depends on its location, access, facilities and charges. Two aspects of location are important: the distance by sea from other ports and the nature of the port's hinterland. The success of Larne in the 1980s and early-1990s demonstrated the importance of distance by sea from other ports. As it is situated only 30 nautical miles from Lochryan (where the ports of Cairnryan and Stranraer are situated), Larne permits a high frequency of service to be offered economically. Dublin Port's strategically attractive location in the main centre of population and economic activity gives it a different natural advantage.

The ports in the Republic of Ireland are generally under direct State ownership. The two exceptions are Greenore which is privately owned and Rosslare which is owned by CIÉ, the state public transport company. In the UK a number of ports are owned by ferry operators; Stena Line owns the ports of Stranraer, Holyhead and Fishguard, while P&O owns the ports of Larne and Cairnryan, and Sea Containers owns the port of Heysham. Access to berths, especially in the RoRo sector, is a significant determinant of the openness of the industry to service development by existing operators and new entrants. It might, therefore, seem that ownership of ports by ferry operators is likely to lead to artificially high barriers to entry. However, EU competition law, to which ferry operators have had recourse on a number of occasions, has more recently served to prevent abuse of their position by the integrated port/ferry operators. In fact, the ownership of ports by ferry operators owes more to their history, in particular the involvement of the rail companies in ferry operations, than to any deliberate efforts by the ferry operators to achieve vertical integration.

Ports provide a number of revenue-generating services. In return for access to berthage and terminals they charge ship dues (based on the gross tonnage) and cargo and traffic dues (per tonne of cargo or per vehicle or passenger). In addition, they charge for services such as pilotage and towage. Some port authorities also act as a stevedore (i.e. the provider of handling services for cargo traffic). This is the case, for example, in Rosslare. In ports such as Dublin and Belfast, there are a number of licensed, independent stevedores who provide services to the shipping companies by arrangement. For the most part, ferry companies tend to provide their own stevedoring service, which in their case simply involves tying up and letting go ships and marshalling vehicle traffic.

The high capital cost of providing LoLo and RoRo terminals encourages port operators to want them used as intensively as possible. However, a look at the schedule of RoRo services, for example between Dublin and the UK ports of Holyhead and Liverpool, neatly illustrates the pressure on ports to provide single-user facilities. The services tend to cluster around departure times from Dublin of 21.00-23.00 and arrival times in Dublin of 06.00-07.30. These 'time windows' are so firmly established that no ferry operator would feel confident of operating a profitable service outside these windows. The only exception to this trend is the HSS service on the Dún Laoghaire-Holyhead route which as mentioned above has, by virtue of its speed, attracted a substantial flow of freight traffic on daylight sailings. But its single most popular freight sailing remains the 04.10 departure from Holyhead which, because of the craft's speed, offers the last early morning sailing from Holyhead and the first arrival in Ireland at 05.50. This is what has happened in Dublin where each of the RoRo operators, P&O, Merchant Ferries, Irish Ferries and Stena Line, use individual terminals. However, the berths remain multi-user facilities, with particular operators having individual berthing times at which they have priority. In the case of Rosslare, the port authority provides a single terminal with four berths where each of the operators has its own berthing slots. To the extent that a ship will fit on a berth, operators in Rosslare can also make use of different berths if necessary.

Until recently, the commercial port sector was governed by old legislation which had little relevance to modern trade, namely the Harbours Acts 1946-1976 and the Pilotage Act 1913. This legislation defined the ports as quasi local authorities with primarily an administrative role. Its restrictive nature curtailed the commercial freedom of the ports to the extent that they had to seek ministerial approval for the fixing of dues and charges, the acquisition and disposal of property and the implementation of infrastructural improvements. The port boards were very large (up to 28 members in one instance) comprising representatives of various constituencies such as the local authority, the local chamber of commerce, customers and ministerial nominees. Connellan (1996) notes that by the very nature of their composition, such boards were potential sources of conflicts of interest and their members were more likely to identify with their constituency than with the port.

Throughout the 1980s, there was strong criticism of the commercial constraints being placed on ports by outdated legislation. Eventually, in October 1990, the government established a review group chaired by the industrialist Patrick Murphy to recommend a more appropriate legislative structure and policy. The review group's report neatly encapsulated the problem when it noted that "Ireland's ports have been severely constrained in their ability to respond commercially because of the restrictive legislation under which they operate".[1] The solution it proposed centred on the establishment of separate State companies to run the principal commercial ports. While the review group considered the option of port privatisation, it thought the timing for such a move was unrealistic, but recommended that it remain an option for the future. It also considered and rejected the options of a single management company for all of the ports (much like the Irish airports authority Aer Rianta) and the amalgamation or regionalisation of ports. Despite the obvious appeal of amalgamating ports such as New Ross and Waterford or the Shannon Ports and Foynes, which are so close geographically, the Review Group rejected this just

---

[1] Government of Ireland (1992)

as they rejected the option of a single management company because they felt these options would reduce competition.

The Review Group's report was published in June 1992 and the Harbours Act 1996 implemented many of its recommendations. It provided for the establishment of twelve commercial State companies with smaller boards and gave the ports much more commercial freedom while also imposing some additional obligations. As commercial companies, the ports are now covered by the Companies Acts. The 1996 Act emphasises the obligation of the port companies to make a profit and a return on capital employed. But the Minister, as the single shareholder, still retains power to sanction borrowings, to approve port bye-laws and to determine the remuneration of the CEO. More detailed comment on the performance of the ports under the new regime is contained in Mangan and Cunningham (1999).

Following enactment of the Harbours Act 1996, eight of the ports were "corporatised": Dublin, Cork, Dún Laoghaire, Shannon, Foynes, Galway, New Ross and Drogheda. While the scope of the 1996 legislation included the port of Waterford, it was not established as a commercial port company until January 1999. This delay was the result of the financial difficulties caused by the liquidation of its principal customer, Bell Lines, in 1996 as well as severe storm damage caused to two cranes and the need to clarify commitments regarding a loan from the European Investment Bank. Though it was intended to corporatise the smaller ports of Arklow, Dundalk and Wicklow, this has not yet happened. The ports of Rosslare and Greenore are not covered by the legislation as Greenore is privately owned and Rosslare is owned by CIE.

Writing in the autumn of 1999, it is perhaps a little too early to assess the progress of the corporatised ports. Many of them had begun to experience considerable growth before the new legislation took effect. Some had also begun to modernise their stevedoring services and to develop new areas of business. However, the change in status did not relieve the ports of all difficulties. Some of the ports are overstaffed, but port employees were guaranteed that their jobs would be preserved under the new regime. This makes it almost impossible for a port company to achieve cost savings in a key area. The new port companies are gradually replacing restrictive work practices with more productive ones, but the pace of change is slow. Undoubtedly, the ports have benefited dramatically from the high level of economic growth which Ireland has experienced since 1994. However, their current economic success may be disguising the need for internal reorganisation and a change of culture within some of the port companies.

9.5 ISSUES FOR THE FUTURE

In the last ten years, approximately IR£220 million has been invested in Ireland's port infrastructure with support from a number of EU funds. The purpose of this investment was to reduce the economic disadvantage of Ireland's geographical peripherality by providing better port facilities and improving port efficiency. The tangible target was to secure a minimum reduction in combined shipping costs of 15 per cent in real terms. Certainly port charges in a major port like Dublin have decreased in recent years. For example, passenger dues were reduced by 25 per cent in 1994, traffic dues fell by 5 per cent in 1995 and 1996 and in 1998 tonnage dues fell by 28 per cent.

At the time of writing, the issue of further investment in ports was being assessed as part of the National Development Plan. The ESRI[2] noted that under the next phase of the Operational Programme for Transport "investment in air and sea ports...does not need to reach the levels of the last. It could even be argued that users should pay for these facilities, without further subvention". A study commissioned by the Department of the Marine and Natural Resources from Baxter Eadie (which has not been published) indicated that investment of IR£133 million was needed over the next seven years to ensure that there was sufficient capacity in the ports to meet market demands. They estimated that there would be a shortfall of approximately 9 million tonnes in terms of port handling capacity, most of it concentrated in the ports of Dublin, Cork, Rosslare and Waterford.

Another infrastructural issue is the need to overcome bottlenecks in land access to some of the ports, Dublin being the most obvious example. While a decision had been made to build the Northern Port Tunnel in Dublin, it is unlikely to be completed until 2004.

Much of the discussion on the development of ports focuses on the need for investment in infrastructure. Less attention is usually paid to the 'softer' issue of how that infrastructure is used and managed. In the past, each element of our transport system, including ports, tended to have a territorial approach. This meant that there was little attention paid to the links between the various elements. It is only recently that the organic link between a city-based port, such as Dublin or Belfast, has been taken into account in planning. Another recent development is the recognition that it would be advantageous for an island economy in a peripheral location and dependent on trade to be excellent at logistics. While there are a few logistics 'stars' in Ireland, the country has hardly begun to exploit the opportunities of managing our transport in an integrated fashion. It is Ireland's success in this area that will ensure that the heavy investment made in infrastructure will have been truly worthwhile.

9.6 CONCLUSION

Ireland's maritime transport sector has blossomed in the 1990s in response to the country's remarkable economic growth. Both Ireland's ports and the shipping companies serving them made significant investment in shore facilities, ships and in service development. The ports have also undergone a change in

---

[2] ESRI (1999), *National Investment Priorities for the Period 2000-2006*. Policy Research Paper No. 33, Dublin: Economic and Social Research Institute.

ownership which has given them greater freedom to pursue a more commercial path.

Undoubtedly further improvement is needed to port facilities, some of which are out of date. If no EU funds are provided, it is likely that only the larger ports will be able to fund further investment of substance from their own resources. A number of the principal RoRo operators have ordered new tonnage which will come into service on the Irish Sea in 2000 and 2001. Expansion of LoLo facilities is also in hand. In relation to the management of ports, it is possible that the option of privatisation may be reviewed earlier than anticipated because of government policy on State enterprises and the greatly improved financial position of some of the principal ports.

References and Further Reading

Central Statistics Office, *Statistics of Port Traffic* (published annually) (Ireland).

Connellan, E, *Dublin Port- A New Era* A paper presented to the Chartered Institute of Transport in Ireland (15 April 1996).

Department of Economic Development, *Trade at the Principal Ports* (Northern Ireland).

Government of Ireland, *Report of the Review Group on Commercial Harbours and Pilotage Policy and Legislation* (Dublin: Stationary Office) 1992.

Mangan, J and F Furlong, "Strategies for Developing Port Administration in Ireland" *Maritime Policy and Management* (1998) Vol. 25, No. 4, pp. 349-360.

Mangan, J and J Cunningham (1999) "Government Reform and Change Management in Irish Port Administration", European Case Clearing House (Reference 399–124–1).

Mangan, J, *Land Access to Sea Ports* Round Table 113. Paris: European Conference of Ministers of Transport (ECMT) November 1998.

Chapter 10
Road and Rail Transport

John R Harvey
Iarnród Éireann

10.1 EARLY DEVELOPMENTS

From the earliest times, humans have struggled to solve the problems of transporting themselves and their property. Transport has always been implicitly understood to be a prerequisite for everyday living. People and materials must be brought together in an efficient manner to accomplish the common good. Production and trade can flourish only where the appropriate means of transport have been developed. Developments in transport enhance the success of commerce as opportunities for further trading are made possible by innovations in the way people and goods are moved. Those who, at the dawn of history, discovered the wheel and harnessed animals in the service of transport knew all of this intuitively.

Efficient transport is dependent on the provision of appropriate infrastructure and the design of vehicles to travel over it. The Romans certainly were aware of this fact. Their prowess in road building is legendary. At the height of their power, the Romans had constructed 50,000 miles of roads traversing their empire! These roads were the commercial and military arteries of the empire and no doubt help explain their prosperity and their dominance for so long. However, from these early times until the end of the 18th century, development in land transport was slow. The basic technology of transport remained unchanged. The 18th century road was not unlike the Roman road, neither was the 18th century horse drawn wheeled wagon very different to its forerunner which had moved along the Appian Way in Roman times.

Whilst few improvements had been made in the technology of transport up to the end of the 18th century, a particular development from the world of mining was eventually to prove to be of pivotal importance. This development was a 14th century European transport innovation relating to the use in mines of primitive railways with wagons hauled by horses. In these mines, the rails were originally constructed from timber, as were the wagon wheels. The impetus for this development was the reduction in friction achieved and the consequent reduction in the tractive effort required to haul a given tonnage. Such railways were introduced into the coalmines of Newcastle and Durham before the middle of the 17th century. Over time, the wooden rails and wheels were replaced by cast iron flanged plateways and wheels and then by wrought iron rails and flanged wheels. By the end of the 17th century plateways and railways of this type were common in mining areas. The basic concept of the railway as a low friction, guided way was thus born.

The speed of land transport was tied to the speed at which vehicles could be hauled by horses. For heavy freight traffic, the horse drawn wagons moved at walking pace. For faster passenger vehicular travel the stagecoach concept was developed. This improved the average travel speed to about ten miles per hour. Early in the 18th century, stagecoach services for passengers commenced operations in Ireland from Dublin to Kinnegad (1718), Dublin to Drogheda, Kilkenny and Athlone (1737) and Dublin to Belfast (1788). In 1789, mail coach services were inaugurated from Dublin to Cork and Belfast. The mail coach service expanded rapidly so that by 1834 there were 28 mail coach routes in Ireland and 40 coaches were operating out of Dublin. Open coach services known as "long cars" or "bians" were operated by Charles Bianconi, who commenced operations between Clonmel and Cahir in 1815. He soon extended his operations to link the principal towns in the south and west of Ireland where large areas were not served by stage or mail coach services.

Canals were developed as a response to the practical difficulties of hauling heavy freight in horse drawn wagons over poor road infrastructure. As a transport mode, the canals were even slower than the roads on account of the time it took to traverse the canal locks. Nevertheless, the horse drawn canal barges were capable of conveying much higher freight tonnages than the horse drawn road wagons of the time simply because the frictional forces opposing forward motion were far less by water than by road.

In Ireland canal construction work commenced in 1731 with the Newry Ship Canal. In 1750 construction work commenced on the Grand Canal and continued into the following century. The Newry Ship Canal was completed in 1769, the Grand Canal in 1811 and the Royal Canal in 1817. In addition to the conveyance of freight traffic, flourishing passenger services developed on the canals, so that by the mid-1830s the number of passengers travelling on the Royal and Grand Canals exceeded 150,000 per annum. By the mid-1850s canal passenger services had ceased, unable to compete with the new railways. The canals in Ireland were moderately financially successful in their time and continued in operation for many years, until the unalterable slowness of the mode finally resulted in their abandonment by commercial users.

The railways came to dominate the transport scene during the latter half of the 19th century. However, at the end of the 18th century, the speed of land transport had hardly changed beyond that which prevailed in ancient times. To an observer at that time it must have seemed that the speed of land transport was irrevocably linked to the speed of the horse and that little could change to alter that basic fact. However, things were about to change! The steam engine was about to reinvent the transport industry!

10.2 THE STEAM ENGINE AND STEAM LOCOMOTION

The steam engine was the basis for the technological transformation of land transport. The first practical steam engine was constructed in England by Thomas Savery in 1698, and improved upon in 1712 by Thomas Newcomen. Newcomen's engine was used widely for pumping water out of mines. In 1769,

James Watt redesigned Newcomen's engine, patenting his improved station-ary steam engine. Watt went on to invent further improvements in steam en-gine design. The development of the steam engine powered the Industrial Revo-lution and this, in turn, generated a greatly increased demand by factories and mills for raw materials and by the public for manufactured goods. Traditional transport methods were perceived to be slow and inefficient and inadequate to meet the increased demands brought about by the Industrial Revolution. The need for new and improved methods of transport soon became apparent.

Towards the close of the 18th century, Richard Trevithick, a mining ma-chinery engineer, had the vision to combine the idea of the stationary steam engine mounted on a wheeled vehicle with that of the low friction guided rail track. This synthesis, coupling steam power to vehicle wheels, created the first self-propelled vehicle, the first steam locomotive. In 1804, Trevithick success-fully demonstrated the first steam locomotive operating on rails at the Pen-y-Darren ironworks near Merthyr Tydfil in South Wales. This event was of piv-otal importance to the science of transport. It marked the boundary in time between ages past when transport was dependent on the physical effort of man and animals and the future when transport would be mechanised. The age of the train was born and with it mankind stepped into the new age of mechanised transport! Trevithick was quickly followed by other locomotive engineers in-cluding George and Robert Stephenson, each of whom improved upon the original design by achieving reductions in overall locomotive weight, a fea-ture which had resulted in rail breakages during the 1804 trials.

Eventually, in 1825, the first effective steam hauled railway commenced regular freight operations between Stockton and Darlington. The Stockton and Darlington Railway (S&DR) was also operated by horse drawn vehicles for passenger traffic until the operating and cost advantages of steam traction tri-umphed. In 1829 the Liverpool and Manchester Railway (L&MR) was opened. This was the first passenger and freight railway to be worked entirely by steam traction.

Apart from being mechanically efficient transport modes, the S&DR and the L&MR were profitable ventures and the prospect of increased returns on capital stimulated investors to back railway construction in Britain, Europe and North America. The rail mode soon dominated the transport market in these regions. The history of land transport during the rest of the 19th century is largely concerned with the extension of the railway system throughout the world.

10.3 THE INTERNAL COMBUSTION ENGINE

The first self-propelled road vehicle was steam powered and dated back to the time of Trevithick. However, the weight of early steam powered vehicles made them cumbersome and impractical for road use. Despite the success of the rail mode the quest for a practical power source to propel road vehicles continued during the 19th century. The perseverance of those involved was rewarded in

1876 when Nicolas Otto and Gottlieb Daimler developed and patented the Otto-cycle internal combustion engine. This petrol engine made the development of the motor car possible. The road motor vehicle had arrived! Some years later, in 1896, Rudolf Diesel invented the oil engine named after him. The diesel engine has a higher compression ratio than the petrol engine requiring heavier construction. It is used in some cars and (almost universally) to power road freight vehicles and buses.

The first cars appeared on the roads in Ireland from the mid-1890s onwards. The Motor Car Act governing Irish motoring was passed in 1903. By 1911, there were 9,169 registered motor cars, buses, lorries and motor cycles in Ireland. This figure was set to increase rapidly in the following years as the public and transport operators became aware of the flexibility of road transport. By 1965, the total number of mechanically propelled vehicles had risen to 447,129. By 1997, it was 1,432,330. Table 10.1 contains details of licensed mechanically propelled vehicles in Ireland. It indicates the inexorable increase in road vehicles in Ireland over a long period of time. Every category of vehicle, except motor cycles, experienced rapid growth. In the case of private cars the increase is equivalent to an annual average increase of 4 per cent over the 12-year period from 1985 to 1997.

Table 10.1: Mechanically propelled vehicles 1923 –1997

Year	Private Cars	Motor Cycles	Goods Vehicles	Public Service Vehicles	Other Vehicles*	Total
1923	9,246	n.a.	3,507	n.a.	n.a.	12,753
1935	38,007	n.a.	8,744	n.a.	n.a.	46,751
1965	281,448	51,968	47,909	5,019	60,785	447,129
1975	510,651	36,711	52,367	6,220	75,202	681,151
1985	709,546	26,025	93,369	7,653	78,165	914,758
1997	1,134,429	24,424	158,158	16,185	99,134	1,432,330

Note: * includes tractors, excavators, dumpers, exempt and other vehicles etc.

Sources: Tribunal of Inquiry on Public Transport, 1939; Irish Bulletin of Vehicle and Driver Statistics, 1990 and 1997; Department of the Environment and Local Government.

The increase in car ownership is linked to Ireland's growing prosperity since joining the EC in 1971. Ireland's strong economic growth, as indicated by annual average increases in GNP of up to 7 per cent during the 1990s, accounts for the particularly rapid rise in car ownership during this decade. The increase in the number of goods vehicles since 1985 represents an annual average growth rate of 4.5 per cent. Again, the buoyancy of the Irish economy can be cited as the underlying reason for this growth. The continual increase in the number of road vehicles over many years has resulted in the fact that the road mode is the principal means of inland transport in Ireland today. Car travel accounts for 78 per cent of all road vehicle miles of travel in Ireland. Table 10.2 gives a detailed breakdown of the vehicle miles of travel for all types of vehicle.

Table 10.2: Millions of vehicle miles of travel in Ireland in 1995

Vehicle Class	Total Rural	Total Urban	Grand Total	per cent
Pedal Cycle	290	123	413	Not incl.
Motor Cycle	119	54	173	0.87
Car	12550	2876	15426	78.08
Light Goods	2034	393	2427	12.28
Farm Tractors	262	8	270	1.37
Buses	178	43	221	1.12
Rigid Trucks	634	156	790	4.00
Articulated	329	50	379	1.92
Truck/Trailer	42	4	47	0.24
Miscellaneous	19	5	24	0.12
Grand Total*	16167	3589	19756	100.00

Note: *excludes Pedal Cycle. Table gives total vehicle miles by all mechanically propelled vehicles.
Source: *Traffic Station Counts and Road Travel for 1995* National Roads Authority (1996).

The increase in the numbers of road vehicles over the years has given rise to serious problems of traffic congestion, air pollution and traffic accidents in Ireland. The concomitant neglect of the railway mode during the 1970s and 1980s has further exacerbated these problems.

The National Roads Needs Study (National Roads Authority, 1998) examined the future requirements for roads in Ireland for the period 2000 to 2019, taking cognisance of future traffic growth rates. These depend on population growth, average income growth, projected car ownership levels and truck fleet levels. The study estimated that expenditure of £6 billion will be required during the period 2000-2019 to ensure that the national primary and secondary road networks can accommodate existing and projected traffic volumes at an acceptable level of service.

The study's projections for future car ownership levels in Ireland indicated that car ownership levels will increase from 23.9 cars per 100 inhabitants in 1992 to 48 cars per 100 inhabitants in 2015. It estimates that light vehicle traffic (passenger car) levels on national and secondary roads will increase by a factor ranging between 2.0 and 2.2 by the year 2020 using 1995 traffic levels as the reference level. On secondary roads, not used by tourists, the traffic levels will increase by a factor of 1.7. Heavy vehicle traffic on national and secondary roads will increase by a factor ranging between 1.7 and 1.9. The prospect of traffic levels increasing as per these predictions should force transport planners to rethink strategies based solely on road options. What price will have to be paid in terms of road accidents, urban congestion, air pollution, noise pollution and other environmental damage if these predictions are permitted to come to pass?

Road Costs

With regard to road accidents, NRA (1998) indicates that, in 1997, 472 persons were killed in 424 fatal accidents and 13,115 persons injured (of whom 2,182 were seriously injured and 10,574 received minor injuries) in 8,072 injury accidents on Irish roads. In addition, there were 22,364 material damage accidents (where no deaths or injuries occurred). In this publication, the NRA have estimated that the cost of a fatal accident in 1997 was £886,000, while costs of £110,000, £10,500 and £1,148 apply to serious injury accidents, minor injury accidents and material damage accidents respectively. Using these NRA accident cost estimates, the total cost of road accidents in Ireland in 1997 was £795 million. Assuming the same level of accidents in 1999, and by applying consumer price index increases to this 1997 figure of £795 million to update to 1999 prices, it is estimated that the total cost of road accidents in Ireland in 1999 is £830 million. If unreported, uninsured and/or underinsured accidents are estimated at 20 per cent of the total, then the total cost of road accidents in Ireland in 1999 approaches £1 billion per annum.

In 1997, the Department of Environment and Local Government published the Government Strategy Document *Sustainable Development – A Strategy for Ireland*. This report quotes OECD and EU estimates for the external costs of road transport, "OECD and EU estimates suggest that the external costs of land transport (e.g. congestion, noise, air pollution and accidents) can be up to 5 per cent of GDP – a significant cost to the overall economy". GDP in Ireland in 1998 was £59.637 billion. The Central Bank estimate[3] for GDP in 1999 is £66.945 billion (Central Bank of Ireland, 1999). Using the half of the above OECD/EU estimate of 5 per cent for external costs, i.e. 2.5 per cent, the total estimated cost of road transport externalities (including road accidents) in 1999 is estimated to be £1.67 billion.

The high annual cost associated with road transport externalities ought to focus transport planners minds on policies designed to lessen rather than increase our reliance on the road mode. It now seems to be the appropriate time to consider further rail proposals designed to meet Ireland's future transport needs related to minimising the effects of peripherality whilst reducing the negative externalities associated with the road mode.

10.4 THE RAILWAY IN IRELAND

In 1834, the first railway in Ireland commenced operations between Dublin and Dún Laoghaire (then Kingstown). The Dublin and Kingstown Railway (D&KR) was the first ever commuter railway, linking Dublin to its growing suburban residential areas and to the port of Dún Laoire. In the following years, the railway system in Ireland was gradually extended to serve every major town in the country. The rail network reached its maximum size in 1920 when it comprised of 5,500 route kilometres.

As had occurred in Britain, the railway in Ireland became the dominant transport mode for passenger and freight traffic. Other transport modes, such as the stage/mail coaches and the canals, were unable to sustain their financial viability in the face of the competitive advantages of the rail mode in respect of its speed, safety, reliability and comfort.

The success of the railways in Britain and Ireland during the 19th century brought with it considerable economic power in matters of trade and commerce. In the absence of competition, railways became monopolies in the realm of transport. In order to curtail possible monopolistic abuse by the railway companies and in order to ensure public safety, governments enacted various Railway Acts designed to regulate the rail industry. The Railway and Canal Traffic Acts of 1854 and 1894 made it illegal for railways to discriminate unfairly between freight customers in respect of rates for similar services. A Railway Commission was set up under the 1873 Regulation of Railways Act to monitor and prevent such unfair discrimination. With regard to safety, the Regulation of Railways Act of 1889 enforced the use of the absolute block system of railway signalling thus ensuring a high standard of safety for the rail mode.

With the advent of the railway, people began to travel in large numbers for the first time. The railway offered easy access to transport at affordable prices and greatly increased personal mobility, which had been very limited before the advent of the train. However, despite their success in the 19th century, the railways were to witness a general reversal in their fortunes during most of the 20th century. Just as the railways eclipsed the canals during the 19th century, the railway mode was eclipsed by the road mode in the 20th century. The ubiquitous nature of the road system in Ireland gave the road mode the advantage of greater flexibility in serving the needs of passengers and freight customers, when compared to the fixed infrastructure of the rail mode. In addition, the demography of Ireland favoured the road mode as much of the country was sparsely populated and isolated. This made it difficult to serve it well by rail.

In the aftermath of the First World War, the Civil War and partition, the railways in Ireland experienced financial difficulties. These financial difficulties were due partly to increased wage rates conceded to staff during the war whilst the railways were under government control and partly to growing competition from road traffic. In 1924, the Railways Act was passed forming the Great Southern Railway Company (GSR), by amalgamating 26 railway companies in the Irish Free State. Continuing competition from private bus and truck operators led the GSR to demand government regulation of road transport in order to protect the railway. As a result, the Road Transport Acts of 1932 and 1933 were passed. These prohibited scheduled passenger services, except under government licence, and severely restricted 'for reward' road freight activity. The Transport Acts enabled the GSR to survive, but road competition continued and eroded the railway's market share.

The Second World War saw further restrictions on road transport due to the shortage of fuel, a fact that favoured the railways during this period. Under the Transport Act of 1944 the GSR and the Dublin United Transport Company were merged to form Córas Iompair Éireann (CIÉ), with responsibility for rail, bus and road freight operations within the State. In 1950, CIÉ was nationalised under the Transport Act of that year. In 1957, the Committee of Inquiry into Internal Transport (The Beddy Report) recommended the closure of uneconomic railway lines. The Transport Act of 1958 empowered CIÉ to terminate uneconomic rail services. In the following years (up until 1967) branch line and station closures reduced the CIÉ rail network from the 1958 level of 4,350 kilometres to the 1968 level of 3,080 kilometres.

Despite the closures the financial position of the railway continued to deteriorate during the 1960s as a result of rising inflation. In 1971, the first McKinsey Report, (*Defining the Role of Public Transport in a Changing Environment*) was published. The report was important in that it contained a cost-benefit analysis of the various services provided by the railway. It stated that:

> ... *analysis of social costs and benefits, however, shows that many railway services make a major contribution to the community. It has been concluded that these services should be retained and developed further to play an important continuing role in the future national transport system. Even after the effects of social costs and benefits are included the continuation of some railway services cannot be justified. Restructuring of the railway is necessary, therefore, to eliminate these services and improve the railway financial results* (McKinsey, 1971, p.iv).

This theme was taken up in the internal CIÉ planning document *Railplan 80*, produced in 1972, which translated the overall strategy outlined in the McKinsey Report into action.

In 1980, the second McKinsey Report recommended that CIÉ be reorganised (McKinsey, 1980). In 1984, the Dublin Area Rapid Transit (DART) electric railway was inaugurated. In 1986, the Transport (Reorganisation of CIÉ) Act gave effect to the reorganisation of CIÉ into three separate transport companies, Iarnród Éireann, Bus Éireann and Bus Átha Cliath. The Road Transport Act 1986 deregulated the road haulage industry in Ireland. The Canals Act 1986 transferred the canals from CIÉ to the Office of Public Works. Iarnród Éireann commenced operations in February 1987. Since then, the total number of passengers carried has increased from 24.9 million to 31.8 million in 1998.

10.5 THE OPERATIONAL PROGRAMME ON PERIPHERALITY

Ireland's peripherality has forced transport planners to focus on strategies aimed at minimising the inherent disadvantage of being an island far from the centre of the European marketplace. The strategy has involved obtaining assistance from the European Regional Development Fund (ERDF) under the EU's Community Support Framework (CSF) for Community structural assistance. The objective is to improve access transport infrastructure for sea and air transport modes, and internal rail and road transport infrastructure between the cities, towns, ports and airports.

In 1990, the Operational Programme on Peripherality (OPP) was published. The principal objectives of the OPP were to address and remedy the major trading disadvantages associated with Ireland's peripheral location. In addition, the OPP sought to support the development of industry and tourism at sub-regional or local level by improving access to industrial production facilities and indigenous raw materials and to tourism centres by the implementation of measures to create or improve roads and other transport infrastructure services.

The total planned expenditure for the OPP was £829 million (in January 1990 prices) of which £530 million (64 per cent) was EU Community (mainly ERDF) grant assistance, with the balance of £299 million funded by the exchequer. 82 per cent of the OPP expenditure related to peripherality projects, i.e. national primary roads improvements, airport improvements and seaport improvements; 18 per cent related to sub-regional development projects, i.e. roads supporting industrial development and tourism, the development of rail passenger services in Dublin and rail freight infrastructure in other regional locations. Of the total planned expenditure, £623 million (75 per cent) was allocated to roads. The OPP was successfully implemented and a total of 50 major improvement projects on national primary roads were completed including, *inter alia*, bypasses at Athlone, Newbridge/Kilcullen, Glanmire and Shankill/Bray.

Due of the decision to focus on critical road infrastructural deficiencies, the OPP provided only £36.4 million (4.4 per cent) for public transport. However, in 1992, the EU approved grant aid under the OPP for the first phase of the upgrading of the rail infrastructure on three mainline railway routes, *viz.* Dublin to Belfast, Dublin to Cork and Dublin to Waterford. The EU approved co-financed expenditure (at a grant aid rate of 75 per cent) of £9 million on the Dublin to Cork railway line, £3 million for track upgrading on the Dublin to Waterford line and £10 million on the Dublin to Belfast railway line as part of the Trans-European Network of High Speed Rail and Combined Transport. This latter project was a joint Iarnród Eire/Northern Ireland Railways project, supported by the Irish government and the Northern Ireland Office. The Dublin to Belfast project involved track upgrading, signalling system renewal and the acquisition of new rolling stock. The upgrading of track and signalling was continued with grant aid assistance under the Cohesion Fund (1993-1999) and new rolling stock was acquired with grant aid assistance under the Operational Programme for Transport (1994-1999). Other railway projects included the rail connection to the new Waterford Port at Belview, the construction of the Lavistown Junction Loop, the acquisition of gantry cranes at rail freight terminals and the development of diesel rail commuter services. The total co-financed railway expenditure under the OPP amounted to £48.2 million.

The OPP did not resolve all of the difficulties facing access and internal transport in Ireland, but very substantial physical progress was achieved during its implementation. The OPP was a good beginning to the ongoing programme of investment in Ireland's transport infrastructure.

10.6 THE NATIONAL DEVELOPMENT PLAN AND THE OPERATIONAL PROGRAMME FOR TRANSPORT 1994-1999

The *National Development Plan 1994-1999*, published in 1993, built on the success of the EU Community Support Framework (CSF) 1989-1993 under which the OPP was implemented. The National Development Plan (NDP) contained an analysis of the many remaining deficiencies in access and internal transport infrastructure of the country not addressed in the OPP. In particular, the NDP highlighted the major areas of concern affecting land transport in Ireland. The NDP analysis confirmed that, in contrast with the other EU Member States at the centre of the Community, Ireland's internal transport system was still relatively under developed and generally of poor quality.

The NDP analysis noted that rail conveyed significant volumes of bulk and other freight traffic, much of which was unsuited to transport by road. Up to 85 per cent of rail freight was import/export traffic. The NDP analysis concluded that severe constraints on railway investment in the past had led to significant under-investment in railway asset replacement and railway infrastructural renewal with the result that most of the locomotive and rolling stock assets and track infrastructure had exceeded its normal life expectancy. The NDP estimated, in 1993, that investment of approximately £800 million over a 30-year period would be required to restore the railway network to an adequate operational level.

It was realised that the above transport system deficiencies were having serious negative impacts on transport costs which were higher than in other EU countries for domestic and inter-state trade. The future competitive position of the country would suffer unless a strategy for transport infrastructural improvement was devised. In the age of 'just in time' (JIT) transport logistics, good transport services can only be delivered in circumstances where journey time variances are predictable. This was not the case in many parts of Ireland prior to the implementation of the investment programme set out in the NDP.

Few towns had bypasses and traffic congestion and long delays were the norm for motorists, bus services and road haulage operators going about their business.

Total expenditure on transport proposed in the NDP for the period 1994-1999 was £2.6 billion. Over 66 per cent was proposed for road development and improvement. However, the NDP recognised that the national railway system had an important role to play in the development of efficient land transport in Ireland. This recognition was reflected in the level of expenditure that was proposed, which compared well with that allocated under the OPP and represented a positive re-evaluation of the importance of the railways.

The NDP outlined a series of objectives and achievement targets for national primary roads, toll roads, national secondary roads, non-national roads, mainline rail, Dublin Transportation Initiative, State airports, regional airports and ports. With regard to the national primary roads, four key corridors, namely north/south, southwest, east/west, western, were to be developed and an average inter-urban travel speed of 80 kph to be attained by 2005. The National Roads Authority (NRA) was established with statutory responsibility for the management of the national road development programme from January 1994. The NRA was given power to levy tolls on national roads or enter joint venture agreements for toll-based private investment. With regard to national secondary roads two key cross country routes were to be developed linking Dundalk to Nenagh (along the N52) and Athlone to Rosslare (along the N80). Both of these cross-country routes were identified as being commercially important as they provide interlinks to key national primary routes, *viz.* the N2, N3, N4, N6, N7, N8, N9 and N11. With regard to non-national roads, regional and local non-national roads of importance in the generation of jobs in industry, tourism, fisheries, forestry or rural areas were to be developed.

Investment in the Mainline Rail Network focussed on the railway lines proposed for inclusion in the Trans European Network of High Speed Rail. Implementation of the Dublin Transportation Initiative (DTI) would include a light rail system for Dublin, ten quality bus corridors, the upgrading of suburban services on existing railway lines, integrated ticketing, completion of the Dublin ring road, an efficient access route to Dublin Port, improved traffic management measures and improved facilities for cyclists and pedestrians. Investment in State airports would be concentrated in Dublin, Shannon and Cork Airports. Investment in ports would be concentrated in Dublin, Dún Laoghaire, Waterford, Cork, Rosslare and the Shannon Estuary Ports.

The objectives of the NDP were given effect in the *Operational Programme for Transport 1994–1999* (OPT), published in 1994, and currently being implemented. The total planned transport expenditure for the OPT was £2.6 billion (in 1994 prices) of which £1.137 billion (43.55 per cent) was to be co-financed by the ERDF fund. The total planned OPT expenditure by measure was as shown in Table 10.3.

Table 10.3: Operational Programme for Transport 1994–1999

Measure	Expenditure	Percentage of total
National Primary Roads	£1,099 m	42.09
National Secondary Roads	£114 m	4.37
Mainline Rail	£275 m	10.53
State Airports	£225 m	8.62
Commercial Seaports	£77 m	2.95
Non-National Roads	£442 m	16.93
DTI and Other Public Transport	£356 m	13.63
Regional Ports	£17 m	0.65
Technical Assistance	£6 m	0.23
Total Proposed Expenditure	£2,611 m	100.00

Source: Adapted from Operational Programme for Transport 1994-1999 (p. 8).

Of the total planned investment of £1,099 million in national primary roads proposed in the OPT, £401 million would be co-financed by the ERDF and national funds, £599 would be co-financed by the Cohesion Fund and national funds and the balance of £99 million would be co-financed by national resources and would receive no EU co-financing. The per cent rate of aid for national primary roads projects co-financed by the ERDF was 75 per cent. For national secondary roads projects co-financed by the ERDF the per cent rate of aid was 65 per cent.

Of the total planned investment of £275 million in mainline rail proposed in the OPT, £59 million would be co-financed by the ERDF and national funds, £124 million would be co-financed by the Cohesion Fund and national funds and the balance of £92 million would be financed by national resources and would receive no EU co-financing. The percentage rate of aid for mainline rail projects co-financed by the ERDF was 50 per cent. The percentage rate of aid for the Dublin Transportation Initiative co-financed by the ERDF was 65 per cent.

The OPT set specific targets for projected time savings for road and rail investments. For example, travel time savings of 28 minutes were projected between the Border and Dublin, savings of 12 minutes between Dublin and Wexford and savings of 22 minutes between Cork and Rosslare. Rail passenger journey time savings of 15 minutes were projected between Dublin and Cork and 10 minutes between Dublin and Limerick. Passenger journey time savings were also projected for the other mainline rail routes proposed for upgrading. These journey time savings reflect the fact that the upgrading of the railway lines as a result of the OPT will permit higher maximum rail speeds to be attained. Large sections of the Intercity network were upgraded from old jointed track on wooden sleepers to new continuous welded rail (CWR) on concrete sleepers. The maximum rail speed on the Dublin to Cork and the Dublin to Belfast lines is 160 kph. Planned maximum rail speeds on the Dublin to Limerick, Sligo, Galway, Tralee, Waterford and Rosslare lines will be 145 kph. Iarnród Éireann's target is to upgrade the entire Intercity network to CWR as funding becomes available. Railway projects funded by the OPT during the period 1994-1999 include track and signalling upgrading on the Intercity network, extension of DART electrification between Bray and Greystones and between Howth Junction and Malahide and the acquisition of new DART carriages and diesel railcars.

Assessment of Programmes

At the time of writing, the OPT is drawing to a close. The effects that this investment programme has had on inland transport in Ireland have been very significant. Irish transport has been transformed in a way unimaginable prior to the OPP and the OPT. However, DKM (1997) noted that the pace of economic expansion in Ireland since 1993 had the effect of stimulating higher than expected traffic growth resulting in greater demand on transport infrastructures than projected in the OPT. This rapid growth rate and the failure to meet some OPT implementation targets, particularly in the areas of road construction and in light rail and bus projects in Dublin, were cited as "exacerbating the perceived adequacy problems with the road system which were evident in 1993". As a result, DKM concluded that congestion on some transport networks had not been reduced to the extent proposed in the OPT.

Nevertheless, new road infrastructure provided under the OPT has improved inter-urban road journey times. Railway line upgrading has likewise improved rail journey times. The primary objective of the OPT was to minimise the effect of Ireland's peripherality by improving its transport infrastructure. Great progress has been made towards achieving this objective. However, as indicated above, the task of upgrading Ireland's transport infrastructure is not yet completed. Future investment programmes are currently being planned to eliminate remaining infrastructural deficiencies. ESRI (1999) identified two principal priorities for future transport expenditure: national primary and secondary roads, where many inadequacies remain and in urban public transport in Dublin, Cork, Galway and Limerick. With regard to public transport, the ESRI Report states that:

> *Due to the delay in the completion of public transport projects in Dublin under the current programme, and the rapid growth in traffic, the situation in the city is increasingly critical. Public transport investment, on a scale not hitherto contemplated, is now unavoidable in Dublin* (ESRI, 1999, p.157).

The options for public transport investment in Dublin include light rail (LUAS), suburban rail, bus development and the completion and/or the construction of major road developments such as the C-ring and the Port Access Tunnel. In view of the fact that the bus system carries 90 per cent of public transport passengers in Dublin, the ESRI Report advocates the provision of better rights of way for buses in the city via provision of more bus ways, quality bus corridors, bus only streets and bus priority measures. The report also advocates the consideration of transport demand management measures (e.g. review of road tax, fuel tax, road tolls, parking charges) to reduce pressure on road capacity. In view of the population growth in Dublin and the adjoining fringes in counties Meath, Kildare and Wicklow, the ESRI Report also recommends additional future investment in suburban rail lines serving these areas in order to alleviate the rapidly growing traffic pressures on the city.

Under a new £430 million safety investment programme, 640 kilometres of radial railway lines from Dublin will be upgraded to CWR on concrete sleepers by the end of 2003. This programme also involves investment in signalling, level crossings, bridges and track maintenance. The railway system is no longer being overlooked in deciding the shape of future investment programmes.

10.7 CONCLUSION

The principal objective of transport planning during the past decade has been to improve or provide access and land transport infrastructure, to ensure that Ireland will not be disadvantaged relative to its EU partners due to its insular and peripheral location. The OPP and OPT programmes have made it possible to bring this objective within reach. Major airport, seaport, road and rail infrastructural improvements have been implemented throughout Ireland under these programmes. The insular nature of the country has been minimised by the provision of efficient air and sea transport services. The improvement of Dublin Airport and Rosslare Europort under the OPT examples of access infrastructure development. Land transport within Ireland has been transformed during the 1990s. Modern road systems have been constructed and have reduced the time taken to travel between cities and towns. Bypasses have been constructed around many cities and towns further reducing travel times.

The rapid economic growth during the 1990s could not have occurred without the transport infrastructure to support it. As industry has grown so too has road transport, both private car and freight haulage. The problems associated with road transport have also grown. These problems are becoming critical and must soon be addressed. Easy access to cities and towns is a prerequisite for industry to locate in a region. Industries have been encouraged to locate throughout the country partly as a result of the improved road infrastructure. The railway system in Ireland has also been transformed during the 1990s. Mainline track upgrading and new rolling stock on Intercity and suburban rail lines have greatly improved the speed and quality of rail transport. The railways witnessed a general reversal in their fortunes during most of the 20th century. Just as the railways eclipsed the canals during the 19th century, the railway mode was to be eclipsed by the road mode in the 20th century; but the analogy ends there. In the 19th century the canals failed to survive as they could not adapt and compete with the technology of the railways. In the 20th century the railways did survive precisely because they could adapt and compete with the technology of the road mode. At the close of the 20th century, railway technology has equalled, if not surpassed, road vehicle technology in terms of speed, safety, comfort, and the capacity to move people and goods. Modern rail transport has much to offer in terms of beneficial economic and environmental attributes compared to road transport, i.e. lower energy consumption, lower land use requirement and lower air pollution. The fact that the rail mode has the capability to resolve many of the problems associated with road transport and road transport externalities is now beginning to be recognised and appreciated by transport planners.

After almost a century of decline, the rail mode has re-discovered its competitive advantages in fast, mass passenger movement and bulk freight transport. Rail transport can never supplant road transport in Ireland, but it can serve the country well particularly in the areas of fast inter-city passenger rail transport, rail commuter services to/from and within urban centres and rail freight movements. Transport planners should note the potential of the rail mode and through appropriate investment strategies develop its future role in transport in Ireland. A new balance must now be struck between road and rail transport in Ireland in order that as we enter the new millennium we do not carry with us our old mistakes of concentrating on road transport to the neglect of rail and thereby create for ourselves, as we have done in the past, more traffic jams, more congestion, more pollution and more accidents. Wisdom dictates that it is time to maximise the use of the rail mode. Let the transport planners create the opportunity for this to happen by making wise decisions.

References and Further Reading

Allen, G, *Railways: Past, Present and Future* (London: Orbis Publishing) 1982.

Central Bank of Ireland, *Quarterly Bulletin*, Autumn, 1999.

Department of Environment and Local Government, *Sustainable Development – A Strategy for Ireland* (Dublin: Stationery Office) 1997.

DKM, *Operational Programme for Transport: Mid Term Evaluation* (Dublin: DKM Economic Consultants) 1997.

ESRI, *National Investment Priorities for the Period 2000-2006* (Dublin: Economic and Social Research Institute) 1999.

Government Publications, *Operational Programme on Peripherality, 1989-1993* (Dublin: Stationery Office) 1989.

Government Publications, *Operational Programme for Transport, 1994-1999* (Dublin: Stationary Office) 1994.

McKinsey, *Defining the Role of Public Transport in a Changing Environment* (Dublin: McKinsey & Company Inc. 1971.

McKinsey, *The Transport Challenge: the Opportunities in the 1980s* (Dublin: McKinsey & Company Inc. 1980.

Nowlan, K, *Travel and Transport in Ireland* (Dublin: Gill & Macmillan) 1973.

NRA, *National Road Needs* Study, *1999-2019* (Dublin: National Roads Authority) 1998.

NRA, *Road Accident Facts, 1997* (Dublin: National Roads Authority) 1998.

O'Connor, K, *Ironing the Land* (Dublin: Gill & Macmillan) 1999.

O'Riain M, *On the Move* (Dublin: Gill & Macmillan) 1995.

Chapter 11
Access, Transport and Tourism Development

Sheila Flanagan
Dublin Institute of Technology
and
Kevin Hannigan
Irish Management Institute

11.1 THE TOURISM INDUSTRY

Tourism is the world's largest industry with a gross output in 1996 of US$3,600 billion, equivalent to 10.7 per cent of the global economy. It is the largest generator of jobs, employing 225 million people globally, 19 million of whom work in the EU. It has created an additional 154 million jobs world-wide over the past ten years and is responsible for 10.6 per cent of the world's employment. International arrivals more than trebled between 1970 and 1993, from 165 million to 500 million. Within the same time period, international tourism receipts experienced an 18-fold increase from US$17.9 billion to US$324 billion. It is forecast that the number of international arrivals will reach 964 million by 2010.[1]

According to the World Tourism Organisation (WTO), tourism markets are becoming increasingly competitive as more and more destinations look to tourism as an economic generator to create new employment and income or to replace existing industrial infrastructure or agriculture. Global demand is also changing with an increased awareness among consumers regarding the potentially damaging effect of tourism development on the environment. There is also increasing interest among travellers in visiting and maintaining environmentally sound destinations. These trends underline the point that, whilst tourism can be viewed as an industry that exploits a renewable resource, sound management and careful monitoring of its impact on the environment is essential. Otherwise, that delicate balance that renews the resources would prove fragile indeed.

A quite distinct fundamental change is also occurring in most major generating markets as the population of these countries age, particularly in those countries that experienced a significant post-war baby boom. There is also a trend in greater interest in cultural tourism and products (WTO, 1988b). Each of these trends presents opportunities for development and underline the importance of building the industry along carefully planned lines.

In 1996, international tourism increased by 5.5 per cent for arrivals and almost 8 per cent for tourism receipts (excluding international transport). WTO

---

[1] Data from ITIC (1998) and WTO (1998a).

(1998a) suggests that tourism in 1996 seemed to have entered a consolidation phase, a development favoured by a certain revival in consumer confidence. However, international tourism in 1997 grew more slowly world-wide with greater volatility among the regions. Those regions increasing their share of tourist arrivals since 1975 include East Asia and the Pacific, Africa and, to a lesser extent, the Middle East. East Asia and the Pacific has also expanded its share of global tourism receipts over this time period.

European Tourism Performance

In 1997, international arrivals in Europe grew by 3.2 per cent to almost 362 million. This represents close to 59 per cent of total arrivals world-wide, making Europe by far the most important destination. This is not surprising given the large number of geographically proximate, independent and wealthy states that comprise Europe. Tourist receipts were estimated at more than US$223 billion, an increase of 0.9 per cent over 1996 and representing almost 50 per cent of world tourism receipts. (WTO, 1998b). However, while tourism is far more important in Europe in terms of sheer volume than any other area of the world, growth forecasts for all EU countries in 1999, at 2.3 per cent per annum, are well below the world average. The only exceptions are Ireland (5.8 per cent), Denmark (3.3 per cent) and Austria (3.1 per cent).

Lower growth means that although Europe continues to maintain its overall dominance as a tourist destination, it has experienced a significant loss of 10.2 percentage points in its share of arrivals since 1975. America remains a distant second in overall share of arrivals with 19.4 per cent of the market in 1997, a loss of 3.1 percentage points since 1975 (ITIC, 1998b). It is forecast that Europe will remain the largest receiving region up to the year 2020, although its below average rate of increase will result in a continuing overall decline in market share. The more mature European destinations will need to strive continuously to seek product and market differentiation to avoid obtaining a tired image in generating markets. The focus needs to be on new types of product development and niche marketing. On the upside, European tourism will be boosted by increased tourism development and marketing in the former Soviet bloc countries of Eastern Europe. These countries have the potential to become Europe's tourism tigers in the period up to 2020.

11.2 IRELAND'S TOURISM GROWTH

The performance of the Irish tourism industry over the past decade has been impressive. Following a protracted period of stagnation, growth emerged in the late-1980s and continued throughout the 1990s. Overseas tourist visits to Ireland grew from 4.3 million visitors in 1994 to 6.1 million visitors in 1998. Irish tourism is now a £2.5 billion industry when domestic trips are included. Its success is also evident in the number of jobs supported by tourism. In 1998, the industry provided over 120,000 full-time equivalents, equal to 8.8 per cent of the Irish workforce. This compares with 51,700 jobs in 1987 (Bord Fáilte, 1998).

Table 11.1 shows the growth that has taken place in recent years and the relative importance of source markets. Traditionally, the UK had been by far the most important market in terms of numbers. However, visitors from the US were always important since expenditure per person was generally much higher than the UK. This remains the case and is a particularly important point in an industry that is experiencing strains on capacity in some areas. In effect, non-UK visitors represented a higher value-added market, on average. Within this characterisation there are exceptions, but the key point is that the industry must strive to increase revenue, rather than numbers and, ideally, revenue per visitor per day. This point is particularly important where capacity constraints on access transport infrastructure and nodes are relevant.

Figure 11.1: Overseas tourism to Ireland: numbers and revenue (1988-1998)

		1988	1994	1995	1996	1997	1998	Growth (per cent) 1988-98
Britain	(000's)	1,508	2,308	2,285	2,590	2,850	3,199	112.1
	£M	267	452	501	574	683	749.6	180.7
Europe	(000's)	408	988	1,101	1,177	1,168	1,255	207.6
	£M	123.7	371.6	414	466.6	457.7	467.2	277.7
Germany	(000's)	113	269	319	339	303	310	
France	(000's)	111	231	234	262	250	270	
Italy	(000's)	21	121	112	119	111	141	
Benelux	(000's)	58	121	147	169	204	205	
Other European	(000's)	105	246	290	289	302	330	
North America	(000's)	419	494	641	729	777	858	104.8
	£M	165.5	213.4	275	316.6	348.2	384.4	132.3
USA	(000's)	385	449	587	660	718	858	
Canada	(000's)	34	45	54	69	60	69	
Rest of World	(000's)	90	159	204	186	213	221	121.0
	£M	37.6	77.2	96.5	93.8	99.7	103	173.9
Total Overseas	(000's)	2,425	3,696	4,231	4,682	5,007	5,534	128.2
Visitors	£M	594	1,114	1,286	1,451	1,588.6	1,704.2	186.9

Source: Bord Fáilte, *Tourism Facts* 1988-1998

One of the most significant developments of the current period of growth has been the increasing importance of the European market. From 1988 to 1995, visitors from continental Europe increased by 170 per cent, from under 17 per cent to over 26 per cent of the total. This trend has since eased with traditional markets performing strongest. In 1997, the number of visitors to Ireland from Britain grew by 10 per cent, with North America growing by 7 per cent and visits from other long haul destinations increasing by 15 per cent. Although mainland Europe showed a decline, this masks a strong performance from some countries, with the Netherlands (+20 per cent) and Belgium/Luxembourg (+22 per cent) showing particularly strong growth. The importance of each market to the Irish tourism industry between 1988 and 1998, in terms of numbers and revenue, is outlined in Table 11.1.

The performance of Irish tourism is all the more remarkable when compared to the recent experience of tourism in Europe, which has seen more modest growth of 3.2 per cent in tourist arrivals and a 0.9 per cent increase in revenue. In fact, statistics produced by the World Tourism Organisation in 1996 showed that "Ireland was one of the fastest growing tourism industries in Europe" in the period 1988-1998. A strong point of the Irish industry is that revenue grew faster than arrivals, 149.5 per cent compared to 128.2 per cent, when inflation is removed. As a result, each individual visitor was worth more, on average, in 1998 than in 1988. The main reason is that expenditure per visitor from Europe is higher than from the UK and that this market has grown faster. This is important since it means that the potential returns from investment in new facilities to accommodate or to transport these visitors will be higher. The return per visitor is explored further in Table 11.2.

This data show that American visitors remain the most valuable. However, when allowance for inflation is made, the real value of expenditure by American visitors, on a per capita basis, has declined. Expenditure per UK visitor has risen while there has been a slight decline in the European figure. Of course, this is only one half of the picture and it is likely that American visitors may also require a greater input of resources. For an economy such as Ireland facing input constraints in terms of infrastructure and labour, these trends raise a number of important issues for consideration in the development of a strategic blueprint for the industry.

Table 11.2: Expenditure per visitor by origin (1998 and 1988)

	American	European	British
1998	448	372	234
1998 at 1988 prices	358	298	187
1988	395	303	177

Source: Calculated from Bord Fáilte, *Tourism Facts* 1988-1998 and CSO *Economic Series*

The tourism industry has grown considerably faster than many other sectors of the economy. The direct and indirect effects of tourism are spread widely, with more than 41 sectors across the economy identified as benefiting form tourist activity. The industry's foreign earnings – tourism accounts for 5.3 per cent of exports – make a greater net contribution to the country's balance of payments than does any other sector (ITIC, 1998). Because the wealth generated by tourism is almost totally retained within Ireland, the industry has an important impact on economic activity beyond the direct expenditure of visitors.[2] Earnings are re-spent on other Irish goods and the people who are employed in tourism spend their incomes on further goods and services. As a result, the total effect is a multiple of the initial direct expenditure. The relationship between the direct and final impact is known as the tourism multiplier. The multiplier gives a better idea of the true impact of growth on the economy than would be obtained from including direct expenditure only. Based on the multiplier for 1995, it is estimated that tourism in 1998 accounted for 6.3 per cent of Irish GNP.

Bord Fáilte have estimated that, for every pound spent by out of state tourists, 57p eventually ends up with the government through VAT, excise duties, PAYE and other taxes. This means that government revenue, through taxation of overseas and domestic tourism expenditure, generated £1.4 billion in 1998, of which £1.1 billion came from foreign tourism.

In 1997, there was an estimated 1,359,000 people at work in Ireland. The latest update of information derived from commissioned research carried out by Deane and Henry indicated that over 51 jobs are supported for every £1 million of out of state tourism expenditure and 36 jobs per £1 million of domestic tourism expenditure. As a result, tourism accounted for about 8.8 per cent of jobs – or more than one in twelve. One further point is also important; because tourism is characterised by the fact that consumption takes place where the service is available and tourism activity is often concentrated in areas that lack an intensive industrial base, the industry is credited with having a regional distributive effect.[3] However, this feature also means that, in addition to facilities at access points, tourists also require considerable facilities within the country.

11.3 THE FACTORS OF CHANGE

The performance of Irish tourism since the mid-1980s has been impressive relative to the remarkably weak performance of the previous fifteen years (Deegan and Dineen, 1997). This has happened as a result of a number of important policy and market developments. Building on the belief that tourism

---

[2] Tourism has an import content of less than 10 per cent compared to that in other key sectors which ranges from 44-55 per cent.

[3] Bord Fáilte (1998). Bord Fáilte estimates are based on information from the CSO's Country of Residence Survey(CRS) and Bord Fáilte's Survey of Overseas Travellers (SOT).

has a central role to play in Ireland's economic development since the mid-1980s, new policy instruments have been developed and applied. In this period, tourism has generally obtained a much higher profile than previously.

Financial Incentives

The most notable drivers of tourism growth include the availability of EU support through Structural Funds. These resulted in strong and consistent product development and increased destination marketing through initiatives such as the Overseas Tourism Marketing Initiative (OTMI), the Domestic Tourism Marketing Initiative (DTMI) and Tourism Brand Ireland. Over £2 billion has been invested in product development in the tourism industry over the past decade. There is a strong view within the tourism and financial services industry that without grant aid and tax incentives much of the recent investment would not have taken place. IR£288 million in grant aid resulted in a total investment of IR£1.04 billion in tourism products. Nearly 70 per cent of this has been dedicated to accommodation and visitor attractions.

Targeting Niche Markets: Short Stay/City Breaks

Dublin has begun to realise its potential as a major European city destination. According to ITIC (1996), a significant part of this increase in tourism to the city is 'destination specific' and the growth to Dublin should not be viewed as displacement tourism (in other words occurring at the expense of other regions). The dramatic growth in Dublin and its hinterland is due to increased demand for city tourism and the growing number of visitors using Dublin as a gateway. The marked increase in the share of Ireland's tourists visiting and staying in the city reflects an increase in two categories of holiday visitors: city tourists and gateway tourists. In the case of city tourists, the sole or principal motivation is to visit Dublin. The capital is currently Ireland's only urban destination that can compete effectively with other high profile UK and European cities.

Dublin has tapped into one of the fastest developing sub-sectors with tourism. According to the Irish Tourism Industry Confederation (ITIC, 1996), the trend has been towards short-stay holidays since 1989. Short stay breaks to Dublin, of one to three nights, almost doubled between 1993 and 1996 to 252,000. Since these breaks are generally additional to the main summer holiday, this also contributes to the alleviation of the seasonality problem in the Dublin region. Among tourism analysts, Dublin is now recognised as one of the most popular cities in Europe for short-term visitors and weekend breaks. Despite appearances, the city is not just attractive to English stag party organisers. The developing 'street tourism' in such areas as Temple Bar has been a critical factor in enhancing the capital's appeal. A wider range of tourist attractions and their greater accessibility by virtue of longer opening hours has made Dublin "an 18 hour per day tourist city" according to Tom Coffey of the

Dublin City Centre Business Association.

The popularity of city breaks, or urban tourism in general, has most certainly been boosted by the growth in the number and range of package programs on offer since the beginning of the 1990s. Two important factors affecting urban tourism are access and accommodation. In terms of visitor accommodation, national room capacity increased by 40 per cent between 1989 and 1994. As shown in Table 11.3, the total number of approved rooms (hotels, town and country, self-catering and hostel) increased by 49 per cent from 7,475 in 1990 to 14,500 in 1997 and the trend continues.

Table 11.3: Approved accommodation Dublin (number of rooms)

1990	1991	1992	1993	1994	1995	1996	1997	Growth
7,475	8,220	8,767	9,308	11,137	13,000	13,721	14,500	94%

Source: Dublin Tourism

Marketing and Promotion

Initiatives such as the Overseas Tourism Marketing Initiative (OTMI) and Tourism Brand Ireland, as well as increased and more effective promotional spending undertaken by carriers, product providers and overseas operators, have been very successful. A significant proportion of this marketing investment has focused on creating new demands for Ireland as a destination. Bord Fáilte and the Northern Ireland Tourist Board launched the first major advertising of the whole of Ireland as a single destination, in the US in 1994. Since then a single media campaign has been operating under the aegis of OTMI. Much of the achievements were made in an increasingly competitive environment.

Northern Ireland Peace Dividend

The possibility, however remote, of any contact with conflict or political instability is one of the most damaging developments for any emerging tourism destination. However, the ending of conflict can lead to a remarkably rapid rehabilitation of the destination. It is as though tourists are anxious to travel to destinations once perceived to be out-of-bounds, but only if there are considerable reassurances forthcoming. Ireland has proven to be a good example of this general trend. Holiday visitors to Northern Ireland for all markets increased markedly during the 1994-1996 ceasefire. The peace process has shown that the absence of conflict in Northern Ireland can be a stimulus for the growth of visitors to both parts of Ireland.

Fashionability

Just as the damage from media coverage of the Northern Ireland conflict was extremely damaging, the benefits from positive exposure in the international press, should not be underestimated. The 'Celtic Tiger' economic performance image has depicted Ireland as a modern, economically creative and progressive nation. When promoted in tandem with the country's acknowledged physical attractions and unspoiled way of life, this newly acquired 'high-flying' image, has been a significant factor contributing to visitor growth and investment. The attraction of Ireland as a getaway place for film stars, and the ensuing publicity from the success of high profile films with Irish connections, have generated an interest in Ireland and made it a chic destination. This has been complemented by the success of numerous artists, musicians and the achievements of Ireland's much lauded literary giants.

However, no matter how attractive the country may appear, there will be little benefit if it remains inaccessible if it is unduly expensive to travel to. As a result, much of the credit for the boom in Irish tourism must be given to improvements in transport facilities. Improvements in access routes by air and sea and enhanced facilities at air and sea ports, liberalisation of air transport and an industry focus on destination development and competitiveness have all been identified as key drivers of growth. This viewpoint is mirrored by Bord Fáilte (1994) who identify a combination of factors which influenced Ireland's tourism performance within the past decade. While marketing and promotion, availability of finance, fashionability and the Northern Ireland peace dividend are important factors, access transport developments are recognised as being a key influence which has impacted on tourism growth.

11.4 THE ROLE OF TRANSPORT IN IRELAND'S TOURISM BOOM

Air Transport

The biggest impact of all has been as a result of the liberalisation of air routes. Demand for foreign travel is highly price sensitive among holidaymakers. Between 1978 and 1986 numbers on the Dublin-London route fell by 6 per cent. Liberalisation, however, has allowed for significant growth and the emergence of new entrant airlines into the market in Ireland. Liberalisation of Anglo-Irish routes in 1986 allowed for a 107 per cent growth rate in traffic between 1986 and 1988 (Barrett, 1991). Over the same time period, fares fell by 42 per cent in real terms. Ryanair played a significant role in lowering the cost and frequency of air transport and secondly, as a result of a change in government policy, direct flights to and from the USA were permitted. The growth that has occurred is illustrated for a variety of scheduled services in Table 11.4.

Table 11.4: Scheduled air capacity

Routes	1997	1993	% increase
Dublin to London	4,758	3,082	54
Dublin – UK Provincial	3,515	1,467	140
Dublin to Europe	2,566	1,621	58
Cork to UK	980	551	6
Shannon to UK	743	460	62
Shannon to Europe	105	38	176
Ireland – US	1,060	650	63

Source: Aer Rianta

Passenger traffic at Dublin Airport increased from 2.6 million in 1985 to 11.6 million in 1996, an increase of almost 350 per cent. Aer Rianta are predicting an extra one million passengers for Dublin Airport in 1999 to a level of 12.6 million. Dublin is now the fastest growing airport in the world and the Dublin-London route is the busiest at 4.1 million in 1998. This is expected to rise to 4.5 million by the end of 1999. The extent of the growth in traffic through Dublin Airport in recent years is indicated by the data in Table11.5.

Table 11.5: Traffic flows through Dublin Airport 1991-1998 (000s)

1991	5,278
1992	5,808
1994	6,980
1996	9,091
1998	11,600
% Growth	**120**

Source: Aer Rianta

This dramatic expansion of access transport has been described by tourism industry leaders as the single most important driver of growth in tourism (ITIC, 1998). Both new entrants and established operators, following the liberalisation of air transport within Europe, have also supplied additional air capacity on a variety of European and transatlantic routes. For example, the amount of scheduled capacity operating to/from Ireland through the three State airports of Dublin, Cork and Shannon has increased by approximately 70 per cent since 1993. Airlines have devoted significant levels of investment to acquiring additional aircraft capacity, especially since 1993, while considerable expenditure has also been attributed to upgrading and expanding airport facilities.

Airports can influence traffic development and not just respond passively to growth. In recent years, market research on the potential of a variety of routes into Dublin has been carried out. A very detailed route profitability model has been developed to enable Aer Rianta to assess the likely viability of particular routes. This model has been used to work with other airlines and airports within the route network with a view to introducing new services. Examples where such a proactive approach has led to the introduction of new services to Dublin include the annual Icelandic charter services in autumn/winter, the new direct service to Helsinki, and the recently introduced direct Singapore Airlines 747 cargo service between Dublin and Singapore. Indeed, the latter service has been so successful that Singapore Airlines has recently doubled the capacity on this route by adding a second weekly 747 service.

Because of the huge surge in passenger volumes (especially over the past three years when traffic has increased by 50 per cent) facilities have been stretched to capacity at Dublin Airport. Aer Rianta has in place a comprehensive development plan for Dublin Airport called "Airport 1 – Creating the Best Airport" which involves investing £170 million in new facilities at Dublin Airport over a 5-year period. Many of the new projects have been completed, including the following.

- Multi-storey car parking complex (1996).
- Major new taxiway systems (1994-1996).
- New surface car-parking: 5,000 spaces (1997).
- Departure lounges in Pier A – Phase 2 (1997).
- Departure lounges in old Central Terminal Building (1997).
- New check-in area on Arrivals Road (1997).
- Terminal extension/new Pier C (1998).
- New Great Southern Hotel at Dublin Airport (1998).
- Additional Apron/Taxiway (1997/1998).
- Main Runway Extension (1999).
- 6-Bay Extension of Main Terminal (2000).

These projects, when completed, will increase the capacity of the existing site at Dublin Airport to about 14 million passengers per annum with the possibility of additional expansion, if required, on the present site. In addition to facilitating growth in the tourism industry, the benefits derived from an investment programme of this magnitude include increased employment in the construction industry and extra spending power. However, it should be remembered that this implies the use of scarce Irish resources. It is important that the benefits obtained, particularly from the resulting growth in the tourism industry, are adequate to ensure that there is a reasonable and acceptable return on this investment. This cannot be assessed accurately with reference to the whole industry and each phase of development must show a positive net return. However, on one point we can be confident. The boom in the Irish economy, and particularly the huge fall in unemployment, means that previously under-utilised resources have now become scarce. The result is that the cost of investing resources in tourism instead of elsewhere in the economy has risen. This means that the returns must also rise. This is a natural progression in the development of the economy and is in keeping with a rising standard of living. However, it inevitably implies that the tourism product offered must be capable of selling as a luxury product – as distinct from a mass tourism product – and that the facilities produced must be utilised to the fullest extent possible. The need to follow this development path is reflected in the discussion on future challenges in the final section of this chapter.

Sea Transport and Port Developments

Total passenger capacity on sea routes between Ireland and Britain has increased by 15-20 per cent since 1993, while there has been a decline in passenger capacity on European sea routes. While the expansion of passenger capacity on sea routes has been less dramatic than on air routes, surface carriers have experienced frustrated demand for car and coach tour traffic at peak times. Sea transport ferry facilities have therefore been upgraded by the replacement of older ships on both the central and southern British corridors with new, larger and more modern conventional vessels and high-speed services. As a result weekly car capacity on the Ireland-Britain routes has increased by over 30 per cent since 1993 (ITIC, 1998).

Table 11.7: Passenger capacity to/from Ireland on Stena/Irish Ferries sea routes

Routes	1997	1993	% Change
Dublin-Holyhead	7,472	7,120	5
Rosslare-Fishguard	2,500	2,000	25
Rosslare-Pembroke	2,254	1,735	30
Ireland-Britain Total	12,226	10,855	13
Ireland-France	308	665	–54

Source: Stena Line and Irish Ferries.

Within the Republic of Ireland, vessel and port investment over the time period 1994-1998 is estimated at £230 million. The high speed service (HSS), introduced by Stena, has a turn round time of 90 minutes between Dún Laoghaire and Holyhead. In 1997 the new ferry terminal in Dún Laoghaire harbour opened offering further potential for increased capacity and speed of transfer. Over the time period 1991-1996, sea traffic on the routes operated out of Dún Laoghaire by Stena increased by 139 per cent. Similar daily capacity growth has occurred on routes out of Dublin Port operated by Irish Ferries, with passenger capacity increasing by 153 per cent between 1992 and 1999. In the same period, Irish Ferries increased its car and freight capacity by 318 per cent and 307 per cent respectively. All of these investments in port development have resulted in faster, more frequent and more comfortable access by sea to Ireland.

Just as in the case of air transport, value-oriented campaigns to increase market share, substantial infrastructural investment and increased competition resulting in significant fare cuts on key routes in the sea transport industry have contributed in a major way towards the growth of inward travel. In addition, the larger ports, in conjunction with Bord Fáilte, have formed a marketing company called 'Cruise Ireland' for the purpose of attracting cruise ship business to Ireland. This is a growing business sector for Irish ports with over 100 cruise ship calls per annum to Irish ports. Cruise ship passengers tend to be high yielding and so the economic benefits of this traffic to the port hinterland are quite significant.

11.6 INFRASTRUCTURAL CAPACITY UTILISATION: PROBLEMS OF CONCENTRATION AND DISPERSION

Seasonality

Research into the Irish tourism industry during the 1980s identified poor value for money and a lack of quality product as major obstacles. These were caused, to a great degree, by a lack of investment due to the prospect of low returns. One of the main causes of the low return on investment was identified as the highly seasonal nature of the Irish industry. This is a common problem in tourism, but as Price Waterhouse (1987) found, the problem was particularly acute in Ireland. ITIC (1992, p.72) concluded that, in Ireland:

> *Excessive seasonality is the biggest barrier to tourism development and the most pervasive problem in the industry.*

In addition to low profitability arising out of low capacity utilisation, seasonality also leads to high prices and physical congestion in the peak season, capacity problems in transport and a poor range of holiday types. As a result, the government decided that a major aim of the Second Operational Programme would be to improve the seasonal distribution of visitors (Government Publications, 1994). The target set was that, by 1999, 66 per cent of holidaymakers would arrive outside the peak July-September period, compared with 60 per cent in 1994. By 1998, this figure had risen to 62 per cent, thus underlining the intractability of this problem.

Because the main problems are caused by congestion and poor utilisation in the low season, the problem is best described by visitor numbers rather than revenue. In fact, peak season pricing means that the seasonal profile of revenue is even more highly peaked. However, this also means that visitors are paying a higher price for scarcer resources in the summer. The seasonal distribution of arrivals in Ireland means that 28 per cent of visitors arrived in the peak months of July and August in 1998. As shown below, the peak was considerably higher in some regions of the country. This compares with 25 per cent in the UK. The problem in Ireland is made worse by the fact that visitors in the peak period also stay longer and because up to 65 per cent of domestic holidays are taken in these months. In addition to the two peak months, the shoulder periods of May-June and September also accounted for 30 per cent of the total. In contrast, the period from January to March accounted for only 14 per cent of arrivals. The extent of seasonality in Irish tourism is indicated by Figure 11.1. While there has been growth overall since the late-1980s, the figure shows that this has resulted in very high peaks in the summer months.

Figure 11.1: Overseas visitors by quarter 1990-1999

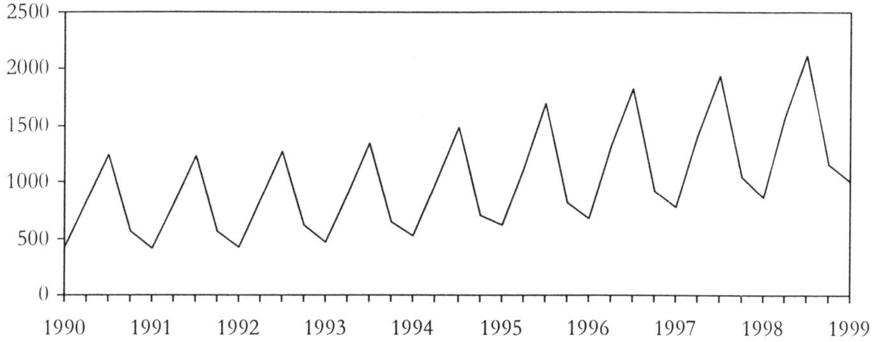

Source: Bord Fáilte.

Figures for the seasonal distribution of arrivals are not available for many European countries, but the OECD publish bed occupancy rates in hotels as an indication. These also show Ireland is highly peaked by international standards. In addition, the high numbers of visitors to Ireland who are visiting friends and relatives (VFR) tend to arrive in the peak season, but do not stay in hotels. This means that figures based on hotel occupancy are underestimates of the degree of seasonality in Ireland.

Three main factors determine the degree of seasonality in the industry. These are:

• the type of product on offer;
• the degree of seasonality in principal markets;
• the proportionate origin of visitors.

There are a number of reasons why the problem has proven so intractable in Ireland. Major investment in facilities has meant some improvement in low season attractions, but the product is essentially outdoor based. The low percent of business visitors, a market which is not seasonal, is also a reason why the Irish industry remains more highly peaked than the UK. The UK market is seasonal, particularly among VFR visitors, although minor peaks occur around Easter and Christmas. However, this is not a market that is easily influenced by product development or marketing. The growth in importance of the European market, particularly in the late-1980s and early-1990s, also meant that while Ireland improved the seasonal profile of visitors from traditional markets, this was hidden by the increased importance of the highly seasonal European market.

The lesson would appear to be that while some marginal improvements in seasonality are possible, future growth, in terms of the number of arrivals, will remain concentrated in the already busy periods. Dublin is a possible exception to this having developed as a short stay destination. However, the difficulties experienced in improving the profile suggest that the solutions to the problems caused by this high peak must come from the transport and tourism operators rather than as a result of an overall plan for the development of the industry.

Regional Distribution

Similar problems to seasonal concentration can be caused by excessive regional concentration. As noted above, tourism has an inherent ability to transfer resources to areas that lack an alternative economic base. Thus, major benefits may be gained from the development of tourism in such areas, while growth in already busy areas would risk congestion and logistical difficulties. Table 11.8 shows that although over 50 per cent of visitors include Dublin in their itinerary, and many of these do not proceed to travel elsewhere in the country, the Irish industry is quite well spread with 50 per cent of revenue going to the western regions.

One aim of recent policy has been to improve this distribution, but Dublin has been growing at much the same rate as the west. The strong performance of the north west in the period 1993 to 1997 is evidence of the beneficial impact of the ceasefires in Northern Ireland. While the Irish tourism industry is beneficial from the point of view of its distribution, the impact of this is lessened somewhat by differences in the seasonal profile of the industry in some regions. Figure 11.2 uses a simple ratio – the number of overseas visitors who arrive in the period April to September divided by the number in October to March – to compare different regions. Seasonality is clearly a greater problem in western regions than in the east.

Table 11.8: Regional distribution of overseas tourism 1993-1997

	Number of Visitors		Revenue	
	% of total	Growth	% of total	Growth
Dublin	52	71	30	38
South East	17	28	9	26
South West	30	41	19	40
Shannon	20	29	12	42
West	23	37	12	29
North West	11	20	7	50
Midlands/East	16	40	9	37

Source: Bord Fáilte *Perspectives on Irish Tourism: Regions 1993-1997*

Figure11.2: Ratio of visits in high to low season by region

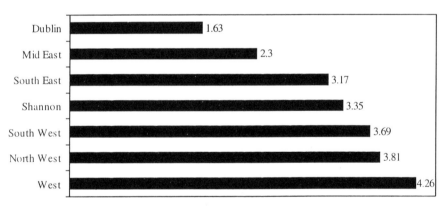

Source: Calculated from Bord Fáilte (1998).

The problem is that resulting employment in the regions will tend to be temporary and part-time. Furthermore, for the reasons already discussed, organic growth in the west will be more difficult to achieve.

One other issue is worth noting: a very high proportion of visitors travel to more than one region. This means that, for the holidaymaker, Ireland remains essentially a touring destination. In this it is unlike the package holiday destinations of southern Europe. This has various implications. A benefit is that, to a large extent, tourists can merge into the landscape and the benefits can be accessed directly by local communities without needing to be filtered down from areas of large concentration. A more negative implication is that tourism growth has an impact on the whole country, rather than on controlled areas.

Environmental difficulties could arise in the absence of careful planning and monitoring. Furthermore, from a transport point of view, tourism growth is not just an issue at the point of access. Problems of logistics arise in transferring visitors to the various parts of the country. Other problems arise, often in the most remote areas, where strong local bases for touring have been established. The result is that logistics problems in Irish tourism are multi-dimensional and must be tackled at a number of levels. This is discussed further in the final section of this chapter.

11.7 FUTURE TOURISM CHALLENGES

The Global Tourism Industry

The World Tourism Organisation's *Tourism 2020 Vision* (WTO, 1998c) provides an overview of global 'megatrends' for the period up to 2020 and offers predictions for opportunities into the next century. The main predictions include the following.

1. By 2020, there will be 1.6 billion international tourist arrivals world-wide spending over US$2 trillion. This compares with 613 million international arrivals in 1997 and receipts of US$ 418 billion. However, with only 3.5 per cent of the world's population engaged in international tourism, the industry is in its infancy.

2. Europe will remain the largest receiving region, though its below global average rate of increase between 1995-2020 will result in a decline in market share from 59 per cent to 45 per cent. East Asia and the Pacific, increasing at 7 per cent per annum will overtake America as the second largest receiving region.

3. Most industrialised countries will come close to their ceilings for domestic tourism in respect of the proportion of their populations engaging in it and the incidence of their participation. It seems highly likely that the existing ratios of domestic to international tourism activity will be maintained.

4. The top ten tourist receiving countries will see a major change with China (currently not in the top ten) becoming the leading destination by 2020. Hong Kong will also become one of the main destinations. The Russian Federation will also enter the top ten. Fast growth in Asian destinations such as Thailand, Singapore and Indonesia along with South Africa will increase their importance. The corresponding top ten generating countries will also see a major impact, with China entering at fourth place. The Russian Federation will also become a major outbound tourism country.

The study also identifies a number of major determinants and influences on international tourism activity during the period 1995 to 2020. These many factors, summarised below, in combination will produce a polarisation of tourist tastes and supply, so that large-scale, mainstream, smaller volumes and individualised tourism will all grow.

Economic factors

- Continued moderate to good rates of global economic growth.
- Above average economic performance of the Asian Tiger economies.
- Emerging importance of new Tiger economies, such as China, India, Brazil and Indonesia.
- Widening gap between rich and poor countries.
- Spread of harmonisation of currencies.

Technology

- Information technology development.
- Transport technology advances.

Political factors

- Removal of barriers to international travel.
- Transport and other forms of deregulation.

Demographic developments

- Ageing population and contracting work forces in industrialised countries leading to more south–north migration.
- Erosion of the traditional Western household.

Globalisation

- Growing power of international economic and market forces and consequent reduced control of individual states and non-global corporations.

Localisation

- Conflict in developing countries between identity and modernity.
- Demand from groups defined on ethnicity, religion, and social structures to be recognised in their own rights.

Socio-environmental awareness

- Boosted public awareness of socio-cultural and environmental issues.

- Greater media reporting on major global problems (e.g. decreasing water supplies).

Living and working environments

- Growing urban congestion both in the industrialised and (especially) developing worlds.

Change from 'service' to 'experience' economy

- Focus switching to delivering unique experiences that personally engages the consumer.

Marketing

- Use of electronic technology to identify and communicate with market segments and niches.

In this changed environment, the key priorities identified for National Tourism Organisations will be:

- increased, more focused and more aggressive marketing;
- improved competitiveness through product differentiation, quality and price;
- growing recognition of the need for sustainable tourism development to ensure long-term prosperity.
- less state control, and more state/private sector partnerships.

Challenges Facing the Irish Tourism Industry

Fitzpatrick Associates (1997) in their mid-term evaluation of the Operational Programme for Tourism (1994-1999) raise a number of issues in relation to the product investment programme. The absence of genuinely innovative products funded under the Operational Programme for Tourism and the lack of success in reducing the seasonal nature of tourism are noted. The need for selective action to improve the spatial or regional tourism distribution is emphasised together with the need for the diversion of funding resources into the area of marketing and the development of visitor management plans. This viewpoint is mirrored by the Irish Tourism Industry Confederation in their *Strategy for Growth Beyond 2000 – A Strategic Framework for Irish Tourism*. This points to the need for a policy of selective incentives for product development in disadvantaged regions and the need to address the problem of seasonality.

Tomorrow's customers are likely to be more educated, sophisticated and more experienced travellers according to ITIC; increasingly they will look for high standards of delivery and service in destinations and activities. This points to a need for investment in training. Within the tourism sphere, and in particular in relation to the growing sophistication of visitors, management training is a priority in this regard. In any future investment programme, the guiding principles should be:

- economic, social and environmental sustainability;
- addressing the seasonality of Irish tourism (in particular outside of the Dublin region);
- regional spread or distribution of tourism;
- maximising yield to ensure the economic viability of investments.

Issues relating to access should not be ignored. Convenient access is a key determinant of visitor numbers and is critical to achieving some of the objectives outlined above, including season extension and greater regional spread. The key strategic access challenges facing the tourism industry include:

- The continued need for marketing support for carriers who are critical partners in destination marketing.
- The development of clear national policy on access. Particular attention needs to be paid to the west with a view to achieving the core objective of regional spread.
- Encouragement of better access to the regions through perhaps the growth of scheduled services at regional airports. A need also exists to encourage more direct ferries from mainland Europe so as to attract more mobile European tourists to the regions.
- Internal access needs to be improved, particularly inter-modal travel (air/coach/train) in order to facilitate integrated access.

11.8 CONCLUSION

As this chapter has shown, rapid growth in tourism, while of great benefit to the economy, brings with it a number of problems related to the transport of visitors at entry points and within the country. Logistics solutions are required, but the nature and applicability of solutions depend on decisions at three distinct levels. These arise form the fact that tourism is not a single product but a composite of a large number of products and of the country as a whole.

The first level of decision-making relates to the overall strategic plan for the industry and, indeed, for the economy as a whole. If further growth in the tourism industry is to continue to benefit the Irish economy, it is important that Ireland can access high-value markets. This requires continued investment in high quality facilities and the implementation of appropriate policies in sectors of the economy that have close linkages with the industry. The liberalisation of air transport is the best example of the latter. Failure to extend this lesson will lead to a poor return from the investment that has occurred to date. However, as a result of the development of the car-hire business in Ireland and the growth of privately operated bus charters, it is arguable that tourists are better served regarding transport than is the domestic population.

The second level arises from the fact that the composite nature of the 'product' introduces a considerable degree of flexibility on the part of producers in relation to the product that is produced. Of course, the lack of any single attraction of international standing – Dublin as a single attraction being a possible exception – means that Ireland will continue to produce a product that requires visitors to travel around the country. However, the development of niche products to overcome regional and seasonal concentrations is vital if the impending logistical problems of further growth are to be avoided. Sport tourism and 'grey' attractions – for older age groups – are examples where there have been some successes, but most potential remains untapped. Regional festivals are also important. However, there are much greater benefits from out of season events, such as rugby weekends in Dublin or the Wexford Opera Festival, than from the more usual mid-season festivals such as the Rose of Tralee. Out of season events have the potential to grow the industry without congestion, while the latter accentuate existing problems.

The third level for problem solving is at the level of commercial operators. In this regard, tourism operators are faced with two problems in addition to those experienced in other industries. Firstly, supply chains within tourism are not as well defined as in other industries and the complexity of the product means that the important linkages are difficult to model. The industry requires world class efficiency in areas as diverse as the supply of fresh ingredients for high class restaurants to stuffed leprechauns for souvenir shops. Secondly, transport in tourism intrinsically involves the customer in a way that is uncommon. In fact, for some types of tourism, transport is the product. Since services cannot be stored, tourism stretches the just-in-time system to its extreme, where inventory is zero and production and consumption take place simultaneously. This means that logistics managers in tourism can learn from other industries but, ultimately, there are few ready-made solutions that can be transferred.

The current challenge is to ensure that the achievements in the growth and development of Ireland's tourism industry over the past six years are consolidated and built upon beyond the year 2000. All the indications are that the boom in global tourism over recent decades will continue. However, continued growth will place considerable strains on facilities, particularly at access points. Investment in creative and effective marketing, product development and access will all have a crucial role to play in keeping Ireland on a growth path in a highly competitive marketplace.

References and Further Reading

Barrett, S *Transport Policy in Ireland In the 1990's* (Dublin. Gill & Macmillan) 1991.
Bord Fáilte, *Perspectives on Irish Tourism: Regions 1993-97* (Dublin: Bord Fáilte) 1998.
Bord Fáilte, *Developing Sustainable Tourism* (Dublin: Bord Fáilte) 1994.
Davidson, Thomas Lea, "What are Travel and Tourism: Are they really an Industry?' in

William F Theobald (ed.), *Global Tourism – The Next Decade* (Oxford: Butterworth Heinemann) 1995.

Deegan, J and D Dineen, *Tourism Policy and Performance: the Irish Experience* (London: International Thomson) 1997.

Dublin Tourism, *Tourism Facts for the Dublin Region* (Dublin) 1998.

English Tourist Board & Jones Lang Wooton, *Retail, Leisure and Tourism* (London) 1998.

Fitzpatrick Associates (1997) Mid-Term Evaluation of the Operational Programme for Tourism 1994-1999.

Go, F and R Pine, *Globalisation Strategy in the Hotel Industry* (New York: Routledge) 1995.

Government Publications, *Operational Programme for Tourism 1994-99* (Dublin: Stationery Office) 1994.

ITIC, *Strategy for Growth Beyond 2000 – A Strategic Framework for Irish Tourism* (Dublin: Irish Tourism Industry Confederation) 1998.

ITIC, *Changing Distribution of Ireland's Tourism* (Dublin: Irish Tourism Industry Confederation) 1996.

ITIC, *A Strategic Framework for Tourism Enterprises* Report prepared for the Irish Tourism Industry Confederation by Tansey Webster Economic Consultants, Dublin (1992).

Jansen-Verbeke, M, "Leisure and Shopping Tourism Product Mix" in G Ashworth & B Goodall (eds), *Marketing Tourism Places* (London: Routledge) 1990.

Law, Christopher, *Urban Tourism: Attracting Visitors to Large Cities* (place of publication: Mansell Publishing Ltd) 1993.

Lickorish, Leonard J, 'Tourism Facing Change' in M Quest (ed.), *Horwarth Book of Tourism* (London: Macmillan Press) 1990.

Mills, Stephen, "The Development of New Tourism Products" in M Quest (ed.), *Horwarth Book of Tourism* (London: Macmillan Press) 1990.

Price Waterhouse, *Improving the Performance of Irish Tourism* (Dublin: Stationery Office) 1987.

WTO (1998a), *Tourism Highlights 1997* (Madrid: World Tourism Organisation) 1998.

WTO (1998b), *World Tourism Statistics 1997* (Madrid: World Tourism Organisation) 1998.

WTO (1998c), *Tourism 2020 Vision* (Madrid: World Tourism Organisation) 1998.

Chapter 12
Logistics and Manufacturing

Brian Fynes
University College Dublin
and
Sean Ennis
University College Dublin

12.1 INTRODUCTION

In this chapter we address the relationship between manufacturing and logistics management. Firstly, we examine the evolution of manufacturing and the emergence of lean production/world class manufacturing (WCM) in recent times. In doing so, we identify the fundamental differences between the traditional and emerging theories of manufacturing and logistics. We then proceed to explain how 'world class' can be measured and examine the practices companies can adopt in order to proceed in this direction. Case histories of the implementation of WCM and its impact on logistics in two multinationals located in Ireland, Microsoft and Dell Computers, are then recounted to illustrate how leading-edge companies have improved performance by fundamentally changing the way they do business.

12.2 EVOLUTION OF MANUFACTURING: IMPLICATIONS FOR LOGISTICS

Advances in our understanding of manufacturing management are of relatively recent vintage. The central theory, which has underpinned traditional mass production, is the Economic Order Quantity (EOQ) Model (Figure 12.1). As order size increases, the costs associated with carrying the increased level of inventory also increases. Conversely, as order size increases, fewer orders need to be placed and ordering costs (or set-up costs in a production context) fall. The basis of the theory is that there is an optimum production batch size (EOQ) which minimises total costs. This batch size is based on achieving an equitable *trade-off* between production set-up costs and inventory carrying costs. This concept of *trade-offs* subsequently became a central assumption of both manufacturing and logistics management. The relationship between quality and cost is a frequently cited example of a trade-off: if you wanted a BMW 525i, you have to pay for it

Figure 12.1: The Economic Order Quantity (EOQ) Model

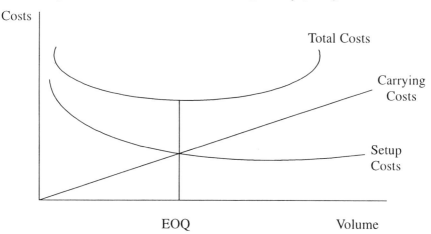

The manner in which manufacturing subsequently evolved in the final century of the second millennium is illustrated in Figure 12.2. Using the automobile industry as an example, one can see that at the start of the 1900s there was a very wide range of products on sale. Each vehicle was a one-of-a-kind and custom built to the requirements of the owner. Volumes, however, were quite low since cars were only purchased by those with high incomes. This was the era of *craft production*, which is still epitomised in the fashion industry by the made-to-measure customised suits that are tailored for the rich and famous on Saville Row.

However, the application of a more scientific approach to manufacturing quickly led to the emergence of *mass production* as the dominant way of producing goods. Mass production was based on three basic principles: specialisation of labour, standardisation of parts and ownership of the entire supply chain. Using these principles, Henry Ford developed and manufactured two million units of the Model T per year. Mass production was characterised essentially by economies of scale: by producing in large batches, manufacturing costs were spread over a greater number of units in a marketplace that was dominated by considerations of price. Competition was primarily cost-focused. At the same time, product variety fell to just a few dozen offerings: "you can have any colour as long as it's black". However, while this approach was acceptable in the less-consumer oriented markets of the first half of the century, it is not likely to satisfy the fashion-conscious user of colour co-ordinated mobile phones at the turn of the millennium.

**Figure 12.2: The progression of product variety and production volume
in the auto industry**

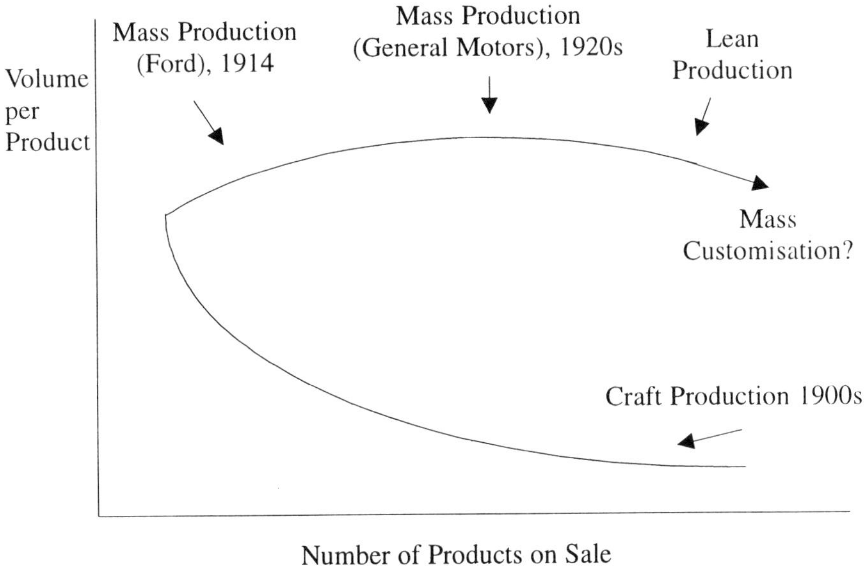

Volume
per
Product

Mass Production
(Ford), 1914

Mass Production
(General Motors), 1920s

Lean
Production

Mass
Customisation?

Craft Production 1900s

Number of Products on Sale

Source: adapted from Womack *et al.* (1990)

Alfred Sloan at General Motors responded to the emergence of consumer needs
and tastes . By the late-1920s, General Motors gained significant market share
by offering greater variety (different models and extra features). This trend
away from standardisation and towards customisation was to culminate with
the emergence of the Japanese car industry and their *lean production* or world
class manufacturing strategies. Such strategies were based on the notion of
using less resources to offer far greater choice. Based on an international research project in the automobile industry,[1] the term 'lean', although often loosely
used in management jargon, was defined in terms of a two-to-one performance
gap. The lean organisation is twice as efficient and as effective as its more
traditional competitor: it uses less of everything (with the exception of knowledge and information technology). It takes half the time and effort to design its
products, half the human effort and tooling to make it with half the level of
inventories and level of defects. As a result, the customer can be offered twice
the number of products (product range flexibility) that can be built in half the
normal volume (volume flexibility). Thus, economies of *scope* with both volume and variety advantages had come to replace economies of scale as the
basis of competition. Likewise, logistics, which means having the right quality
product in the right pace at the right time at the right price must also be correspondingly lean.

---

[1] Womack *et al.* (1990).

What does the future hold with respect to the evolution of manufacturing? Product diversity has increased as products have grown more complex and differentiated, while simultaneously product life cycles have shortened dramatically. At the same time national markets have become increasingly similar, particularly for intermediate goods. Accordingly, companies have been able to extend their global market presence as a result of more flexible manufacturing and distribution methods and better communications and logistics technologies. Some commentators have suggested that in many industries this represents the era of *mass customisation*.[2] Using flexible manufacturing systems (FMS), companies adopting this approach allow the customer to design and configure his/her product order to a personalised specification. For example, the US shoe retailer Custom Foot, does not carry any inventory in its stores; instead it stocks examples of styles, accessories, leathers and colours. Customers effectively *design* their own product from amongst the available options and have their foot dimensions accurately scanned, recorded and an order dispatched to the Italian manufacturer which is filled within three weeks at a highly competitive price (Christopher, 1998).

The competitive advantage in terms of quality, cost, flexibility and speed-to-market accruing to such lean or world class organisations is crystal clear. They can compete on not just one, but on *all* the order-winning criteria in both global and local marketplaces. This ability to compete across a number of competitive fronts represents a fundamental shift in the trade-off assumption which traditionally has underpinned both manufacturing theory and practice. As already noted in the case of the EOQ model, this assumption is based on the proposition that trade-offs between measures of manufacturing performance occur because factories are technology based systems that are limited in what they can do by their equipment, materials, information systems and management systems. As a result, trade-offs must and will occur (Skinner, 1992).

However, competing on multiple fronts represents an entirely different approach to manufacturing. This competing explanation has been labelled the 'sandcone' theory by Ferdows and De Meyer (1990) and is based on the proposition that competencies are *cumulative* rather than *mutually exclusive*. They suggest that lasting improvements in performance always involve the same sequence of, at first, quality improvement, followed by dependability, speed and finally cost efficiency (see Figure 12.3).

Furthermore, in addition to describing a specific sequence of manufacturing improvements, the 'sandcone' structure represents diminishing returns on efforts to improve manufacturing performance. Thus, while the quality 'platform' which forms the foundation of manufacturing is relatively straightforward to establish, improving performance in dependability, speed and cost requires increasing dedication of resources if one is to get to the top of the sandcone because diminishing returns apply.

---

[2] Westbrook and Williamson (1993).

Figure 12.3: The Sandcone Theory of Manufacturing

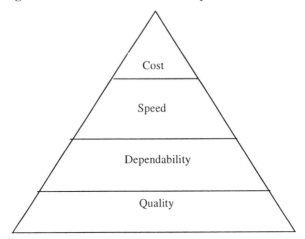

Source: adapted from Ferdows and De Meyer (1990).

The relationship between this conceptual framework and business logistics is also important. From an operational perspective, the adoption of best practice can lead to improvements in both manufacturing *and* logistics performance (Figure 12.4). However, what the terms quality, speed, dependability, cost and flexibility actually mean is open to interpretation. Quality could be defined as conforming to specification (a manufacturing perspective) or customer service (a logistics perspective); speed could be defined as how long production takes (a manufacturing perspective) or the time taken to expedite delivery of spare parts (a logistics perspective); flexibility could be defined as the capability to produce a wide range of goods (a manufacturing perspective) or the capability to deliver at different times (a logistics perspective).

Whatever the definition, the practices companies can adopt to do things right, fast, on time, flexibly and efficiently are a central consideration. These practices are considered in the following section.

12.3 WORLD CLASS MANUFACTURING: PRACTICE AND PERFORMANCE

Before examining the specific components of world class manufacturing, it is prudent to inject a cautionary note into the discussion. Terms such as 'WCM', 'manufacturing excellence' and 'lean production' are pejorative because they convey a vague, simplistic notion about what is required on the part of manufacturing strategy to achieve such positions of eminence. A key prerequisite for understanding such terminology is that it is aspirational in nature and, as a consequence, the onus is on the firm to place a strong degree of emphasis on continuous improvement in products and processes (what the Japanese call

Figure 12.4: Best practice and operational performance

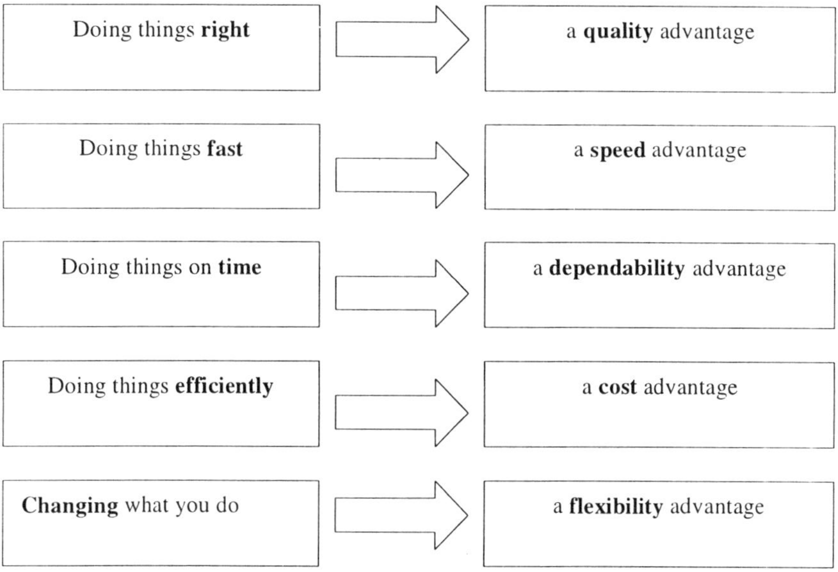

Doing things **right**	a **quality** advantage
Doing things **fast**	a **speed** advantage
Doing things on **time**	a **dependability** advantage
Doing things **efficiently**	a **cost** advantage
Changing what you do	a **flexibility** advantage

Source: adapted from Slack *et al.* (1995).

kaizen). Indeed some commentators have gone so far as to suggest an interesting aspect of manufacturing excellence is that, if such a thing is attainable at all, it will be by those who realise that the target is continually moving (Hall, 1987).

Many of the early promoters of WCM suggested it was based on the core principles of just-in-time (JIT) manufacturing and total quality management (TQM). JIT manufacturing is a disciplined approach to improving manufacturing performance and focuses on the cost-effective delivery of the right quantity of goods at the right place, at the right quality at the right cost. Based on the notion of simplifying production and eliminating waste and unevenness, core JIT practices include kanbans or 'pull-based' production control signals; mixed model sequencing or producing a mix of products daily; set-up reduction to facilitate quick production batch changeovers and JIT supply. The latter is particularly important from a logistics perspective as the ability to supply a customer with small, frequent deliveries and engage in subcontracting (and even product development) requires suppliers to be streamlined in terms of managing and operating within sophisticated supply chains. Likewise, the application of TQM practices has implications for the management of logistics. Traditionally quality control (QC) and quality assurance (QA) was the preserve of manufacturing and focused on conforming to production specification. However, the 'total' in TQM requires quality management practices such as process control, interfunctional teams, customer monitoring, supplier quality control and quality-oriented leadership to be deployed throughout entire organisation. In addition, its remit includes *service quality* oriented functions such as logistics management. As such, it is difficult to disentangle the management of manufacturing from that of logistics.

More recently, a number of studies have attempted to define and measure best practices more precisely.[3] Drawing on the sporting analogy, they have argued that the adoption of best practice can improve business performance (Figure 12.5). While it is acknowledged that factors other than the adoption of best practice can influence performance (e.g. investment in new technology), empirical evidence confirms that more than half of the improvement in business performance can be explained by the adoption of best practice.

Figure 12.5: The practice performance approach

Operations Practices	Operations Performance	Market Performance
TQM Lean Production JIT Concurrent Engineering Logistics Manufacturing Systems Organisation/Culture	Quality Rapid Product Design Low Inventory Fast Response Short Lead Time Low Cost Improved Productivity Employee Satisfaction	Customer Satisfaction Market Growth Profit Growth ROI Growth

Source: adapted from Voss *et al.* (1995).

The inclusion of both operations and market performance as key indicators of world class status are the significant feature of the practice-performance approach. Companies can now assess themselves in order to measure not just practice adoption, but also performance improvement. Furthermore, it is particularly significant that many of the measures of operations performance are logistics-related: low inventory, fast response, low cost and short lead-times.

Companies that self-assess the adoption of best practice and performance can in turn benchmark how they compare with other companies. Indeed, this provides companies with a framework to measure 'world class' status. Figure 12.6 continues with the sporting (boxing) analogy in this regard.

Figure 12.6 is based on the *Made in Europe* survey of 663 manufacturing sites across Europe. Although, the categorisations are somewhat notional, they mirror the empirical approach of Womack *et al.* (1990). The questionnaire used in the *Made in Europe* survey was subsequently adapted as a self-assessment instrument called MICROSCOPE.[4] This framework can be applied to both logistics and manufacturing performance. Companies that score less than

---

[3] See Voss *et al.* (1995) and Hanson (1996).
[4] London Business School/IBM (1997).

Figure 12.6: Measuring world class

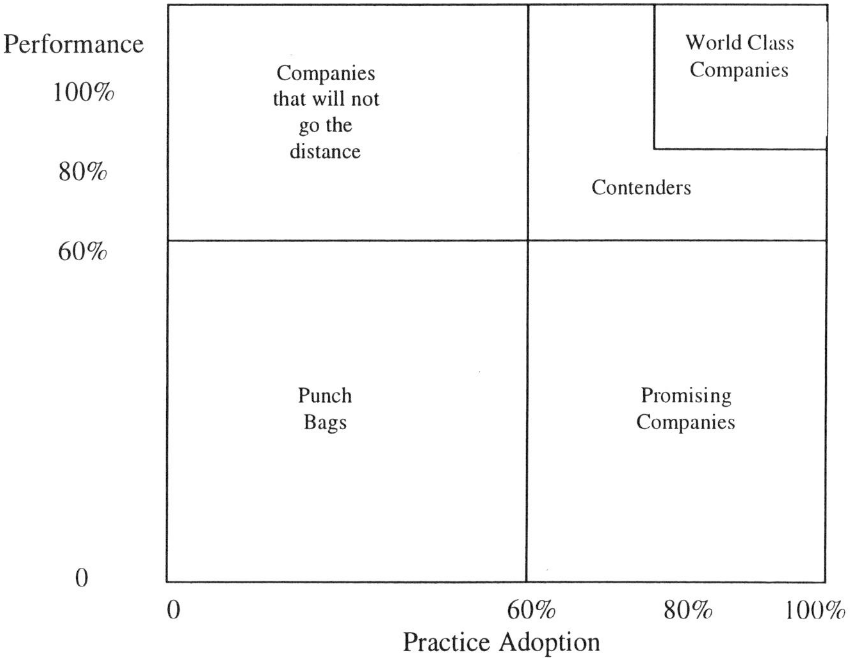

Source: adapted from Voss *et al.* (1995).

60 per cent on practice and performance are essentially 'punchbags' and have difficulty even identifying where to start their improvement programmes. Companies scoring more than 60 per cent on practice but less than 60 per cent on performance are 'promising': whilst they have adopted best practice, implementation problems have meant that performance has not improved commensurately. Companies that score more than 60 per cent on performance but less than 60 per cent on practice adoption have not adapted to changing business circumstances and may 'not go the distance': frequently they are companies that have historically enjoyed good performance because of a monopoly position. Companies scoring between 60 per cent and 80 per cent on both practice and performance are real 'contenders' and are clear about the path forward. Finally, companies scoring more than 80 per cent on both practice and performance are deemed 'world class'. As in any sport, such champions are an elite group with empirical research suggesting that less than 2 per cent of companies fall into this category (Voss *et al.*, 1995).

In the next two sections we examine two such world class companies: Microsoft Ireland and Dell Computers. Both cases illustrate the interplay between manufacturing and logistics strategies in the fast-moving computer industry.

12.4 MICROSOFT IRELAND: FROM LEAN PRODUCTION TO LEAN LOGISTICS

Founded by Bill Gates in 1975, Microsoft emerged in the 1990s as the most important single force in the entire computer industry. Microsoft Ireland is the European manufacturing base of the company. From this facility the company supplies software packages to all major European markets.

When initially established in Ireland, the plant was allocated direct responsibility for manufacturing and shipping to UK and European destinations. Marketing, customer service and technical support were provided by each national sales subsidiary. The manufacturing process at Microsoft Ireland involved two stages. The first stage was the duplication of software packages from master disks while the second stage of the process was the assembly of the finished software package. The assembly process was labour intensive and consisted of placing the duplicated disks, manuals, licence agreement and packing material in the appropriate carton. These were then shrink-wrapped to await shipment.

Initially, Microsoft operated like most other manufacturers: long production runs, large inventories, lengthy set-up times, quality control problems and multiple suppliers, i.e. the manufacturing process was based on traditional production principles. This traditional approach was based on the primary objective of minimising costs associated with long set-up times. Such a process necessitated bulk deliveries of raw materials from their suppliers and required a warehouse of 40,000 square feet capable of housing eight weeks of inventory with associated storage costs. At the end of a production run, the finished goods were moved back to the finished goods warehouse where they awaited shipment. Delivery to customers occurred at the end of the month. This approach resulted in a 3-week order cycle and lent itself to stockouts as production capacity was locked into a given line for considerable periods of time.

The structure of the distribution channel at this time was typical of the industry in general. Microsoft Ireland would ship large batches intermittently to the warehouses of the thirteen sales and support subsidiaries around Europe which were responsible for onward logistics. For example, in Britain, Microsoft Ireland shipped product directly to the UK subsidiary's warehouse. From there, Microsoft UK would ship to a mix of about 200 distributors and dealers using contract delivery for large distributors and couriers for smaller orders to dealers. Backorder (unfilled) rates were typically of the order of 15 per cent of total orders

Microsoft Ireland decided to confront these problems of working capital tied up in inventory, quality and product availability. They commissioned a study which highlighted that, on average, Microsoft's process lead-time was 151 days: 60 days in raw material, 1 day in work-in-progress and 90 days in finished goods. On the other hand the product received value for only four minutes (the time it took the package to be assembled on the line) during a normal production run. Faced with a value-added to non value-added ratio of four minutes to 151 days, the company's response was immediate: emphasising throughput, a policy decision was taken to manufacture smaller lots more frequently. The objective was to receive supplies daily and build (assemble) daily. The company prioritised four critical dimensions of WCM for implementation.

1. Supplier reduction

The company's supplier base included indigenous printing companies (manuals), packaging manufacturers, disk manufacturers and freight forwarders. Microsoft decided to initiate a process of selecting strategic partners. In return for providing their suppliers with a long-term commitment, standardisation of product design and rolling sales forecasts, Microsoft received assurances with regard to mutual cost reduction and daily deliveries. These commitments were not based on legally binding contractual agreements but, rather, on the basis of 'gentlemen's agreements' coupled with quarterly reviews. The result of cutting its supplier base by 70 per cent led to a significant reduction in transaction and communication costs.

2. Production batch sizes were halved

To facilitate shorter production runs, lower inventories and the assembly of all products on a JIT basis, set-up times had to be dramatically reduced. Set-up involved ensuring that all the disks, manuals and packaging were available at the appropriate work-station for assembly. The company came up with an imaginative and novel approach to eliminating lengthy set-up times. While many exponents of JIT suggested that U-shaped production lines facilitated the process, Microsoft replaced the traditional assembly lines with fifteen dual-level carousels or 'round-tables' (see Figure 12.7). While operatives assembled from one level of the carousel, individuals who had completed their tasks for that run set-up the other carousel for the next production run. In addition to eliminating set-ups, quality control was facilitated by this approach. For example, in a production batch of ten units, it became immediately obvious at the end of the process if any disks or manuals were not included in the carton as they would remain highly visible on the carousel. By producing in smaller batches, quality problems were immediately and clearly identified.

3. Employee Involvement

The solution to overcoming resistance to change on the shop floor required a radical change in the way individuals were managed. The company identified employees who they felt would be suitable facilitators in the training of operatives in JIT/TQM techniques. Employees were now to be paid on the basis of the number of new skills they acquired by way of in-company training. Considerable resources were devoted to education and training. Quality focused teams were introduced to brainstorm on how the manufacturing process could be improved.

Figure 12.7: Manufacturing cells with carousels

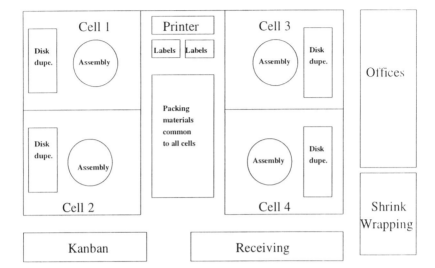

4. Focused Factories

Wickham Skinner (1992) pioneered the concept of focus in manufacturing in the 1970s. He argued that a plant would perform better if it limited itself to a focused number of tasks, processes or products. Within Microsoft, it was decided that a customer-driven approach must form the basis of organising 'factories within the factory'. The requirements of the marketplace were now to have a more significant impact on the manufacturing process and, more specifically, plant layout. Since the geographic destinations of the software packages were language-related, four factories within the plant were introduced: Britain and English language products (Euro), Germany, France and the rest of Europe (multilingual).

Each focused factory was now charged with dealing with specific geographic markets and had its own independent manufacturing cells, production equipment (duplicating machines and carousels) and work teams (see Figure 12.8). In addition the possibility of extra paperwork and administration was eliminated by extending the concept of focus to suppliers. A printing supplier would now typically deliver to only one focused factory. The national flags of the destination markets were in evidence at focused factory, highlighting the market-driven nature of the approach.

Within months, cost of goods sold had been reduced by 25 per cent, while inventory levels in the plant had been cut by 70 per cent and, more importantly from the customers point of view, lead times could now be reduced to just one day.

As the radical changes in operations in the Dublin plant were beginning to impact positively on manufacturing performance, a series of developments

Figure 12.8: Plant Layout with Focused Factories

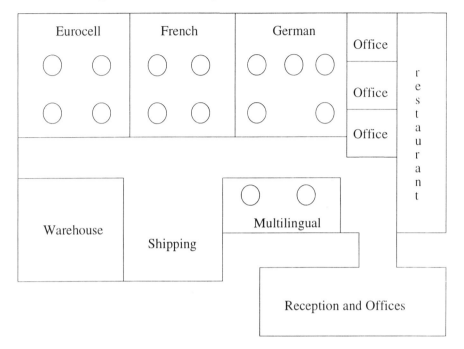

and trends began to emerge with respect to the channels of distribution. Firstly, Microsoft UK (the sales and service subsidiary in Britain) decided to relocate its headquarters to a new site in the south-east of England. As there was a lack of suitable warehousing space at this new headquarters, the parent company felt it was now opportune to evaluate the future warehousing requirements for the UK. There was some concern that the phenomenal growth rates being experienced in the industry could lead to customer service problems and have significant cost implications for the company. As a result, the company decided to evaluate the possibility of separating the warehousing function from the marketing and technical support functions currently being performed by Microsoft UK.

Secondly, newer low cost channels of distribution began to emerge. For example, approximately nine major distributors accounted for 80 per cent of Microsoft's business in the UK. The remaining 20 per cent included smaller dealers, educational establishments and original equipment manufacturers (OEMs). A notable feature of the computer industry is that channel structure has been based historically on the computer hardware sector. In the mid-1980s, distributors concentrated on the sale of personal computers (PCs), where high margins were readily obtained. However, this situation changed considerably in the early-1990s as low cost equipment began to appear on the market. The mystery surrounding the use of PCs began to evaporate gradually, especially when combined with the emergence of user-friendly graphical interfaces such as Microsoft Windows. Hardware manufacturers began to use more direct forms of distribution to customers as lower cost distribution channels became the norm.

In the light of these developments Microsoft Europe felt it was timely to examine logistics strategy with particular emphasis on warehousing requirements and changes in the nature and structure of the channels of distribution. Following a comprehensive analysis of possible future options with regard to logistics strategy, Microsoft Europe's eventual decision was to relocate the UK distribution hub to the manufacturing plant in Ireland. While this might appear to have been a very radical decision in terms of locating at a more peripheral and distant site, the selection highlighted the need to view the decision in the wider context of logistics and channel strategy rather than just simply warehouse location. This broader rationale for selecting Ireland included the following.

1. The realisation that there were significant logistical implications arising from the application of rate-based manufacturing: *the ability to manufacture on a daily basis now offered the opportunity to deliver on a daily basis.*

2. Locating the UK warehouse in Dublin facilitated the adoption of 'one-touch' inventory, i.e. once finished goods were shipped from the production line in Dublin (one-touch), there was no further intermediate stocking points at Microsoft UK.

3. The emergence of the more direct, low-cost channel structure, coupled with a rationalisation of the company's distribution network in the UK from two hundred down to just nine major distributors, immediately facilitated direct shipments from the Dublin plant. It is both feasible and more efficient to ship directly to a small concentration of distributors as against a large number of geographically dispersed dealers.

4. The implementation of lean production principles with JIT delivery from suppliers released an extra 40,000 sq. ft. of warehouse space (by default rather than design) at the Dublin manufacturing site (Figure 12.8). Previously used for storing raw materials, this space could now be used for managing the distribution hub.

Microsoft Ireland were conscious that the relocation of the UK warehouse to Dublin presented the company with a number of inter-dependent challenges associated with supplying the large UK market from a seemingly peripheral site. One of the major factors that had to be considered was the perceived loss of control by Microsoft UK over the entire warehousing function. Concern had been expressed about separating the sales and warehousing functions and the implications this might have for customer service levels in Britain. In addition to a perceived loss of control, any physical relocation of the UK warehouse could potentially eliminate inventory visibility for Microsoft UK. Warehouse managers and supervisors generally prefer to be able to actually see current inventory levels for all stock-keeping units (SKUs). Some means of counterbalancing this 'fear factor' with a 'comfort factor' in the event of relocation needed to be examined. The issue of customer service was addressed by following a phased implementation plan, initially allowing Microsoft UK to define customer service measurements and levels. In addition, the 'comfort factor' was provided by daily e-mail updates between Ireland and the UK. Finally, any manufacturing-marketing interface difficulties relating to customer service that arose were addressed at weekly problem clinics at the UK headquarters.

Within a year, the impact of leaner logistics (relocation, direct shipment and one-touch inventory) on performance was as significant as that achieved when the company adopted world class manufacturing principles. In a marketplace where rapid product introductions and revisions mirrored the importance of time-based competitive strategies, the company were able to record the following improvements in logistics performance:

- delivery lead times were cut to just one day;
- inventory savings of the order of £3 million were achieved in the first year of operation;
- backorder levels fell from 15 per cent to just 5 per cent of total orders.

Furthermore, from Microsoft UK's perspective, they were now able to devote greater attention and resources to their core competence: marketing and technical support.

The Microsoft Ireland experience illustrates how the management of logistics service was transferred to a geographically remote manufacturing location, but with a significant improvement in performance and service levels. While logistics decisions have often been a source of conflict in the often times adversarial relationship that exists between marketing and manufacturing, Microsoft's experience demonstrates that it is possible for manufacturing and sales personnel to understand their respective functional requirements. A key element in this understanding is trust: the sales and service subsidiary were confident that logistics could not only be effectively managed by manufacturing, but effectively managed from a peripheral location.

The case also illustrates the interaction between distribution channel developments and the management of logistics. There is, in fact, a whole range of channels of distribution to be serviced by Microsoft, each requiring different approaches. For instance, direct sales and downloading of software over the internet have more recently emerged as a key distribution channel. It seems that channels are in far from a steady state, so flexible strategies are necessary.

12.5 DELL COMPUTER: DIRECT ON THE INTERNET

Michael Dell founded Dell Computer Corporation in 1983. Spotting a market opportunity by selling PCs directly to the customer, and thereby eliminating the middleman, Dell has grown to a point where, by 1997, it achieved world-wide sales of $16 billion. It can be described as a company that sells Intel and Microsoft technology through a highly efficient logistics operation. Within its operations, it carries less than seven days stock at any point in time; no fin-ished stock is held as Dell only manufactures to order.

Dell has three plants worldwide: Austin, Texas; Limerick, Ireland and Penang, Malaysia. The Limerick factory handles the European market. More than half of the components are supplied on a JIT basis and a further 40 per cent are held in supplier hubs located within fifteen minutes of the plant. The suppliers are expected to stock their own warehouse and refresh their own inventories (Christopher, 1998).

From a manufacturing and overall business perspective, many commenta-tors initially perceived Dell to be nothing more than that of a niche player in the PC sector. This was viewed as a potentially major problem in the late-1980s as it was felt that the single office-home office (SOHO) market and personal purchasers would be uncomfortable with the idea of buying a high value and potentially complex item over the phone without the 'psychological comfort' of personal advice.

In order to redress this issue, Dell began to develop the retail channel in the early part of the 1990s. This move proved to be a major strategic error. Profits dropped to the extent that a loss was reported in 1993. The strategy backfired because their original competitive advantage of being a low-cost manufacturing and channel operator was seriously threatened as Dell was un-accustomed to the challenges of negotiating margins with the retail sector and trading relationships quickly deteriorated. This negative experience concen-trated Michael Dell's mind on the need for a return to what it did best, i.e. a direct sales strategy.

The Dell concept is based on two critical platforms: low inventory/capital investment and speed-to-market (Hubbard, 1998). In the case of the former, every PC is built individually to order with a fifteen-minute 'call down' from the time that the original order is received. Five days elapse from the receipt of order to shipping and delivery to the customer. For the larger market (e.g. Fortune 500 companies), this duration reduces to 48 hours. Dell also insists, as a matter of policy, that, where possible, suppliers of materials and component parts should be located within fifteen minutes from the factory. This allows it to practice JIT more efficiently, and concomitantly eliminate the need to carry inventory.

In May 1997, Dell launched a website enabling potential customers to order a PC to their own personal specification. This effectively allows the customer to decide on and design his/her own hardware/software package and level of technical support. This new channel initially accounted for over 10 per cent of its sales (the remainder was accounted for by telephone orders). Worldwide, sales from Dell's websites generate $4 million to $5 million per day. The company believes that e-commerce, through the internet, is a logical extension of its original Dell Direct strategy. From a manufacturing perspective, it facilitates *mass customisation* in that the customer can now order a customised product which is manufactured and delivered in a very short lead time *without* incurring the price premium that would normally be associated with such a product/service offering.

When designing the web site, Dell followed a number of basic rules:

- Fast downloading of the site should be possible.
- Customers should never be more than three clicks from something interesting – and that includes making a purchase.
- The *Buy a Dell* icon should be visible at all times across the page.
- It should be able to be replicated across Europe, with multiple languages and local content (by early 1998, localised versions of the site are in operation in Germany, France, Spain, South Africa, Scandinavia and the Benelux countries).

The benefits to the customer include a facility to browse through the pages, choose a configuration, place and pay for an order and consider add-ons that they might not have contemplated buying prior to visiting the site. It is also convenient in that it is open 24 hours. Use of the website also encourages a high level of interaction between the customer and Dell resulting in a strong level of intimacy.

The benefits to Dell are with respect to lower transaction costs and scalability. Ability to attract and acquire customers and retain all information about them online (every computer sold via the internet can be traced to the individual customer) facilitates the building of life-long relationships and customer retention. Dell can also use the internet to send information to purchasers about new product developments in hardware, software, and upgrades. No PC is manufactured until an order is received and paid for. Price changes can be made on the website within three hours: this contrasts with a potential lead time of four to six weeks if advertising space has to be booked in the national press and television. Customised web pages can be designed by Dell and included on the intranet of individual companies, which in turn facilitates centralised purchasing.

For Dell, the ability to forecast demand is a critical aspect of managing the manufacturing and logistics interface. The following extract from a recent interview given by Michael Dell reinforces this view:

> *We see forecasting as a critical sales skill. We teach our sales account managers to lead customers through a discussion of their future PC needs. We'll walk a customer through every department of his company, asking him to designate which needs are certain and which are contingent. And when they're contingent on some event, the salesperson will know what that event is so he can follow up. We can do this with our large accounts, which make up the*

> *bulk of our business. With smaller customers, we have real-time information about what they're buying from our direct telephone salespeople. And we can also steer them in real time, on the phone, toward configurations that are available, so this is another way we can fine-tune the balance between supply and demand.*[5]

The Dell Direct Model exemplifies the growing integration between manufacturing and logistics. Indeed it goes further to incorporate marketing and procurement-related aspects of the supply chain. Virtual integration with its customers allows for much more accurate forecasting. This in turn percolates through the manufacturing and procurement aspects of the supply chain.

The focus on carrying minimal inventory also results in Dell achieving significant savings in relation to its competitors. Because the company does not need to maintain inventory in its factories for a prolonged period of time, it avoids the dangers of having large amounts of money tied up in stock. In addition Dell does not suffer from the problems that arise from the somewhat cyclical and unpredictable cost of certain component parts. Dell buys items when they are needed and avoids the danger of buying inventory at a high price only to discover that costs have dropped over the course of a couple of months.

The challenge facing Dell (as it always has) is one of managing customer relationships in what has become to all intents and purposes, a commodity market. Dell management argues that the internet strategy allows the company to move the customer through the stages that are commonly associated with the 'customer experience': awareness, interest, commitment to buy, advice, order placement and post-sales help.

Nonetheless, a supplementary question arises from this approach. Can Dell sustain its competitive advantage? More specifically, what can prevent competitors from copying the Dell strategy? In fact main competitors, such as Compaq, already operate an online operation. However it can be argued that they have to be more circumspect in the manner with which they develop their direct business. The established competitors also have established dealer and retail networks. They risk the not inconsiderable danger of creating major channel conflict if they pursue the direct route too aggressively. Thus, in the short to medium-term, it can be argued that Dell should maintain its pioneering and 'first-mover' advantage. In the longer term however, it is more difficult to be so optimistic as more and more purchases are made direct. The speed with which the 'digital consumer' emerges will dictate whether companies will ultimately drop traditional channels.

It is not all plain sailing however. Clearly, not every customer is in a position to utilise the internet in order to order a PC. Levels of access to the internet vary widely within Europe. In addition, Dell are more happy to deal with customers that have previously purchased a PC and are familiar with the various

---

[5] Magretta (1998) p.79.

specifications that are outlined on the website. Furthermore, not every visitor to the site actually makes a purchase. The present conversion rate (number of sales as a ratio of number of 'hits') on the Dell UK web page is around 23 per cent (Hubbard, 1998) It is Dell's objective to raise this conversion figure to 33 per cent over the next three years. From a logistics perspective, the greatest potential challenge facing Dell is the ability to deliver the product physically to the end user. They have experimented with a number of third party logistics operators but would admit to some variation in the ability to deliver within the prescribed customer service objectives (five days for small companies and individuals and 48 hours for larger companies).

By any standards, the Dell internet strategy has proved to be very successful. It can be argued that the company happened to be in the right place at the right time when the site was launched. People were becoming increasingly disposed to the notion of buying directly. This trend is graphically illustrated by the fact that nearly half of all PCs purchased in the US go through the direct route. The management structure, particularly in the absence of hierarchies and the empowerment of staff at all levels, allied to the entrepreneurial spirit engendered by Michael Dell himself, has allowed for a smooth development of the internet strategy. It does not require an MBA in business to ascertain that the internet complements Dell's direct business model. In the words of Hubbard "it is a perfect match – at both a strategic and a tactical level".

The Dell case demonstrates many of the virtues of using the internet as a viable and cost-effective channel option. It also adheres naturally to the Dell Direct concept. This has allowed Dell to operate on a *build to order* or mass customisation basis where every PC is built individually and carrying no finished stock at all at its plants in the Republic of Ireland. Dell now engages with its customers and sends them information in a targeted and focused manner. In this way, the company pursues a form of *relationship marketing* which is consistent with streamlined manufacturing and logistics processes, which in turn allows the company to cost effectively manage its supply chain activities.

By the end of 1997, Christopher (1998) observed, Dell was growing at a rate that was more than three times the industry average and had become the world's second biggest PC maker (by unit sales).

12.6 CONCLUSION

In this chapter we have considered developments in both manufacturing and logistics and identified how closely intertwined both functions actually are. The principles of lean production which improve the flow of goods through the factory can be adapted to improve the flow of manufactured goods through the logistics pipeline, and ultimately enhance customer service. Logistics has become increasingly important to overall strategy because products are not just things-with-features: they are things-with-features coupled with services or 'envelopes around a product'.

As in the case of mass customisation, 'tailored logistics' have emerged with the potential as an inventive way of creating value for customers, as an immediate source of savings, as an important discipline in marketing, and as a critical extension of production flexibility. As the scope for gaining further competitive advantage in manufacturing becomes increasingly narrow, the remaining sources of value creation such as the development of logistically distinct businesses serving distinct customers is possibly the next source of competitive advantage. In effect, as has occurred in manufacturing, logistics will become leaner and more menu-driven.

References and Further Reading

Christopher, M, Logistics and Supply Chain Management: Strategies for Reducing Cost and Improving Service (London: Financial Times/Pitman) 1998.

Ferdows, K & A De Meyer, "Lasting Improvements in Manufacturing Performance in Search of a New Theory" *Journal of Operations Management* (1990) Vol. 9, No. 2, pp. 168-184.

Hall, R W, *Attaining Manufacturing Excellence* (Homewood, IL: Dow Jones-Irwin) 1987.

Hanson, P, C Voss, K Blackmon & T Claxton, *Made in Europe 2 – An Anglo-German Design Study* (London: IBM Consulting/London Business School (1996).

Hubbard, P, "Dell and E-Commerce: A Perfect Match" in *Traditional and New Channels: Strategy, Selections and Management* (is this a journal?) March, Materials Handling Centre (1998)

London Business School/IBM, *World Class Manufacturing: The Microscope Tool* (London: LBS) 1997.

Magretta, J, "The Power of Virtual Integration: An Interview with Dell Computer's Michael Dell" Harvard Business Review (March/April 1998) pp. 73-84.

Skinner, W "Manufacturing – Missing Link in Corporate Strategy" *Harvard Business Review* (May/June 1969) pp. 136-145.

Skinner, W, "Missing Link in Manufacturing Strategy" in C A Voss (ed.) *Manufacturing Strategy – Process and Content* (London: Chapman & Hall) 1992, pp. 13-25

Slack, N, S Chambers, C Harland, A Harrison & R Johnston, *Operations Management* (London: Pitman) 1995.

Voss, C, K Blackmon, P Hanson & B Oak, "The Competitiveness of European Manufacturing – A Four Country Study" *Business Strategy Review* (1995) Vol. 6, No. 1, pp.1-25.

Westbrook, R & P Williamson "Mass Customisation: Japan's New Frontier" *European Management Journal* (1993) Vol. 10, No. 1, pp. 38-45.

Womack, J P, D T Jones & D Roos, *The Machine that Changed the World* (New York, NY: Rawson Associates (1990).

Chapter 13

Third Party Logistics and Beyond

Barry O'Grady
IBM

13.1 INTRODUCTION

The adage "information is power" is still true. As the market becomes more informed and demanding, suppliers may nostalgically recall the days when Henry Ford's dictum, "You can have it in any colour you like, as long as it's black", left no one in doubt that the supplier was king. That was then. Now, the well-informed global market expects much more from the suppliers of goods and services. Competition is therefore fiercer, as suppliers seek to be the first to reach the customer. Since the mid-1980s, the notion of "core competencies" has emerged as a key way to sharpen the competitive edge. The theory underlying this management approach is simple: *do what you do best and outsource the rest*. Adopting this principle has fuelled the growth of the outsourcing business culture that is with us now. Third Party Logistics (3PL) is at the heart of this thriving sector, as it soaks up the non-core competencies of its clients.

Third Party Logistics has been an important phenomenon in the Irish economic boom and has played a key role in supporting the development of Ireland as an overseas manufacturing location of choice. This chapter considers the role played by 3PL in addressing the changing needs of their clients. After acknowledging the positive role of 3PLs in reducing supply chain costs, the chapter warns 3PLs not to rest on their laurels. The advent of Fourth Party Logistics (4PL) brings a serious new challenge to 3PLs.

13.2 EVOLUTION OF THIRD PARTY LOGISTICS

Third Party Logistics means that the logistics activities in a supply chain are carried out by an entity that *does not own* the products, whether they are goods or services, being managed.

Does 3PL have definable characteristics or can any freight forwarder claim to be a 3PL provider? Opinions differ on this. However, experts generally agree that the services of a 3PL provider include at least two or more logistics activities. Transport and warehousing are the two most common activities of 3PL, but there are multiple other services, including procurement, order fulfillment, light assembly, call centre management, vendor hub management, return and repair operations and carrier management.

The 3PL industry has experienced a solid growth pattern over the last fifteen years, notwithstanding slowing down in recent times. As we consider the evolution of 3PL, why it began and where it is heading, a word of caution is not out of place. Third Party Logistics is often extolled in the glossy brochures of logistics service providers as if it were a magic formula that will relieve the customer of all supply chain headaches. Unfortunately, 3PL is neither magic nor does it always work. In a recent case in Ireland, an electronics company re-evaluated its outsourced operation and brought it back in-house. However, in the majority of cases it is true to say that 3PL relationships have worked well.

To understand the success of 3PL we need to examine the motives behind outsourcing decisions. A 1994 survey of 50 customers and 20 logistics providers in Northern Europe revealed that the chief motives for outsourcing logistics operations were cost management, service improvement, strategic flexibility and faster implementation (Van Laarhoven and Sharman, 1994). We look at each in turn below.

Cost Management

In the 1980s and early 1990s, most large companies focused their improvement initiatives on cost management and, in particular, cost restructuring within the supply chain. This was due to the increasing emphasis on short-term profitability and the pressure on CEOs to demonstrate effectiveness to an increasingly demanding stock market. Consequently, asset-based activities are high on the agenda for outsourcing. Asset turnover increases dramatically when assets such as facilities and equipment are removed from the books and when the company can avoid investment in expensive hardware and software. Therefore, expensive items such as warehouses, trucks, racking, heavy lifting machinery, conveyor systems and supporting applications are prime targets in the bid to increase asset turnover. Outsourcing the logistics function can also facilitate a reduction of headcount and associated overhead costs. In addition, third party logistics providers are likely to be able to achieve economies of scale by offering similar services to multiple customers and, ideally, passing these savings on to these customers.

Service Improvement

Like Strategic Flexibility and Faster Implementation, the motive for outsourcing is of a strategic nature and has a key role to play in today's market, where consumers are increasingly demanding more from their suppliers. Quality of product or service is already a *sine qua non* in the marketplace. How, then, does a company stay ahead of its competitors in the race to satisfy the consumer? This is where the notion of Supply Chain Management comes in. There is now a recognition that individual companies no longer compete as stand-alone entities, but rather as supply chains (Christopher, 1999). Therefore, optimising performance in the supply chain itself becomes paramount. All players in the supply chain must focus on their own core competencies and outsource other activities to whoever can perform them more effectively. For this reason, many companies have outsourced their logistics activities to third party operators who can give an improved service. When all the players concentrate on their core competencies, the end result is a vibrant supply chain that is in position to serve the consumer. In keeping with its global strategy for using a turnkey manufacturing and distribution model, Microsoft in Ireland outsourced its CD-ROM manufacturing to companies such as Modus Media and, in early 1998, its finished goods inventory management and order fulfillment operations to Walsh Western International.

Strategic Flexibility

Strategic flexibility is another motive for outsourcing. Acknowledging that consumers' demands are changing rapidly, companies want to build flexibility into their supply chain to be capable of keeping ahead of those demands. The idea here is that if demand in the market should change, the company is in a position to set up new 3PL relationships to address the changes and to end relationships that are redundant.

Faster Implementation

Multinational manufacturing companies in Ireland have taken on the expertise of local 3PL providers to facilitate them in getting their operations up and running rapidly. While manufacturing and supporting processes are generally similar regardless of the local environment, it is the area of distribution and logistics that provides country-specific challenges. In this situation, companies rely on the local 3PL providers who have their infrastructures already set up. During the set-up of its Dublin Technology Campus in late 1997, IBM Ireland relied on the distribution, logistics and Customs expertise of Irish Express Cargo.

13.3 EXPERIENCE TO DATE

Have Costs Fallen?

Recent research suggests that reducing costs is still the main reason why companies outsource logistics operations. Over 85 per cent of 250 executives interviewed specified reducing costs as the main driver of their outsourcing initiatives (Logistics Management & Distribution Report, 1999).

Yet has 3PL realised bottom-line savings for these companies? The picture is positive, yet somewhat less so as each year rolls on. A 1998 survey of US manufacturing companies revealed that 59 per cent of 3PL users reported that outsourcing had a positive effect on their logistics costs. This shows a drop from 76 per cent in 1997 and 87 per cent in 1996 (Cooke, 1998). The reason for this may lie in the type of operations that 3PL providers carry out. In the case of standard services such as warehousing and distribution, 3PL providers are able to achieve economies of scale across multiple clients. However, as A.T. Kearney Consulting (1999) pointed out, third party solutions are often too specific and tailored to the individual customer's requirements to leverage across several clients. This situation may become more the norm as customers demand increasingly complex logistics solutions in the endeavour to compete in the tougher consumer market.

Improved Performance?

The 3PL industry has scored particularly highly in terms of improving the logistics services in distribution thanks to the extensive networks that providers have established with other transport companies. In recent years many Irish operators have entered strategic alliances or have been acquired by global distribution companies. Seasky has been bought by Expeditors, MSAS has increased its presence in Ireland by acquiring a majority holding in Cassin and BAX Global acquired part of Reindeer Shipping to develop its network in the Irish market. With these links to almost anywhere on the globe, Irish 3PLs are able to enhance their service offering to their customers. A survey in the US showed that 80 per cent of the client companies questioned renewed their contracts with the same 3PL providers (Van Laarhoven and Sharman, 1994).

In some cases, however, customers complain that they have to initiate improvements in the providers' operations themselves, as their 3PL providers do not come up with proposed enhancements to services (P-E International, 1999). This is an area for alert 3PL providers to steal a march on their competitors, as those who come up with initiatives to enhance their operations to the benefit of the client company are in demand. The idea here is that by focusing on what it does best, the 3PL should be in a position to initiate improvements in its logistics and distribution activities to the benefit of the supply chain as a whole.

13.4 TRENDS IN COMPANIES' LOGISTICS REQUIREMENTS

The volume increase in European freight and logistics is a big opportunity for 3PL providers to expand their range of services to accommodate the emerging needs of companies. Companies facing increasingly complex markets need to re-engineer some of their own processes. Operating in an outsourced environment, they require 3PL providers to support them in meeting their changing requirements.

Pan-European Distribution

In order to develop best practice in purchasing and supply management, companies need to consolidate the number of their suppliers. Hence, there is an increasing demand for suppliers who can provide reliable pan-European land-based distribution services. Transport providers are strong in certain countries and weak in others. This may not be the case for much longer, though, as recent months have seen consolidation efforts among European transport companies in an attempt to extend their networks and achieve superior economies of scale. For example, RMF, traditionally strong in Germany and Northern Europe, has joined forces with Securicor Omega Logistics to strengthen its network throughout the rest of Europe.

Enhanced Traditional Logistics Capabilities

Since the advent of JIT and World Class Manufacturing, inventory has been a connotation for mismanagement. To reduce inventories, companies demand smaller and more frequent shipments and thus are more dependent on speed and delivery performance. In addition, in the manufacturing area, *mass customisation* is in vogue. For example, in the computer industry, PCs and servers are now built to meet customer-specific orders. These companies do not hold finished stock, so in order to cut down the lead time for the end customer, a robust and reliable supply chain is essential, especially in relation to the transport of inbound materials and outbound finished product. Not only do they require fast and reliable transport, they also need to know the status of shipments. Hence the need for shipment tracking technologies. The integrators (DHL, UPS, TNT, Fedex, etc.) were the innovators in this arena by using the Internet for their customers to track urgent shipments. Now, companies expect this service as standard from all 3PL providers. To give its customers visibility of their orders to the point of arrival at their doorstep, Dell in Limerick links its web site to providers' shipment tracking systems.

Value-added Activities

Given the general success to date in outsourcing distribution activities, companies are now looking at what other in-house activities can be released to third party operators. We consider a number of examples below.

In another effort to reduce inventory costs, some manufacturing companies require their suppliers to route raw material through vendor hubs operated by 3PL providers. Only when the materials are released from the vendor hub to the customer's manufacturing line does ownership of said materials transfer from supplier to the customer, hence reducing the need for the customer to tie up money in inventory. One of the early vendor hub operations in Ireland was set up by Irish Express Cargo to feed the Apple manufacturing plant in Cork. This operation substantially reduced Apple's inventory costs. Vendor hubs are now used by most of the computer manufacturers in Ireland.

In an age of customer service, return and repair channels have become more important. Companies increasingly look for 3PL providers to manage these returns and carry out repair operations. Having identified this growth opportunity, MSAS Global Logistics recently opened a logistics centre in Germany to operate return and repair channels, as well as activities such as preinstallation of computers and call centre operations on behalf of manufacturing companies. Already a number of Irish 3PL providers carry out after-sales services on behalf of computer manufacturers. For example, Tibbett & Britten Ireland performs after-sales support for Compaq customers in Ireland. From one of its Dublin sites, Irish Express Cargo provides an emergency parts supply service for IBM customers located in Ireland and Europe.

Order fulfillment is also high on the agenda for outsourcing. In Ireland there are many examples of software companies who outsource their order fulfillment operations to 3PL providers and thus reduce the lead time for the customer once an order is made. An added advantage is that the number of touch points in the delivery process is significantly reduced, minimising the risk of damage during transit. A typical example of this is the software industry in Ireland. Instead of the 3PL picking up the shipment from the software company, bringing it to its own warehouse to prepare the required documentation and then transporting the shipment to the customer, the order itself goes directly to the 3PL who picks and packs the order from warehouse stock and prepares it for shipment with all its necessary documentation. Exel Walsh Western provides this type of fulfillment service for both Microsoft and Novell. Assembly operations at the component level and packaging operations are also being pushed outside of companies to 3PL providers.

A recent survey in Europe showed that companies are interested in *one-stop shopping*, that is, in having fewer 3PL providers to deal with. They want 3PL providers who can look after all their logistics needs (Peters *et al.*, 1998). With less relationships to deal with, companies require less resources to administer these relationships. In response to this, 3PLs need to increase the range of services they offer if they are to be chosen.

13.5 THE LOGISTICS SERVICES PROVIDERS

The good news is that the 3PL industry is responding to demands from companies to expand distribution networks and the scope of services offered. A recent survey in the US reported that almost 80 per cent of 3PL operators interviewed had formed alliances as a means of broadening their service offerings (Cooke, 1998). Alliances also benefit the providers by reducing their capital investment, as each partner of the alliance contributes its own infrastructure, be it distribution networks or warehousing facilities, etc. The most popular form of alliances among 3PL players are in the areas of groupage, warehousing, freight forwarding and information systems. Since they share facilities, these alliances are able to make themselves more competitive in bids for new contracts. Allegro, one of the large consumer goods distributors in Ireland, merged with Gillespie Distribution, a subsidiary of Fyffes, to strengthen its distribution network in the face of increasing competition. Exel entered the same sector in Ireland in early 1999 by acquiring Sydney Cooper Distribution. With the facilities and network it inherited in the acquisition, Exel was chosen by Tesco to manage the warehousing of all non-food and slow-moving goods for its outlets in Ireland.

In relation to finding new business, a reference from satisfied customers is the most powerful bridge to success with prospective clients. Presentations by 3PL providers at professional meetings or conferences has also been an important means of attracting clients. These findings tell us about the emerging needs of customers. Having outsourced many of their operations, customers believe that supply chain improvements of a strategic nature should be coming from the third party providers, as these are the logistics experts and not the customers themselves.

3PL providers need qualified personnel to initiate these strategic improvements in their operations and in their working relationships with customers. This is proving to be a challenge for the providers. Traditionally, the transport industry has not attracted high-level professionals into its ranks. Cooke has cited recruitment and retention of qualified personnel as the biggest problem the industry faces (see Table 13.1 for the problems that 3PL face). In a December 1998 study carried out for the Irish Government regarding labour skills required to sustain the vibrant economy, virtually all segments of the transport and logistics industry were reported to be experiencing difficulty in recruiting and retaining staff (*The Irish Times*, 31 December 1998). The solution is long-term and involves raising the prestige of the industry so as to attract key people. Having identified this problem, third level institutions and professional bodies in Ireland have increased the number of logistics courses on offer. Orla Gregory and John Mangan discuss these issues in more detail in Chapter 17.

Table 13.1: 3PL's biggest problems (in decreasing order of importance)

	Biggest Problems (Weighted ranking of CEOs' responses)
1	Staffing problems
2	IT system development/costs
3	Development of adequate pricing system
4	Unrealistic customer expectations
5	Expensive and complex selling processes

Source: Cooke, 1998

Another problem for 3PL is IT systems development and the concomitant costs of such development. These companies specialise in logistics and not in IT. Yet, as customers demand services that require increasingly complex systems transactions, the result is high costs that cannot be leveraged across multiple customers. To resolve this problem, some providers have teamed up with IT companies to be in a position to offer logistics services with state of the art supporting applications. Exel Walsh Western has used the strengths of UK-based Grosvenor International to offer its clients IT solutions for managing customs duty regimes such as Customs Warehousing and Inward Processing. In a sense, this need for outsourcing IT activities shows that the 3PL industry itself is coming of age and is no longer a peripheral add-on to the supply chain.

13.6 FOURTH PARTY LOGISTICS

With each player, including 3PLs, in the supply chain focusing on its own core competencies and outsourcing the non-core activities, the supply chain is becoming increasingly fragmented. With more activities outsourced, there are necessarily more companies in the supply chain. For these companies to bring about a vibrant and competitive supply chain, they need to co-ordinate their activities. In a word, they need integration. This is where some have advocated Fourth Party Logistics (4PL) as the solution. 4PL is a new force emerging in the industry, which seeks to address the perceived deficiency in the area of supply chain strategy. A 4PL provider is defined by Andersen Consulting (who, incidentally, coined the term 4PL in 1998 and subsequently trademarked it) as "a supply chain integrator that assembles and manages the resources, capabilities and technology of its own organisation with those of complementary service providers to deliver a comprehensive supply chain solution" (Bade *et al.,* 1998). The proponents of 4PL argue that neither shippers nor 3PL are in a position to make supply chain management decisions on their own. What is needed is an entity which has visibility of, and therefore the responsibility for, all parts of the supply chain.

A Fad, or for Real?

It is easy to dismiss this phenomenon as a fad or as the latest idea that consultants have whipped up to make money – easy but also perilous. Although Andersen owns the term 4PL, other large consultants are beginning to provide similar services with names such as "lead logistics provider" (LLP) or "general contractor". We will briefly discuss the rationale behind 4PL and how it is being received by clients and 3PL.

John Gattorna of Andersen Consulting has described the evolution in supply chain management (Bade *et al.,* 1999). Until the 1980s, companies generally insourced their activities, i.e. they carried out all the steps in the supply chain from procurement and manufacturing to distribution. As Figure 13.1 shows, the 1980s focused on core competencies and led to certain activities being outsourced to various 3PLs. In this arrangement, the client company manages a relationship with a 3PL for each activity being outsourced. In the third and currently last step in this evolution, Gattorna proposes that the client company now outsource this relationship management to a 4PL. Instead of managing a myriad of relationships with 3PLs, the client company only deals with the 4PL. The 4PL adds value by integrating the processes of all the 3PLs to the benefit of the entire supply chain.

Figure 13.1 Evolution in Supply Chain Outsourcing

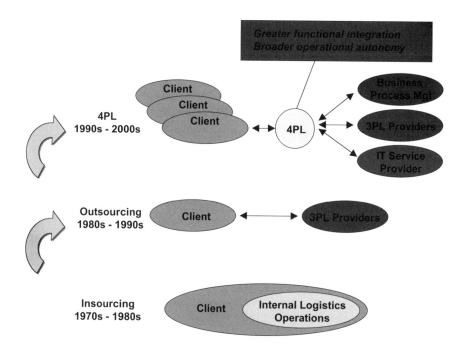

Source: Adapted from Bade *et al.*, 1999

The rationale of these 4PL proponents is that 3PLs lack the strategic expertise and technology to manage the entire supply chain and to integrate all supply chain processes. As experts in warehousing, transportation or other operational activities, 3PLs are able to achieve one-off cost savings. On the other hand, 4PLs are able to achieve more than these one-time savings with their ability to manage all activities in the supply chain. This ability to integrate comes from technology or "in-betweenware", a type of middleware that acts as a go-between among the 3PLs to co-ordinate their activities (Stone, 1999). Andersen Consulting is strong in IT, thus, in its quest to enter the race, KPMG entered a strategic alliance in February 1998 with Manugistics Inc., a leading supply chain management solutions development house. Deloitte Consulting also threw its hat into the ring in 1999 when it poached Douglas Bade, one of Andersen's original 4PL architects. Combining these technologies with their traditional management expertise, these large consulting firms are to be taken seriously.

In addition, the rationale states that a 3PL is unlikely to offer the best combination of technology, warehousing and transportation. On the other hand, a 4PL is in a position to find the "best of breed" provider in each of these areas (Foster, 1999).

Reaction from the 3PL Industry

Understandably, 3PL providers don't agree with these arguments. GATX Corporation, one of the largest 3PL providers in the US, insists that it has the management and technological capabilities to bring about strategic improvements in clients' supply chains. Incidentally, in September 1999, GATX established the GATX Integrated Solutions Group. With this new arrangement, the company will share resources and expertise across its logistics, transportation, liquid logistics, terminals, inventory monitoring and rail divisions to create logistics solutions which focus on optimising clients' transportation and logistics systems worldwide (Transport News, 1999). Clearly, GATX is preparing itself to defend its market from 4PL. In a similar vein, Cardinal Logistics, another large US 3PL, boasts about its "non-asset" logistics solutions and network engineering (Transport News, 1998). This again is an example of a company that sees the necessity of changing the service it is offering in order to compete against the large 4PL consulting firms.

Another problem that 3PLs have with 4PL is cost. The goal of 3PL has predominantly been to reduce cost in the supply chain. In the 4PL model, another (expensive) party enters the model. This extra layer of management, 3PLs argue, is a cost that could be avoided (Foster, 1999).

With the 4PL managing the 3PLs, this latter group no longer has direct contact with the client company. "We don't need anyone getting in the way" is how USCO Logistics curtly puts it (Foster, 1999). Being one step removed from the customer is obviously a disadvantage for any service provider.

Client Reaction

Information on the reaction of clients is sketchy, as few have been exposed to the idea. Nevertheless, clients who want to grab the lead over competitors are generally open to any developments that facilitate them in their endeavours. Integration of the supply chain does seem to be on the agenda. Agility of supply chains has been identified by Martin Christopher (1999) as another work item for logisticians. An agile supply chain is one that is capable of responding in shorter time frames both in terms of volume change and variety change. Agility is becoming more important in order to match the increasing tendency of the consumer market to change its demands in terms of what it wants, when and how much it wants. Agility can only be achieved if all partners in the supply chain operate in harmony with each other. Whether it is 4PLs or revamped 3PLs that will bring about this agility is the question posed here. It will depend on whether 4PL can make the transition from strategic planners to managers and implementers of the supply chain and whether the 3PL industry develops a wider range of technological and management skills to run the supply chain more effectively.

By introducing a 4PL to the supply chain, the client company is further removed from the operational activities of the 3PLs, as Figure 13.1 demonstrated. This in itself could be disconcerting for clients and will therefore most likely be a challenge to 4PLs in their efforts to get customers. Will they be successful? Only time will tell.

13.7 CONCLUSION

To date the 3PL industry has performed well in realising both service improvements and reduced costs for the customer. Both service improvements and costs reductions are consequences of improved operations and economies of scale. However, customers are now demanding strategic improvements that can enhance the competitive advantage of supply chains as a whole. While the 3PL industry grapples with this challenge, the 4PL industry has come into existence as another solution to supply chain management.

References and Further Reading

Anderson, D & H Lee, "Synchronized Supply Chains: The New Frontier" 1999. Located at URL: www.ascet.com.

Bade, D, J Mueller & B Youd, "Technology in the Next Level of Supply Chain Outsourcing – Leveraging the Capabilities of Fourth Party Logistics" 1999.

Located at URL: www.ascet.com.

Burckhardt, P, S Elhence & M Van Rooijen, "European Freight Forwarders: Which Way to Turn?" *The McKinsey Quarterly* (1998) No. 2.
Located at URL: www.mckinseyquarterly.com.

Christopher, M, "Creating the Agile Supply Chain" 1999.
Located at URL: www.ascet.com.

Cooke, J, "Third Party Logistics grows up' *Logistics Management & Distribution Report* (November 1998).
Located at URL: www.manufacturing.net.

Cooke, J, "Outsourcing Report" *Logistics Management & Distribution Report* (October 1998).
Located at URL: www.manufacturing.net.

Foster, T, "4PLs: The Next Generation for Supply Chain Outsourcing?" *Logistics Management & Distribution Report* (April 1999).
Located at URL: www.manufacturing.net.

Foster, T, "Who's in Charge Around Here?' *Logistics Management & Distribution Report* (June 1999).
Located at URL: www.manufacturing.net.

Kearney, A T, "Shippers Turning to Contract Logistics for Operational and Strategic Reasons" 1999.
Located at URL: www.atkearney.com.

Kopczak, L, "Trends in Third Party Logistics" 1999.
Located at URL: www.ascet.com.

KPMG, "KPMG and Manugistics Team Up to Deliver Superior Implementation Services for Supply Chain Management" 1998.

Located at URL: www.kpmg.com.

Lal, S, P Van Laarhoven & G Sharman, "Current Research: Making Logistics Alliances Work" *The McKinsey Quarterly* (1995) No. 3.
Located at URL: www.mckinseyquarterly.com.

Logistics Management & Distribution Report, "Survey Finds Bottom Line Drives Outsourcing" *Logistics Management & Distribution Report* (May 1999).
Located at URL: www.manufacturing.net.

P-E International, "The Changing Role of Third-Party Logistics" 1999.
Located at URL: www.peint.com.

Peters, M, J Cooper, R Lieb & H Randall, "The Third Party Logistics Industry in Europe: Provider Perspectives on the Industry's Current Status and Future Prospects" *International Journal of Logistics: Research and Applications* (1998) Vol. 1, No. 1.

Powell, J, "How to Tell a Forwarder from a 3PL" 1999.
Located at URL: www.logisticstraining.com.

Sabath, R, "Getting Outsourcing to Work in the Supply Chain" 1999.
Located at URL: www.ascet.com.

Stone, S, "Are 4PLs for Real?" *Purchasing Online* (January 1999).
Located at URL: www.manufacturing.net.

Transport News, "Cardinal Logistics Named the Lead Logistics Provider for Textron Automotive Trim Group" *Transport News* (March 1998).
Located at URL: www.transportnews.com.

Transport News, "GATX Forms GATX Integrated Solutions Group" *Transport News* (September 1999).
Located at URL: www.transportnews.com.

Van Laarhoven, P & G Sharman, "Logistics Alliances: The European Experience" *The McKinsey Quarterly* (1994) No. 1.
Located at URL: www.mckinseyquarterly.com.

NOTE

All references to companies, contracts with clients, etc., have been sourced in newspapers and Internet sites which have public access.

Chapter 14
Information Technology in the Supply Chain

Michael Giblin
Icarus e-Com

14.1 INTRODUCTION

The emphasis in this chapter is on electronic commerce as the key Information Technology (IT) that underpins the exchange of information among the members of the supply chain. The participants in the supply chain include manufacturers, suppliers, distributors and their transport and logistics services providers. The logistics industry is the vital central link in the chain, which organises the movement, storage and delivery of product and is essential to making the supply chain work. The focus of this chapter will be to identify the new requirements of manufacturing and how transport must transform itself to exploit the new opportunities presented by these new conditions, which will be largely delivered by IT, and how this can be achieved.

Transport has been, and to a large extent still is, a very traditional and staid industry. Fundamental structural changes in transport are inevitable, and these have already commenced. In addition to its core transport role, manufacturing industry has begun to define and specify in detail those outsourced services it now requires to help it address the new demands of the market. The challenge for transport is to change from the carrier role it has played in the past to being a value-adding partner to manufacturing so as to enable the latter achieve its goals for cost reduction and outsourcing, and at the same time provide improved information and customer service. This chapter looks at the sequence of identifying the market needs, following the evolution of Information Communications Technology as it supports supply chain systems, tracking the parallel developments in transport and describing how two separate industries, manufacturing and transport, can combine to achieve a common objective through integration of information technology.

14.2 GLOBALISATION

Globalisation is a key feature of the modern competitive environment. This is true not only for companies, but also for regions, economies, countries and even continents, since all activities are now exposed to global competition. The emergence of the large trading blocks, e.g. NAFTA, EU and the Asia/Pacific region, combined with highly mobile investment funds, currency and equity dealing and the improved access to the communications of our age *viz.* telecommunications, travel and TV, have telescoped the world and greatly increased the scope for competition. In this environment, investors will compare the target markets and score accordingly.

Global sourcing and distribution, outsourcing and world class logistics are becoming key strategic competitive weapons. Timely and accurate information flows between all trading partners, e.g. from component supplier through manufacturing on to distributors and retail, are essential elements in this new business model. One feature that can make a major difference is the area of supply chain management. The essential ingredients to bind all the elements of the supply chain together are a partnership strategy with respect to suppliers and logistics providers, a co-ordinated approach based on integrated information technology and excellent electronic communications systems.

14.3 MANUFACTURING CLIMATE

It is appropriate to first examine the economic and business requirements of the manufacturing customer. Since the start of the industrial era, business managers, production engineers and accountants have progressively and successfully attacked manufacturing costs. Initially the focus was on labour costs, first in the automation and streamlining of production line processes and the associated issue of having manning levels calculated on a scientific basis. The next identifiable target area was the large capital costs tied up in inventory, particularly in the supply of raw materials, and to a lesser extent the distribution of finished product. Inventory is an area of high investment where improvements in lead times can lead to significant savings. The immediate focus was in more effective management of in-house inventories, and thereafter in the organisation and scheduling of component delivery from suppliers. Occurring simultaneously with the improvements in production processes, work on inventory management led to new concepts being articulated, such as the Japanese Kanban system and Just In Time (JIT) manufacturing. These were first perfected in the car industries of Japan, then in the US and later in Europe. They proved to be revolutionary new ways of working. In addition, new materials and resource planning methodologies and systems were developed, such as MRP and MRP2 (Material and Resource Planning) for reordering and production planning.

Initially all these functions were managed within the 'four walls' of the organisation and could be controlled by local management. However, it became clear there were significant accumulated costs hidden within the actual price of the raw material itself. Typically, the cost of a stock item includes its original value, plus the cost of the layers of separate processes undergone, plus transport, warehousing, brokerage, etc., all occurring outside the factory gate and beyond the control of the purchasing company. Supplier prices could be negotiated but not controlled. Some of these costs were more visible, such as the actual cost of holding the inventory, since even when the manufacturer forced the supplier to deliver on a JIT basis, the vendor's response was often to set up a large warehouse convenient to the manufacturer's factory. While this facilitated the JIT delivery, it often only transferred the cost back to the supplier to be included in the price of the delivered component.

14.4 INFORMATION COMMUNICATIONS TECHNOLOGY

Clearly, the procurement of materials and the management of their supply and delivery could be done more cost effectively through closer business partnerships and by implementing better information systems linking the business participants. This proved to be a very difficult problem to solve, since there were major IT technical and security problems to be overcome. There were also issues of trust between the business partners, which required new partnership agreements, such as setting up open book accounting arrangements. Even multinational subsidiary companies owned by the same parent corporation struggled with the problem of transferring key manufacturing data between their own national companies in different countries. Up to the late 1970s these companies had local systems to address national requirements, and worldwide area networks (WANs) were not yet readily available. It took both time and technological developments in ICT to solve these communications issues. For example, by the early 1980s Philips NV Eindhoven Holland had decided to develop their own proprietary communication protocol and data format standards to address this issue among its own subsidiaries.

Corporations took many different approaches as solutions emerged, with some choosing global Value Added Networks (VANs) to meet their communications needs. Examples of VANs are the IBM Information Network or the GE Information System (GEIS). The function of a VAN is to take business data from one trading partner's computer in a specific file format and deliver it to other partners' computers in a format its computer could process. This usually involves the VAN providing communication protocol conversion and reformatting the files using determined data standards, which are some of the value-added services VANs add to basic communications. There are many other types of VANs, such as global, national and industry-specific, often set up and owned by an industry such as automotive, insurance, etc. In transport there are Cargo Community Systems set up, usually by a specific mode, such as ports/ shipping or aircargo. Examples include FCPS in Felixstowe port, SEAGHA in the port of Antwerp, and CargoNaut (the aircargo system) in Schiphol, Amsterdam.

The ICARUS system in Dublin is one of only two truly multi-modal systems in the world, having started life as the world pilot site for the International Air Transport Association (IATA). Its services have been developed to provide e-commerce solutions for all modes of transport and for manufacturing clients. These include track and trace, bookings, waybill and manifest transfer, proof of delivery for forwarding, shipping, ports, road haulage and logistics providers. In 1998 it was exclusively awarded the networking of the national electronic customs clearance system for the Irish Revenue Commissioners.

14.5 ELECTRONIC DATA INTERCHANGE

EDI is computer to computer transfer of business information in a standardised electronic form without human intervention. This requires that the business document, such as an order or an invoice, is transmitted in a strictly formatted message and according to clearly defined standards. The standards are those developed by the United Nations, known as UN/EDIFACT (EDI For Administration Commerce Transportation). Prior to the intervention of the UN, there was a proliferation of national and industry-specific EDI standards which led to a 'Tower of Babel' of languages, meaning that business transaction messages could not be transferred across international borders or even business sectors. While a company can define its own in-house format or standard, no two firms' hardware and software systems will be precisely similar, so agreement on a common standard is key to EDI communications between bilateral trading partners (one to one). This is even more important if the communications involve more than two parties (one to many or many to many), such as when a manufacturer has many suppliers or a transport carrier has many customer partners, such as forwarders. For example, the airline industry had its own highly successful IATA standards prior to the UN initiative.

In addition to the data formats of the messages, it is also essential that the EDI partners share the same computer hardware communications protocol. As in the case of the UN, on the hardware side the International Standards Organisation (ISO) led the implementation and acceptance of Open Systems (OS) between disparate computers. For both problems – data formats and protocol conversion – a VAN such as ICARUS will resolve the incompatibilities and take files in any format (or even a flat file) from one system and deliver it without intervention to the next computer without manual processing.

EDI facilitated significant benefits to users, especially productivity gains, by minimising data capture, eliminating errors, processing key functions such as orders, waybills, etc. and improving customer service. Since EDI delivers scaled benefit to larger operations, it is therefore of key importance to companies processing significant amounts of transactions. EDI was the technology mainly chosen by the customers of VANs, as described above. In Ireland it has particular application in the retail/distribution supermarket chains (e.g. Tesco, Dunnes Stores, Superquinn, etc.). The great global manufacturing industries, such as the automotive, aerospace and electronics industries, are dependent on it. In the late 1980s it was seen as the business technology of the future, in more or less the same way as e-commerce is now perceived. Smaller companies, however, accepted the technology only when it was a requirement for doing business with larger partners, rather than on a voluntary basis because of its inherent benefits. The main reasons for this were lack of technology expertise and the cost of implementation versus return for small-scale use.

14.6 ELECTRONIC COMMERCE

Electronic commerce is the latest name for electronic business transactions, also previously known as Electronic Trading and Paperless Trading. These were all based on EDI, which has been around for over 25 years and which has provided the model and basis for modern e-commerce transactions. While e-commerce transactions utilise the same fundamental transfer of functional information, the technologies deployed are somewhat different in that the Internet is the new medium. With e-commerce based in World Wide Web (WWW) sites, the traditional marketplace is being replaced by a virtual (i.e. electronic) marketplace.

The Internet can be viewed as a multifaceted channel for education/learning, trading, entertainment, etc. Websites were first used as electronic brochures for the promotion of companies, and for non-trading bodies they were used for promotion of the organisation's services and displayed in pages of static text and graphics. The growth of the Internet is mainly attributable to four factors: the availability of realistically priced high spec PCs, the decreasing cost of telecommunications, the availability of user friendly software and simpler communications protocols. These protocols support both the transmission of e-mail and e-commerce web functionality. These have all combined to produce explosive and continuous growth, which at present looks exponential. The Internet and the web have opened up communications between businesses and consumers, governments to citizens and businesses to businesses. While business to consumer transactions, such as simple book ordering, may be the favoured flavour in the media at present, other areas have far more significance. For example, an Electronic Government is about to be launched, with major developments unveiled such as electronic tax returns by mid-2000. At present, business to business is five times as important as the consumer end, and in terms of value of product sold it is also growing much more rapidly.

The web has evolved to a second generation of interactive websites incorporating database functionality. This has opened up new applications across all business sectors. Functional information such as catalogues, product information, contact details, tracking information and proof of delivery can now be accessed interactively. This in turn means that real time transaction and information can be exchanged between trading partners, both large and small. Allied to this is the development of Digital Certificates. The accompanying enabling legislation will shortly enable secure electronic payments to become a reality for both businesses and consumers. This will herald in a big increase in the demand for suitable transport and logistics services as the channel of distribution changes to a more home or desk-based purchasing model rather than the current store-based model. The supply chain has been at the forefront of using online database systems to provide trading partners and customers with quality logistical information. This has been provided by the express operators and the sophisticated logistics services, but now needs to become the standard rather than the exception, and all transport operators must embrace the technology.

14.7 ENTERPRISE RESOURCE PLANNING (ERP) SYSTEMS

Outsourcing of non-core business activities is another feature of the new manufacturing paradigm. This is an important area and will be discussed in further detail later in the chapter in relation to the development of third party value added logistics providers. The rise in global manufacturing and global sourcing of components as well as the outsourcing of pertinent functions has meant that management and control of these activities has become a very important issue. To achieve this properly there must be integration of associated information flows from external sources into the manufacturing systems of the manufacturing company. Where MRP previously addressed the company's manufacturing and inventory needs, new systems were required to be able to receive, process and integrate these wider information channels. A new generation of totally integrated corporate management IT systems known as Enterprise Resource Planning (ERP) systems have now been developed. As their primary purpose, these integrate critical financial data streams, but they also deliver the capability to link to external gateways. The best known provider of such systems is probably SAP, but there are a number of other offerings such as Baan, JD Edwards, Epicor, Oracle and Peoplesoft.

The concept of ERP systems is to provide a fully integrated enterprise-wide system with each functional activity (business operations such as forecasting, procurement, logistics, manufacturing, quality control, marketing, distribution and even HRM) linked to the finance area, thus providing full visibility, accountability and control. Significantly, these systems are designed with all the inbuilt hooks for communications, such as the ability to send structured data files, which can then be reformatted to Electronic Data Interchange (EDI) standard transactions and output to external interfaces. These provide internal access from within the company, but are also designed so that with the appropriate secure gateways they can be enabled to link to external Value Added Networks, or as appropriate, to the Internet.

14.8 SMALL AND MEDIUM-SIZED ENTERPRISES (SMES)

In this way the larger manufacturing companies committed to the ERP route are well prepared for e-commerce. Large companies will take many different approaches and most will continue to refine and upgrade the historic investment in their in-house legacy systems, and develop them further to address both their internal financial information and accounting needs and their e-commerce strategies. ERP systems are very expensive: they are spoken of in price terms of 7 digit numbers, or multiples of millions for global corporations. They also require customisation and re-engineering of existing business processes to be fully exploited. Clearly this approach is not an option for smaller companies in the SME sector, where there will be a great variety of IT situations. These will range from those at the top end of the technology scale – aware and aggressive companies with their own systems and expertise – to the bottom end of the scale – companies with virtually no IT. At the bottom end of the scale these companies may only have a PC, with perhaps a low-cost basic accounting package, but no IT support for their actual business operations. The middle range of SMEs is the most interesting, but impossible to categorise accurately and will contain companies at the lower and upper levels of the technology ladder.

In general, companies can be divided into two main types, namely technology leaders and technology followers. A typical company in the SME sector would be one with a good in-house system probably developed or provided as a customised package by their software house. This is generally designed to address their operations, sales and accounting functions. In terms of expertise there would be a high dependence on the software house, with perhaps one person, often an accounting person or a junior in the company, trained to look after the database, system management and peripheral equipment items such as printers. There can thus be an undue dependence on the software house for strategic advice, or even an expectancy that the software house will be the arbiter on the nature of technology investment issues, in other words allowing these to be decided on technical rather than on strategic business grounds.

In terms of electronic commerce this is fine if the software house has all the relevant communications and Internet expertise itself. However, many such firms are very strong in applications development, but may not have the skills in communications technology. Commercially, the software house will have a strong interest in upgrading their packaged product while addressing the needs of a single client. There can be difficulties in pricing and also issues of the ownership of Intellectual Property Rights for new developments of a package. This can mean it is necessary to employ a software house with the right communications skills, but companies are extremely reluctant to have two software houses working on their system. In such scenarios, the company is likely to consider three options: a) do nothing, b) turn to expensive consultants to recommend a path, or c) outsource their needs to an electronic commerce provider.

14.9 UPTAKE/APPLICATION OF E-COMMERCE

Although in general larger companies will have a big advantage in terms of technology, it is nevertheless important for SMEs to be aware of options that can be implemented cost effectively and without risk and which will provide them with a solution to allow them to compete. It will be seen that in some cases it will be easier for those companies currently weak in IT to quickly implement successful solutions, whereas those companies with an existing IT investment in hardware, software and expertise may find it difficult to work within their existing framework. There has been a recent blandness in the press about the most exciting new developments in IT involving business solutions. This is mainly as a result of the incessant hype of the media. Rarely, if ever, do we see articles showing a real understanding of business e-commerce issues, containing practical ideas helpful to business people.

Writers are mainly addressing the individual or the business to consumer private user with his own home computer, whereas we have seen that the business to business sector is much more significant. The media can convey the view that for those SME companies without their own IT expertise, one has only to wait and all their problems will somehow be solved, cheaply and without risk (i.e. miraculously) in the coming electronic commerce revolution. Another feature is the stasis engendered where a firm decides not to act, but instead cautiously wait for fear of making an incorrect investment decision. Peer pressure at the company director level rather than thought-out strategy or customer service is often the criteria for the decision.

With events happening so quickly today, these firms tend to wait lest the solution offered today will be outdated tomorrow. This attitude differentiates the followers from the leaders. The individual companies in a supply chain are of course typical of all firms, and most are SMEs. Their IT capability is limited, but the sector they operate in has huge demand for information exchange, possibly greater than in other sectors. It is not, of course, possible in a document such as this to illustrate the full diversity of corporate in-house systems. The focus of this short outline is clearly on enabling technology which links systems to achieve effective electronic business communications.

14.10 SUPPLY CHAIN MANAGEMENT (SCM) SYSTEMS

There are a number of software providers of corporate management systems that address the needs of the supply chain, such as Manugistics and i2. Baan provides a separate suite of SCM within its ERP offering. As in the case of ERP, companies looking at totally new systems have to carefully consider the technical issues and options for further developing their legacy systems, including the limitations that this will have and the perceived risks in going for something new. The year 2000 (Y2K) bug has been a significant consideration, with many companies deciding to go for new systems, but on the other hand it has tied up technical resources and encouraged other companies to await the outcome.

There are many parallels and inter-dependencies in the evolution path of both electronic commerce and supply chain management. Christopher (1998), quoting Aitken (1998), offers a succinct view of what a supply chain is:

> *A network of connected and interdependent organisations mutually and co-operatively working together to control, manage and improve the flow of materials and information from suppliers to end users.*

Information is thus accepted to be of primary importance to the flow of the materials, and the efficient processing and use of data requires a certain level of IT support with a supply chain function and its interaction with other partners requires e-commerce. There is a myriad of information flows between the respective partners in the supply chain. Looking at a hi-tech manufacturer in isolation will give an indicative insight into the flows between partners (Figure 14.1). In examining a simple business transaction such as the processing of a sales order, it will be possible to look at the chain reaction on a micro and macro level. Those manufacturers with ERP can control management and operational flows within their walls since the system has functionality, which allows for sales, forecasting, production, and accounting to be integrated seamlessly. However, in the new world of outsourcing, the manufacturer will want his/her logistics service provider (LSP) to provide the same visibility as provided by their internal system. This information on the inbound supply of components is critical for the company's manufacturing process. Equally important to the company and also to its customer on the distribution side is detailed information on the status of outbound finished product.

Figure 14.1 Supply Chain Information Flows

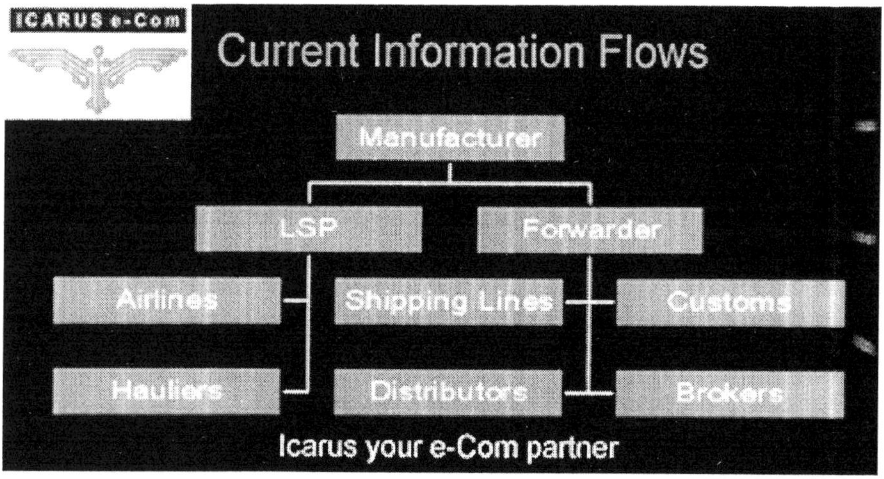

The deployment of e-commerce solutions makes it possible for external information flows to be internalised. When this is implemented with suppliers, logistic partners and distributors, it gives the manufacturer visibility within the total supply chain. For example, a purchase order for components will be electronically addressed to the LSP as a call off, and he/she will arrange the delivery on a JIT basis. The LSP will also simultaneously reorder replacement safety stock from the supplier, arrange transport by sea or air and customs clearance, prepare billings and notify the accounts department of both the supplier and the manufacturer. In the case of finished goods, the LSP arranges the shipment. This may include functions such as sub-assembly, kitting, manuals, picking and packing, transport to a distribution centre or delivery direct to the consignees' door. With smaller shipments this may mean sub-contracting the delivery to an express operator using EDI, or for larger shipments to remote destinations by a haulier. The total visibility required here clearly requires sophisticated IT with e-commerce links.

14.11 TRANSPORT INDUSTRY

Freight transportation as an industry in Ireland and elsewhere has undergone dramatic change over the past 25 years. Various developments in different areas have occurred over a short timeframe and have had a tremendous impact on freight transportation. Examples include containerisation, intermodality, bigger purpose- built ships, roll-on/roll-off ferries, deregulation of trucking creating back loading, GPS and satellite tracking, GSM phones and communications, bar coding, more wide-bodied aircraft, improved aircargo igloo containers, better refrigeration, improved port facilities and road access, new motorways and town bypasses, etc. Despite these impressive changes and improvements in infrastructure, the needs of customers around the world have been changing even faster, so much so that it creates an impression that somehow conventional transport services have been standing still.

In terms of structure, conventional freight transportation has changed little in this period with regard to the role played by different types of companies. This is especially visible in international trade, as an export shipment needs the services of a great variety of transport organisations. These include forwarders, hauliers both for pickup and delivery, consolidators, ship agents. brokers, carriers such as shipping lines and airlines, port authorities, break-bulk groupage operators, stevedores and terminal handlers, customs clearance agents, etc. At destination there can be a similar array of actors. While not all these parties will be regularly involved, each has a legitimate business function, which means that each of those involved will have to capture the shipment information which controls the physical movement of the shipment. This can give rise to costly duplication and even delays due to errors in documentation, as each party in the chain has to re-enter the shipment information into his computer system. A disparate industry with so many interdependent players needs to have a technical information exchange infrastructure, such as a cargo community system, to handle information transfer for efficiency, speed and error reduction reasons. Each of these parties act independently of each other and have their private arrangements for charging out their services, therefore it is not easy for the exporter to have an all-in confirmed price for the complete movement of the goods in advance.

While the majority of transport players listed here still perform basically the same function as they did 25 years ago, at least two service provider groups have responded to the new manufacturing scenario in a most dramatic way. These are express/door-to-door operators and third party logistics service providers, or LSPs. In both cases their market response has been so positive that they have helped the whole market to grow. Indeed, the large express companies actually claim to have created the market for overnight packages, and perhaps with some justification. Economists, the World Bank and governments see both LSPs and express operators as essential ingredients and catalysts for an emerging economy. The success of their product in both cases has been due to the timeliness in addressing an unfulfilled need, at a pricing level which was economic and with levels of service and information that are real and transparent.

14.12 DOOR-TO-DOOR SERVICES

The demand for these services has grown rapidly for very specific reasons:

(1) the increase in frequency of shipments due to JIT manufacturing, with a decrease in shipment size;

(2) a clear need for a door to door product to be provided for a single price;

(3) a reduction in delays and improvement in service through the elimination of the usual conventional transport partners;

(4) huge demand for envelope and small package delivery as the services sector expanded in the 1970s and 1980s;

(5) the partial deregulation of the then inefficient national postal monopolies for small packages.

This need is demonstrated in our cities every day by the motorbike couriers fulfilling a similar need at local level. The international express/courier companies (i.e. Fedex, DHL, TNT and UPS) are known as 'integrated carriers', as they fulfil all the transport partner roles themselves, i.e. pickup, forwarding, carrier or airline, customs broker, and delivery. Creativity in product development to address market demand has been the key to their success. Their service is based on high standards of service, every facet of which is controlled and monitored by their fully branch- networked central computer systems. Their marketing has been brilliant, offering money back guarantees, up to the minute tracking information and continuous new product development well ahead of customer demand. While some of the large companies in this market may have started with envelopes and small packages, they have now matured as an industry and are beginning to make inroads into the conventional 'hard' freight market.

In the heavier shipment section of the market the customer demands were no different, and in the 1980s and early 1990s this opportunity was seized by some of the conventional members of the transport community, mainly those forwarders that provided their own road haulage operations and also some road hauliers. Exporters and shippers up to then were generally more concerned with price rather than service and the conventional industry looked cheaper, at least at first sight. In the past the exporter generally determined the transport routing and the transport mode(s), but as the issue of costs and the introduction of logistics thinking grew, this changed. A number of the critical factors, such as the reduction in total transit time, the elimination of break-bulk and distribution centres, reduced handling providing better product quality and lower claims ratio, have all combined favourably for door to door delivery by road freight service.

The key factors in the success of road haulage were the completion of the European motorway network and the reduction in customs clearance delays at border check-points in the 1980s leading to the creation of the EU open market in 1992. From an Irish and British point of view, another key factor was the introduction of fast roll on/ roll off ferries, permitting an Irish trucker to deliver to a consignee at his factory or depot anywhere in the UK next day, and in the great population centres of north west Europe on the second next day.

14.13 LOGISTICS SERVICES PROVIDERS

Third party service providers are discussed in the previous chapter, and retail logistics in the following chapter, but in this chapter both topics are of interest in the context of their contribution to the supply chain through the medium of IT. In Ireland we have seen the growth of what are termed 'vendor hubs' for the hi-tech manufacturing sector. These occur where offshore suppliers are contracted to deliver on a JIT basis, but rather than set up and operate their own local warehouse they sub-contract this out to a LSP. Typically, this could involve a South East Asian component supplier to an Irish PC manufacturer employing a third party, such as a forwarder or transport partner that he already deals with, to take on this new business activity. This business will have its own requirements separate to the core business, and a key capability will be the IT systems capable of handling stock levels, reordering, customer call-off, pick and pack, reporting, etc. This system will also have to be EDI enabled or have other e-commerce links with both the offshore supplier and the local manufacturer. There are a number of Irish and multi-national companies, such as Exel Walsh Western, Williames Transport, AEI, Expeditors Seasky, Meadows, MSAS, etc., supplying services in this market. One fully Irish-owned company, Irish Express Cargo, has become a world leader in this area through its technology. Its world-class service, based on IT, has been recognised by its customers and it has been appointed the global logistics provider for Hewlett Packard.

14.14 INTEGRATING THE SUPPLY CHAIN

Multinational manufacturers have moved into the era of distributed manufacturing and raw material sourcing on a global basis. In Ireland we have the excellent examples of the hi-tech electronics manufacturing companies such as Dell, Intel, Gateway, IBM and others. The companies in this sector made their decision to invest in Ireland based on a number of positive arguments, such as an educated workforce, tax incentives, etc., even in spite of some negatives, such as the peripherality of the location and acknowledged transport infrastructural problems. Nevertheless, the success of their business demonstrates that they have somehow overcome these problems. This is a tribute to the Irish logistics industry, achieved largely through information technology. Nationally there is indirect confirmation of this as well, as we don't hear the plaintive excuse of peripherality wheeled out to excuse failure anymore. World-class logistics supporting the supply chain with sophisticated IT and communications systems is one of the pillars of the much heralded Celtic revival.

The high-end transport providers, i.e. the LSPs and the express operators, can deliver these solutions for the lines of traffic they handle. In the future, manufacturers will also want a single standard format and an integrated flow from all their transport partners. So far the demand for 'visibility' has been from the hi-tech sector; however, it is just a question of time, in the e-commerce age, that demand will soon come from other sectors. Figure 14.2 is an architecture of how all material information flows from suppliers and intermodal transport partners can be integrated and shared among those entitled to access the information, using the Internet and the web as a common interface.

Figure 14.2 Providing Visibility in the Supply Chain

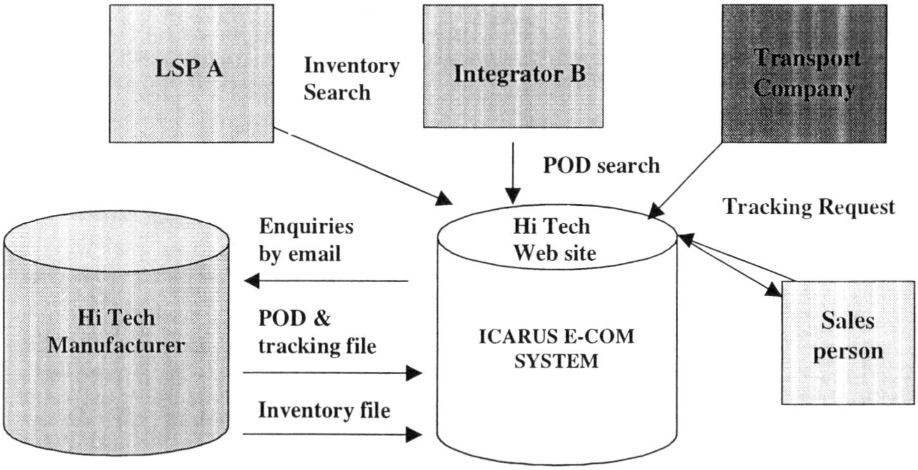

The diagram shows how an e-commerce provider with industry expertise can provide an information Value Added Service (VAS) without the need for individual implementations for each party. Existing EDI connections to carriers can be leveraged to provide the status information. One option that the manufacturer could choose is to create a web-based database of all shipment movements and inventory levels and have this updated by all the transport partners. The information can be sent in a format their system can output and the VAS can do the necessary conversion/translation required. This database could be password controlled and access to it could be authorised in many ways, such as access to own shipments, departments access, supplier access, total access for management and accounting, etc.

14.15 PROGNOSIS FOR INFORMATION TECHNOLOGY IN THE SUPPLY CHAIN

Manufacturing and other industries will take up new technologies as rapidly as they make commercial sense. The question arises as to how quickly transport service providers can respond. The situation described above is unfortunately not typical of all Irish transport companies; indeed, it is quite the exception. There is what one could describe as a first world and third world technology divide in Irish transport. The first world scenario is as depicted above, but beside it we have a third world technology scene covering a very large section of the road haulage sector and significant parts of the rest of the transport industry. Most of these latter companies lack a strategic view, many are without the necessary expert resources and some don't have the confidence to make investment decisions on the nature of their IT. What can be done to help these companies? The Irish government has recognised that there is a problem, and a number of official studies have been carried out, such as *World Class to Serve The World*, the report of the Forfas Transport & Logistics Group, and *Technology Foresight Ireland*, an overview report by the Irish Council for Science, Technology and Innovation (ICSTI) and also published by Forfas. In each of these reports there is a strong case for the support and development of what is referred to as systems logistics. Clearly, Government cannot invest in a company's in-house IT systems, no more than they can invest in their trucks or other essential equipment, but there are quite a number of things that can be done by government agencies by way of awareness, education, demonstration projects, consultancy, etc. As in other matters, Government will not solve business problems – their solution remains a market choice.

There are positive indications that SME transport companies accept the importance of these issues. Companies without the big IT systems are also beginning to realise that the Internet and the web are the new tools which can allow them to compete and that an e-commerce provider can deliver solutions for their customers without the need for major investment in their in-house IT.

Figure 14.3 illustrates that a transport provider can facilitate his customers to have immediate and comprehensive status information on their supply chain, using the most common access references identifiable to the client. It is important that small and mid-range transport operators understand in specific rather than generic terms what the market demands now and in the short-term. They will even be agreeably surprised that, with the right support, this need not require major investment.

Figure 14.3 Status Information

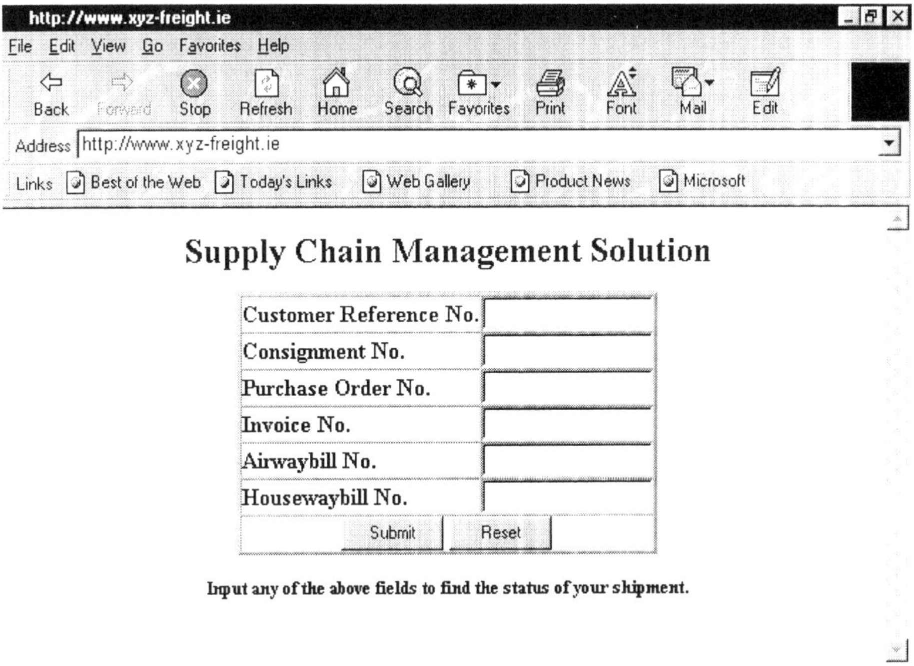

Supply Chain Management Solution

Customer Reference No.	
Consignment No.	
Purchase Order No.	
Invoice No.	
Airwaybill No.	
Housewaybill No.	

Submit   Reset

Input any of the above fields to find the status of your shipment.

In the medium-term, manufacturing will change further as the concept of 'made to order' becomes the next paradigm shift, and customers are encouraged to select and even design their purchase via Internet enabled e-commerce. Another marketing advantage offered to customers will be to specify delivery arrangements, including the time of delivery. New e-commerce enabled call centres, which currently concentrate on the sale of services such as bookings, travel, insurance, etc., will be introduced for products and will become virtual shopping malls on a global basis. In this scenario transport service will be defined by the end customer rather than 'first available' for the supplier and the transport partner. Such 'time definite' transport services will become the service standard of the future, in international as well as domestic markets.

It is easy to see that only e-commerce can effectively deliver this. This will suit the global transport companies, but there will still be a role for SME transport companies locally and by subcontracting from the bigger players, provided they become part of a network of reciprocal operators sharing similar high standards and suitable technology.

In the longer-term the tendency for global brand companies to shed non-core functions will increase. This is likely to mean that more companies, like Swatch and Apple in the case of their new Imac PC, will outsource the manufacturing process and decide to concentrate on their essential core competencies of design, marketing and customer service. As already happened with the arrival of third party logistics providers, virtual logistics service providers will emerge to broker and arrange the manufacturing process, inventory management and distribution, and bind all business functions together in a transparent and seamless fashion.

References and Further Reading

Aitken, J, *Supply Chain Integration within the Context of a Supplier Association* (Cranfield University, PhD Thesis) 1998.
Christopher, M, *Logistics and Supply Chain Management* (London: Financial Times/ Pitman Publishing) 2nd edition, 1998.

Relevant Supply Chain Websites

1. Electronic Commerce Sites
Icarus e-Com	www.icarus-e.com
Aer Lingus Cargo (tracking site)	www.aerlinguscargo.com
Meadows Freight Ltd	www.meadowsfreight.ie
Williames Airfreight Ltd	www.ccs.ie/williames/willt&t.htm
AerGP – Aer Lingus & General Parcels	www.aergp.com
Richmond Logistics	www.richmondlogistics.ie
TwoWay Forwarding & Logistics	www.twoway.ie

2. Global Logistics Providers
Irish Express Cargo	www.irishexpresscargo.com
Exel Logistics	www.exel.com
Expeditors Seasky	www.expeditors.com
Air Express International AEI	www.airexpressintl.com
GeoLogistics	www.geologistics.com
MSAS	www.msas.com

3. Express 'Integrated' Operators
DHL	www.dhl.com
Federal Express	www.fedex.com
TNT	www.tnt.com
UPS	www.ups.com

4. Professional Industry Bodies
Chartered Institute of Transport in Ireland	www.ccs.ie/citi/citi.htm
Institute of Logistics & Transport ROI	www.ccs.ie/ilog.htm
Irish Exporters Association	www.ccs.ie/exporter/iexport.htm
Institute of Freight Forwarders of Ireland	www.ioff.ie

Chapter 15
Retail Logistics and Efficient Consumer Response
Paul O'Reilly
Teagasc

15.1 INTRODUCTION

In recent years, established Irish and European retailers have been operating in an increasingly competitive environment. The need to provide customers with higher service levels at a lower cost while building customer loyalty has provided for a difficult working environment. Not only are there more retail outlets, but many offer similar products. The same brand of soap can be bought at convenience stores, supermarkets, pharmacies and discount stores, and as a result consumer choice puts tremendous pressure on retailers, with many historical leaders struggling in today's tougher environment. In the US, of the fifteen most profitable retailers in 1985, only six remained on the list by 1995 (Dvoark and van Paasschen, 1996). For retailers to survive in increasingly competitive markets, it is no longer sufficient to buy the right goods at the right cost – retailers must also get them to the right place, at the right time, in the right quantity and with the right operational costs. Doing this well requires the best possible logistics, combining the information that determines buying decisions with the product flows that get goods to customers most effectively. This is where retail logistics comes into play. This chapter looks at the trends and stages of development of the retail logistics concept. There is also an examination of the Efficient Consumer Response (ECR) initiative, the focus of current retail logistics strategies. Finally, future challenges facing managers operating in the retail sector are outlined.

15.2 RETAIL TRENDS

A number of trends and developments in the retail sector have contributed to the environment within which logistics managers in the retail sector operate, many of which have had a significant influence on the relationship between various parties within the supply chain. Such trends include concentration, internationalisation, alliances and technology. In addition to these industry trends, the modern-day consumer has also contributed to the manner in which retailers and manufacturers seek to meet their needs in an optimal and efficient fashion. These trends are now dealt with in turn.

Concentration

There has been a growing concentration of retailers in most retail markets in Europe. Analysis shows that the 25 largest retailers account for more than 45 per cent of total European food retail sales (Krishnan and de Wilt, 1995). In the Irish grocery sector the top four retailers account for approximately 70 per cent of grocery retail sales. For many manufacturers, particularly small and medium-sized manufacturers, a single retailer accounts for the majority of sales. On the other hand, a typical supermarket retailer has around 1,000 suppliers, with at least several suppliers in each product category. These high levels of concentration have been a major driver of centralised distribution and are encouraging retailers to seek economies through centralised distribution operations. This trend towards concentration of retailers is not just confined to the grocery sector. Other retail sectors such as home appliances, DIY and clothing are increasingly being dominated by a smaller number of international retailers.

Internationalisation and Alliances

With growth opportunities limited in many countries, retailers are increasingly looking outside their domestic markets to expand their business. Acquisitions are the principal means by which retailers expand, particularly in the grocery sector, although start-ups and franchises are popular means of expansion in clothing and other merchandise markets. International retailers to enter the Irish market in the 1990s include Tesco, Next, Boots, PC World, Currys and Dixons. A second internationalisation feature is the growing use of international buying alliances by retailers. These alliances comprise cross-border collaboration networks, which retailers form among themselves, with the stated aims of co-ordination and optimisation of an ambitious range of activities such as purchasing, market research, quality standards, own label development, logistics and information systems. In addition, the success of vertical alliances, that is, collaboration of manufacturers and retailers in areas such as marketing and logistics, has also influenced the approach of others in the industry.

Technology Developments

Leading retailers are grasping information technologies and putting them to work strategically. Retailers have had to change the method and organisation of communication with the final consumer and become more active in collecting information about the consumer. Access to information and the application of information technology enables co-ordination within the supply chain between supply chain members, management levels and functions. IT is the enabling tool which allows for effective management of different flows of risk, information, product and finance and which also makes new processes possible. Leading retailers have been at the forefront of developing sophisticated and integrated operational and strategic information systems. Examples of technology options being employed include:

- tele-home shopping;

- smartcards and customer cards;
- electronic commerce;
- retail expert systems;
- retail shelf planning software.

Ever-changing Consumer

The market which retailers and manufacturers seek to serve has become more complex than ever before. Socio-economic factors such as higher disposable incomes, smaller households, more working couples, greater ethnic diversity and internationalisation, along with the willingness to accept new technologies, have brought about a new kind of ever-changing consumer. The consumer has become the focus of demand-led supply chains defining the quality, quantity, location and timing of product supply. For a number of well-documented reasons, including changes in the socio-economic environment in Europe, today's consumer is becoming more and more demanding, both in terms of assortment availability and assortment dynamics. The logistics response to these demand-led supply chains is to disseminate electronic point of sale data collected by the retailers and translate this information into optimal assortments.

15.3 DEVELOPMENT OF RETAIL LOGISTICS

Traditionally, the logistics relationship between manufacturers and retailers was grounded in basic physical distribution. Physical distribution was the domain of the manufacturer, with retailers satisfied to focus their attention on merchandising and sales. However, in the late 1970s retailers began to take more interest in the logistical channel and the opportunities that existed within it. The concept of retail logistics emerged from this interest. The development of retail logistics over the last twenty years can be seen in two periods. The first period of retail logistics commenced in the late 1970s and related to transport and warehousing facilities, as solutions were sought for reducing retail store inventory space, simplifying ordering processes and reducing queues of delivery vehicles from outside retail stores. The response of retail logistics was centralised distribution. The second period of retail logistics, commencing in the late 1980s and continuing on to the present day, has seen retailers become more aware of the advantages of controlling and leveraging the logistical channel, especially in light of the emergence of a more volatile consumer. During this second period, retail logistics turned to developing closer relationships between manufacturers and retailers with a view to satisfying consumer requirements in an optimal way.

In the 1980s, retailers' response to the increasingly competitive environment was based primarily on price competition via cost reductions. These were achieved by pressurising their suppliers. In the Irish grocery market, bread and milk were often the product areas targeted, in some cases to the detriment of suppliers. In the early to mid-1990s, retailers began to focus on supply chain management, with the emphasis on optimising back office functions relating to the management of product flows. This focus on supply chain management manifested itself largely on a combination of:

- optimisation of warehousing and transport, for example via centralised distribution facilities and the introduction of increased automation in warehouses;

- better inventory management via reduced stockholdings and more efficient ordering;

- increased use of electronic data interchange (EDI) to transfer information and to simplify and automate administrative processes.

15.4 CENTRALISING THE PHYSICAL NETWORK

An important feature of the way logistics has developed in the retail sector has been the centralisation of distribution facilities. According to a study by Andersen Consulting and the Cranfield School of Management, centralisation of the supply chain has reduced transport, warehousing and inventory costs by an estimated 40-50 per cent in Europe.

Traditionally, the onus has been on suppliers to arrange distribution of their products from the factory through to delivery to the point of sale or retail outlet, i.e. decentralised distribution (see Figure 15.1). Typically this involved small deliveries to many stores and required vehicles to travel significant distances with less than full loads. More significantly, the number of stockholding points in the supply chain was less than optimal. Stock was often held at a number of points in the supply chain – at the manufacturers premises, at local warehouses and at the retail outlet. The growth of retail chains has shifted this bias, as retailers have realised the economies and other advantages to be gained from controlling distribution into stores by having dedicated centralised distribution arrangements. Multiple retailers began to integrate the distribution, inventory control and reordering procedures into one system, comprised of regional distribution centres (RDCs) servicing a given number of retail outlets in the region (see Figure 15.2). These improved systems allowed for shortened order lead times, improved inventory control and more flexible stock allocation between stores. This in turn led to a reduction in the stockholding necessary at retail outlets, thus allowing extra floor area to be released for sales. An additional benefit is less congestion at the stores' back doors as dedicated distribution fleets make timed consolidated deliveries.

Figure 15.1: Decentalised Distribution

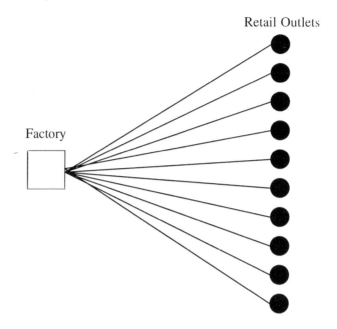

Figure 15.2: Centralised Distribution

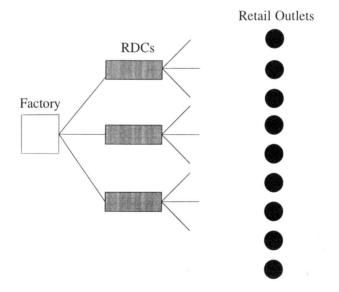

While most quoted examples of centralised operations are in the grocery sector, centralised distribution is in fact a common feature of most retail sectors. Boots, Woolworths, Currys/Dixons, Debenhams and John Lewis all operate regional distribution centres. Additionally, in many cases, retailers are turning to third party logistics providers to organise and manage centralised distribution centres. Manufacturers and retailers are also using third party logistics providers to consolidate product prior to delivery to RDCs (see Figure 15.3). In principle, consolidation centres facilitate 'hub and spoke' type routing patterns. Vehicles arrive at the consolidation centre carrying goods from a given origin and they depart carrying goods for a given destination. Vehicles can be turned around individually, with inbound goods stored temporarily until they are combined with goods unloaded from other vehicles. Cross-docking is a common feature of such consolidation centres. This is where vehicles arriving from the factory are unloaded simultaneously, resorted and consolidated with product from other manufacturers, and the vehicles are reloaded for immediate departure to retailer RDCs or retail outlets. The aim of cross-docking is to create distribution centres which do not carry inventories, thus eliminating stock from this part of the supply chain.

Figure 15.3: Consolidation Centres

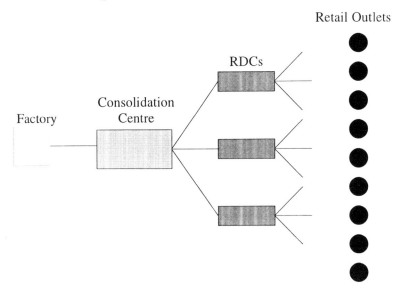

Centalised distribution and consolidation offer a number of benefits to manufacturers, logistics providers and retailers. These are highlighted in Table 15.1.

Table 15.1: Benefits of Centralised Distribution and Consolidation to Supply Chain Partners

Partner	Benefits
Manufacturer	<ul><li>Greater market penetration<ul><li>small firms able to service multiples</li><li>ability to service greater number of RDCs</li><li>enlargement of potential territory</li></ul></li><li>Provides for more cost-efficient full load deliveries</li><li>Ability to focus on core competencies due to single point delivery</li><li>Reduced transport costs</li><li>Higher levels of information received from retailer</li></ul>
Transport Provider	<ul><li>More efficient use of vehicles<ul><li>improved scheduling of vehicles due to standardisation of routes</li><li>reduced miles driven with less than full loads</li></ul></li></ul>
Retailer	<ul><li>Better control of the distribution system</li><li>More efficient use of RDCs<ul><li>greater potential for cross-docking</li><li>maximises full load deliveries into RDCs</li><li>improved labour productivity at RDCs</li></ul></li><li>Lower inventory levels at each retail outlet and improved inventory control throughout system</li><li>Increased frequency of delivery<ul><li>greater product variety</li><li>improved product alignment with customer demand</li></ul></li><li>Shorter time in stock resulting in increased shelf life to the consumer</li><li>Simplified administration</li><li>Improved quality control</li></ul>

Source: Collins, Henchion and O'Reilly (1998)

Perhaps the key feature that underlies the development of supply chains is the increased transparency that now exists. Transparency exists in terms of levels of inventory, collection of information on retail outlets, consumers and costs (particularly inventory and transport costs). This transparency has created a number of opportunities for retailers to work more closely with their suppliers to optimise product and information flow in their supply chains.

15.5 CREATING CLOSE RELATIONSHIPS WITH SUPPLY CHAIN PARTNERS

Darwin's theory of "survival of the fittest" is clearly present in much of modern-day business practice. Yet there is strong evidence, particularly in the retail sector, that true co-operation is the most powerful strategy for sustained success. The retail sector is peppered with case studies and examples of long-term relationships and co-operation between manufacturers and retailers. Behind many of these relationships are efforts to substitute information for inventory.

Forrester Effect

The dynamics of logistics chains, first studied by Forrester (1961), play an important role in determining stock levels and costs. In traditionally organised chains with weak co-ordination, the elements of the chain tend to act independently and defensively, optimising their own performance. In doing so they hedge their response times and build up buffer stocks. Retailers, for instance, often find it difficult to forecast sales accurately and so may experience surpluses in some stock items and shortages in others. When it comes to reordering from the distributor or the supplier, there is an amplification effect, since the new deliveries must not only allow for the lower (or higher) than previously assumed sales level, but also for the surplus in the excess (or shortage of) stock on hand. There may also be a time lag effect due to the time it takes for information to travel. The amplification and time lag effects continue back along the chain, growing in amplitude at each stage and becoming increasingly out of phase. If at the level of retail outlets sales are fluctuating rather than constant, the amplitude effect can lead to widely fluctuating messages along the chain. Inevitably, managers at the various stages begin to adopt protective measures by increasing their safety stocks and, in doing so, increasing the average stock levels along the chain. Faster information flows eliminate these internally created uncertainties that lead to the buffer stocks, thus information serves as a substitute for inventory. Of course, faster information flows require co-ordination and co-operation in the supply chain by all parties.

Rationalisation of Supplier Base

For manufacturers, the search for improved supply chain integrity, coupled with the need to reduce costs from the supply chain through greater control, has resulted in the rationalisation of the supply base. Retailers are seeking now to deal with fewer and larger suppliers. The major retailers increasingly deal with a select few suppliers for key product areas and take every opportunity to pass responsibility for quality control, storage and distribution on to these suppliers, in return for which the chosen few are rewarded with increased volume. Moves by retailers to rationalise their supplier bases have encouraged manufacturers to rethink their relationship with retailers. Once adversarial and confrontational relationships are giving way to greater collaboration and partnership. There is evidence of manufacturers engaging in dedicated product development and capital investment to achieve retailer required cost economies. In return, these manufacturers are rewarded by retailers with fair but competitive prices and assistance with product development, product marketing and research and delivery systems.

In Figure 15.4 below, Christopher (1997) highlights the difference between traditional transactional approaches and the newer partnership approach. Traditionally, the relationship between the two parties to the transaction was a single and potentially tenuous point. Information sharing and collaboration was minimal and business was carried out on a transaction-to-transaction, and sometimes fractious, basis. This fragile connection was vulnerable to competitors. The relationship approach turns the triangle around and increases the number of contact points and the depth of integration between manufacturer and retailer.

Figure 15.4: Closer Manufacturer-Retailer Relationships

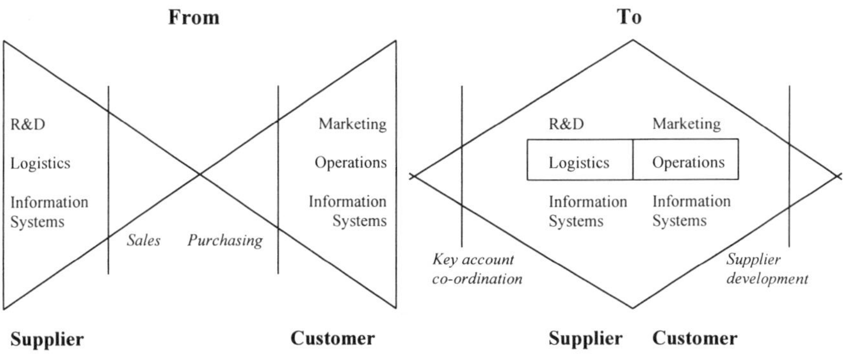

Source: Christopher (1997)

The relationship approach requires significant investment of time and other resources. Therefore, it is not possible for retailers who, in the case of a supermarket chain, are likely to have hundreds if not thousands of suppliers, to develop such a relationship with all of their suppliers. This restraint is forcing some retailers to pass the management of individual product categories to selected manufacturers. These retailers are often referred to as 'category captains'.

Such highly integrated partnerships are very time consuming to establish, thus restricting the potential number of relationships a retailer can develop. This serves to encourage the retailer to rationalise its supplier base and results in higher and more stable volumes of trade for preferred suppliers, ultimately improving operating efficiencies for the supplier and lowering unit price for the retailer.

15.6 IMPROVING THE EFFICIENCY OF THE SUPPLY CHAIN: EFFICIENT CONSUMER RESPONSE (ECR)

Successful co-ordination of supply chain activities by companies such as Walmart and Proctor and Gamble convinced many other retailers and manufacturers that significant cost reduction and other benefits were possible through improved co-ordination of logistics activities between supply chain partners. In 1988, distribution costs at Walmart were 3 per cent compared to 8 per cent at Sears, their major rival (Sellers, 1988). Through analysis of their logistics activities, many manufacturers and retailers found that they had become complacent about the efficiency of their supply chains and, in doing so, had inadvertently supported business practices that served to add time and cost to their supply chain without creating consumer value. This encouraged manufacturers, wholesalers and retailers to set about developing collaborative programmes to improve production, distribution and marketing efficiency. A major initiative, called Efficient Consumer Response (ECR), emerged in the US grocery sector with an objective to streamline and automate the distribution system from the production line to the checkout line (Kurt Salmon and Associates, 1993). The overall goal of ECR is for suppliers and retailers to work closely together to bring better value to the grocery customer (Figure 15.5). A retailer-manufacturer working group in the US devised a set of guiding principles that concisely articulate the ECR strategy:

- Constantly focus on providing better value to the consumer: better product, better quality, better assortment, better in-stock service, better convenience with less cost throughout the total chain.

- ECR must be driven by committed business leaders determined to achieve the choice to profit from the replacement of the old paradigms of win/lose trading relationships with win/win mutually profitable business alliances.

- Accurate and timely information must be used to support effective marketing, production and logistics decisions. This information will flow externally between partners using EDI and will internally affect the most productive and efficient use of information in a computer-based system.

- Product must flow with a maximisation of value adding processes from the end of production to the consumer's basket so as to ensure the right product is available at the right time.

- A common and consistent performance measurement and rewards system must be used that focuses on the effectiveness of the total system, clearly identifies the potential rewards and promotes equitable sharing of those rewards.

Successful implementation of the ECR principles allows for information about consumer purchases to be used by stores, wholesalers and manufacturers. Product flows will match purchase rates and, ideally, items will reach the shelf just before the consumer arrives to make the purchase.

Figure 15.5: The Efficient Consumer Response Initiative

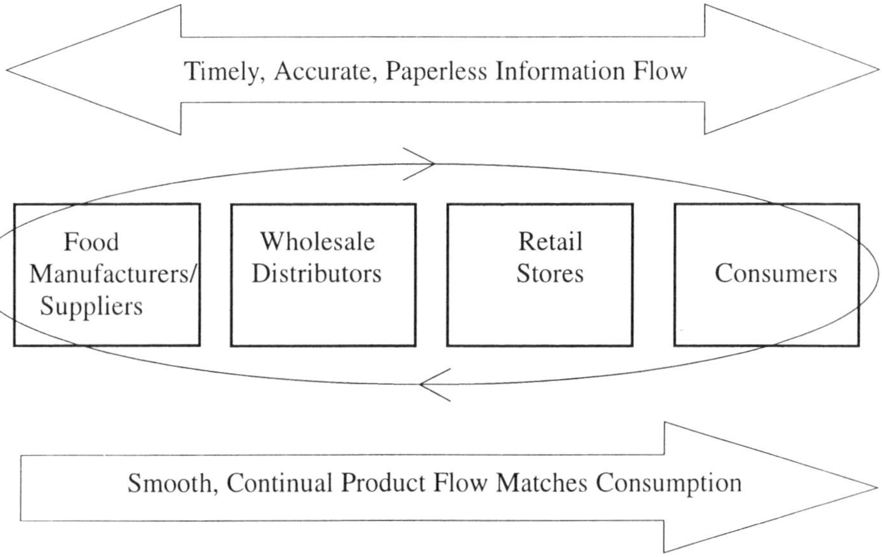

Timely, Accurate, Paperless Information Flow

| Food Manufacturers/ Suppliers | Wholesale Distributors | Retail Stores | Consumers |

Smooth, Continual Product Flow Matches Consumption

Source: *Kurt Salmon and Associates* (1993)

The ECR initiative is often divided in two different ways. One approach highlights three core areas. The first core area deals with merchandising and marketing. By restructuring promotional deals, ECR proponents hope to reduce forward buying of inventory and diverting of products (i.e. buying in low-priced areas and transporting and reselling in high-priced markets). Improved management of shelf space and variety of assortment is sought to reduce warehouse and store costs. Better account management, customised promotions, account profitability analyses and multifunctional selling teams will also improve system efficiency.

The second core area of ECR covers replenishment, logistics and product flow. The intent is to co-ordinate and integrate the approaches used by manufacturers and retailers to speed delivery, reduce unnecessary handling and lower costs. Recommended industry changes include:

- joint inventory management to minimise warehouse costs;
- cross-docking operations to eliminate unnecessary storage locations (i.e. moving cases between manufacturer and retailer trucks without stopping in the warehouse);

- packaging enhancements to reduce product damage.

The third core area of ECR includes changes in administration and technology. Standardised bar coding of boxes and pallets help improve efficiency. Shared point-of-sale (POS) data is critical. If harnessed to its full potential, POS data can deliver breakthroughs in market analysis as well as the benefits associated with automated sales and inventory management programmes. Common POS and ordering systems are required to record this data and shared IT systems are required to communicate this information to supply chain partners.

The ECR initiative can also be divided into four strategies. The first is efficient store assortment. This strategy addresses the use of shelf space and is designed to improve store space utilisation. Experts suggested that if retailers made store-specific category and space allocations, made timely adjustments and considered profit margins when making the allocations, increased sales of 8 to 10 per cent could be expected (Coopers and Lybrand, 1996).

The second strategy is efficient replenishment, providing the "right product, to the right place, at the right time, in the right quantity, and in the most efficient possible manner" (Kurt Salmon and Associates, 1993).

The third ECR strategy is efficient promotion. By simplifying trade promotion deals, offering alternative deals to meet distributor needs, managing consumer and store advertising, improving in-store promotions, keeping accurate deal files and reducing the costs to distribute and handle discount coupons, costs can be saved.

The final strategy is called efficient product development. The flood of new products has added large costs to the distribution system. A typical supermarket carries around 30,000 different products. In 1996, about 19,572 new grocery products were brought to the US grocery market, more than three times the number in 1983 (Food Institute Report, 1997). Research conducted before the ECR initiative found that supermarket buyers reject nearly 60 per cent of new products presented to them and, even when products are accepted, their odds for success are not great. Product failures hurt the bottom lines of both manufacturers and retailers. Better information on consumer preferences and on product attributes could be used to improve the new product success rate.

The cost savings from ECR affect all distribution channels. Some firms have expressed some reservations because many of the programmes initially reduce profit margins. Most of the ECR costs are immediate, while most of the benefits are long-term and less certain. Other firms are concerned about inequities between those who bear the costs and those who reap the benefits.

Successful Implementation of ECR

Successful implementation of ECR-type initiatives requires:

- the commitment of the top management team and adequate resources;

- overcoming organisational and cultural issues, particularly by the formation of cross-functional teams and regular communication;
- the recognition that ECR initiatives are about organisational and business issues, which often involves changing systems and processes;
- the internal and external integration of systems and processes, especially IT;
- an agreement of objectives;
- the appointment of an ECR champion as project leader within each organisation;
- the implementation of a pilot project to establish new business processes and support systems;
- the adoption of a long-term horizon (upfront investment can be significant but returns are over the long-term).

It is the need to overcome cultural and organisational issues and the incompatibility of information systems that are generally regarded as the biggest barriers to the successful implementation of ECR concepts.

Logistics Implications of ECR

Whilst each of the four pillars of ECR have an impact on logistics-related activities, it is the adoption of efficient replenishment that has the greatest impact on product flows, and hence on logistics. There are three physical elements that must be in place for the successful implementation of continuous replenishment:

- appropriately configured production facility;
- integrated IT systems;
- appropriate logistics networks for both the manufacturer and the retailer.

15.7 FUTURE CHALLENGES FOR MANUFACTURERS AND RETAILERS

Ultimately, the logistics challenge faced by retailers and manufacturers is how to optimise product and information flows throughout the supply chain. Integrated IT systems are key drivers in achieving the total integration of the supply chain by optimisation of information, and hence product flows, and in developing value-added services which provide companies with competitive advantage. Overall, retailers and manufacturers must achieve integration of the physical logistics infrastructure and IT both internally (within the organisation) and externally (with other supply chain partners) in order to meet these challenges. In this context, the biggest barriers are the lack of IT integration, especially by manufacturers, and organisational and cultural issues. Shared point-of-sale data is pivotal. If harnessed to its full competitive potential, POS data can deliver breakthroughs in market analysis as well as the benefits associated with automated sales and inventory management programmes. Suppliers who are not privy to POS data could be placed, like competitors, at a competitive disadvantage.

Increasing use of home shopping and electronic commerce and the use of new and alternative distribution channels are among the other challenges for logistics managers working in the retail sector over the next decade.

Third party logistics companies can play a key role in helping consumer goods manufacturers and retailers meet the logistics challenges they face, primarily by helping them to realign their logistics networks and by the provision of value-added services, such as assisting with postponement strategies. The principle of postponement holds that costs can be reduced by postponing changes in the form and identity of products to the most downstream possible point in the chain, thus differentiating the product closer to the customer where demand is more easily forecast.

Other trends and important developments that will impact on retail logistics in the future will be in the following areas:

- a reduction of purchases from retail stores;

- the use of IT for competitive advantage;

- growth in strategic partnerships between retailers and suppliers;

- continuing concentration of major retailers by both organic growth and takeovers;

- the increase in the importance of reverse logistics, especially recycling.

Successful retailers in the future will be those that are willing to work closely with their suppliers to satisfy ever more demanding consumers. To do this there will have to be a greater willingness on the part of retailers to share all necessary information with their suppliers and logistics providers. It has been established by various commentators in the area, including Christopher (1997), that marketing and logistics have aligned themselves. There is little doubt that this trend will continue.

References and Further Reading

Christopher, M, *Marketing Logistics* (Oxford: Butterworth-Heinemann) 1997.

Collins, A, "The UK Grocery Supply Chain" *Journal of Food Products Marketing* (1997) Vol. 4, No. 2, pp. 3-21.

Collins, A, M Henchion & P O'Reilly, "Efficient Replenishment: The Impact of Coupled-consolidation", *Supply Chain Management* (Spring 1999).

Coopers and Lybrand, *European Value Chain Analysis Study* (ECR Europe) 1996.

Dvoark, R & F van Paasschen, "Retail Logistics: One Size Doesn't Fit All" *The McKinsey Quarterly* (1996) Vol. 2, pp. 120-129.

Forrester, J W, *Industrial Dynamics* (Boston, MA: Massachusetts Institute of Technology Press) 1961.

Krishnan, T & H de Wilt, "Supply Chain Management" *European Retail Digest* (Spring 1995) pp.33-52.

Kurt Salmon & Associates, *Efficient Consumer Response – Enhancing Consumer Value in the Grocery Industry* (Washington: Kurt Salmon & Associates) 1993.

Sellers, P, "Why Bigger is Badder at Sears" *Fortune* (5 December 1988) p.82.

Chapter 16
E-Business and the Supply Chain

Brendan Ryan
United Drug

16.1 INTRODUCTION

The development of rigorous methods for gathering and analysing
outside information will increasingly become a major challenge
for businesses and for information experts.

Peter Drucker, *Harvard Business Review* (September 1997)

Developments in telecommunications and computing have occurred side by side over the last 50 years. They are now converging, with the Internet becoming the first manifestation of a unified channel. Very soon, virtually all information technology investment will be part of networked communication systems, whether internal to a business, between businesses, between businesses and individuals or simply between individuals. The Internet and e-business is already becoming a major conduit for commerce. Traffic on the Internet has been doubling every 100 days for the past three years. In 1996, 40 million people around the world were connected to the Internet, and more than 100 million were connected by the end of 1997.

In order to meet this demand, organisations are aggressively investing to build out the Internet. Hundreds of new firms are starting up around the world to help businesses use the web effectively. They design sites and advertising banners, create online catalogues, build security tools, create and track direct marketing campaigns, provide consulting services and develop technology to speed the flow of data and information across the network.

Many of the threats and opportunities of today's business environment are caused by the growth of e-business and the Internet. While much attention is focused on the possibilities offered by direct selling to consumers over the Internet, it is the realm of supply chain management where the real benefits of e-business can be found. Organisations can no longer rely on internal efficiencies to be competitive – they have to extend the reach of efficiency to external companies and they have to monitor thousands of external data points along the supply chain to be responsive to consumer requirements. Whereas Electronic Data Interchange (EDI) was application-to-application technology and, as such, was a closed system, the Internet offers person-to-person and person-to-application interactivity, and at a lower cost. The Internet facilitates communication for all members of the supply chain.

The primary advantage of e-business is that it provides real time information about customer behaviour. Organisations are increasingly seeing the benefit of having the right information in the right place at the right time. E-business facilitates efficiency and competitiveness through improved logistical decision-making. Shell, for example, uses a new automated replenishment system called supplier-managed inventory, whereby manufacturers supplied by Shell no longer place orders. Instead, Shell anticipates demand and proactively replenishes inventory. Customer and supplier share operational information in an atmosphere of mutual trust and mutual gain. Dell's Virtual Integration model is another example and, although few companies can boast of similar systems, there is every indication that the foundations, technical and cultural, are now in place for e-business.

16.2 THE GROWTH OF THE INTERNET AND E-BUSINESS

Over the last few years, the US economy has performed beyond expectations with a shrinking budget deficit, low interest rates, a stable economic environment, expanding international trade and effective private sector management. The dramatic improvements in computing power and information technology appear to have been a major force behind this trend. In 1997, the US generated 85 per cent of total global Internet revenues, though only 62 per cent of users were domiciled in the US. Thus, the US, where electronic trading has become established with the assistance of proactive government measures, is a net exporter of goods purchased over the Internet. Some economists suggest that these advances will create a 'long boom', which will take the US economy to new heights over the next quarter of a century.

In Europe, however, the picture is different. Corporations and Governments have not embraced electronic trading with the enthusiasm of their North American counterparts. There are many well-documented reasons, ranging from a smaller wired-up customer base, higher hardware, software and telecom costs and greater fears over security, and cross border issues such as languages, currencies and VAT rates. Despite the successful best efforts of technology and research companies and the obvious threat of US competition, there remains a general lack of motivation in the marketplace, inertia in management circles and lethargy in government to the full implementation of e-business.

In the case of Ireland, there is no doubt that e-business can offer significant international opportunities for our economy. The opportunity to develop e-business software applications coupled with Ireland's potential to offer an e-business base to indigenous and multinational companies might well provide an extra impetus to our vibrant economy. The establishment of the high-powered Telecommunications Advisory Group, supported by Mary O'Rourke, Minister for Public Enterprise, should ensure that a leading edge telecommunications infrastructure supports this mission. The provision of a young, educated, multilingual workforce to support both the growing telecentre market as well as the e-business market is another well recognised prerequisite for the successful attainment of this expectation.

16.3 E-BUSINESS EVOLUTION & EDI

Although EDI has been in place for over 25 years, small and medium-sized firms all over the world are finding it difficult to implement or to maintain EDI. E-business involves the exchange of digital information using a combination of structured EDI, unstructured data (e-mail) and database access across the entire range of networked technologies. The Internet is a ubiquitous network to which any organisation can connect and, for this reason and in contrast to EDI, the Internet has been a catalyst for the growth of e-business.

E-business implies electronic links between dispersed sources of information and the Internet clearly provides low entry costs and huge potential for quick returns on investments. The flexibility of the Internet also means that switching costs are always low if a business requires change and, unlike EDI functionality, a single PC can support extensive trading relationships across open networks and standards. However, technology is not the only issue, because true competitive advantages are gleaned from the judicious use of information and the adaptation of the culture that comes with the Internet and associated technology. Accordingly, organisations must view the supply chain as a complex planning challenge and organisations must recognise the need for simplicity and user friendly support mechanisms to facilitate the growth of e-business. The challenge for most companies must be to prevent the complexity of their own operations making e-business implementation unworkable.

Organisations must also appreciate that e-business is more than just a technology. E-business is all about building new kinds of relationships: relationships with suppliers, customers, business partners, regulators and every other participant in business life. The application of e-business is thus no longer perceived to be limited to niche companies communicating on closed proprietary networks. E-business has a more widespread and common appeal and, in fact, growth in e-business is predicted to rise at an exponential rate similar to the growth pattern of web use. However, many technological, business and market place milestones will have to be reached before e-business is accepted as the ubiquitous everyday method of conducting and transacting business.

16.4 E-BUSINESS – DRIVING THE FORCES OF CHANGE

In today's competitive market, companies can no longer rely solely on improved internal efficiencies to be competitive. Margins are continuously being squeezed and the rate of change in the market is constantly accelerating. R&D cycles are faster, product updates are continuous rather than staged, just-in-time (JIT) techniques speed up order processing, share prices reflect management decisions instantaneously and business processes are in constant flux to meet changing market demands.

Successful businesses of the modern market have moved from vertical integration models to horizontal supply chains that are more flexibly integrated. Computer giants like Dell and Gateway, for example, are eliminating inventory by building to order, while companies like BMW and Stella Artois that own the customer relationship rather than the supply chain are tailoring customer solutions and focusing on intangible assets. The case of Nike similarly comes to mind because it outsources 100 per cent of production and merely manages the brand.

The seamless flow and integration of information through all disciplines and functions within the supply chain provides companies with a genuine competitive advantage, helping decision makers to respond quickly to trends and changes in customer demand. Again, the key to profit generation is having timely access to the right information at the right time!

The Internet and other enabling technologies mean that it is now possible and much more cost effective than ever before for companies to know exactly what is happening in their supply chain. Technology in the 1990s has been all about connectivity: connecting people inside and outside the business, in supplier and customer organisations. The growth of the Internet is a demonstration of the benefits of this connectivity. The future of e-business is a function of this optimism.

16.5 E-BUSINESS – REPLACING INVENTORY WITH INFORMATION

In today's consumer environment, performance standards have increased and the historic latitude in response to consumer demand is no longer good enough. Shelves must be stocked with goods required by their customers. In effect, information has replaced inventory and the 'just in time' policy has replaced the 'just in case' policy. Excess stock is no longer tolerable and is now considered symptomatic of an operation that is out of control. In order to achieve such standards, collaboration and sharing of information between companies and their respective trading partners is commonplace.

Traditional make and sell strategies, tied to the annual budget, are increasingly being replaced by faster, real time consumer response strategies like Efficient Consumer Response (ECR). The most successful companies in a networked world are those that rely on collecting data and then quickly fulfilling these needs with customised products and services. The traditional competitive background of forecasting customers' long-term commitments has been replaced so that lead times have collapsed and supply chains have become flattened.

E-business has thus given rise to the concept of 'prosumer economics' and the prosumer marketplace, whereby the gap between the point of production and the point of consumption is continuously collapsing. This emergence of prosumer economics marks the beginning of a significant paradigm shift from physical to electronic and from a real to a virtual marketplace that will facilitate commercial decisions and which will enable business to take place at any time and at any place.

Corporate supply chains are moving from the back dock to the boardroom because e-business can facilitate the management of inventory that is neither visible nor owned by these companies. Companies with high base manufacturing costs are embracing e-business as a mechanism to drive cost out of the delivery and overall cost of finished and delivered products, thus allowing them to compete on the basis of being the lowest cost deliverer within the supply chain. Small enterprises have the opportunity to exploit novel and cost effective ways to promote their goods and services on a global level. Entrepreneurs can respond more quickly to new information and position their products and services accordingly.

16.6 E-BUSINESS AND LOGISTICS

IBM: Re-engineering of the Supply Chain

In the Electronics Industry, IBM is an example of a world-class organisation which has reconfigured its logistics operations and has reset its customer and marketing expectations because of the potential of e-business and the requirement for improved communications. IBM has optimised its distribution network and in the process has eliminated unnecessary channel members. This strategy has brought improved transparency to the operation, has eliminated unnecessary cost and has increased competitiveness in a highly volatile and global market.

In the case of IBM server products, manufacturing was originally organised in accordance with brands so that the AS400 product was manufactured in both Rochester (US) and in Santa Polomba (Italy), while the high end server S390 was manufactured in both Poughkeepsie (US) and Montpellier (France). Under this structure, manufacturing performance and response to customer demand was tardy, bureaucratic and inefficient. Today, IBM employs a leaner and more agile model so that manufacturing has been restricted to the parent sites of Rochester and Poughkeepsie respectively and worldwide distribution emanates from the new fulfilment centre in Dublin. This is a more responsive model, and the success of the Dublin fulfilment centre will most probably lead to the development of a similar fulfilment centre in China, thereby positioning IBM closer to the end customers in both Europe, the Middle East and Africa (EMEA) and the Asia Pacific (AP) markets respectively.

Under this new strategy, IBM can operate a 21-day global logistics model from the point of parts procurement to the final execution of finished product delivery. It's an impressive operation considering the complexity of the server product and the possible combinations of end product configurations. The purpose of the strategy is to achieve higher customer satisfaction ratings through increased responsiveness to business partners and global customers through the effective deployment of a leaner, more agile and cost effective supply chain. The success of the strategy is dependent on real time information shared across the globe.

The deployment and roll out of e-business will provide appropriate material planners and schedulers with real time global access and visibility of parts in the legacy systems of the respective sites of IBM. The concept is that the Internet contains sufficient security and adequate protocol for individuals to drill down, via the Internet, into individual stand-alone and legacy systems of the respective brands. In a model where manufacturing service requirements are very demanding and on-time delivery of parts is essential, online query and access to parts inventory is necessary. In an environment characterised by peaks in sales patterns at month and quarter ends (referred to in industry as skewed demand) and where the high dollar value of parts places a heavy responsibility on key management to carry limited stocks, lines down situations are a constant threat. Accordingly, contingency planning and collaboration between sister sites is essential for effective transportation of critical parts during emergency situations. The logistics model is thus a network of communications. Through e-business developments, IBM can offer the final customer 24-hour Customer Quick Ship and 48-hour Premier Response programmes with increased confidence.

United Drug PLC – Integrated Logistics

United Drug Plc, an Irish Plc company, manages outsourced activities on behalf of healthcare manufacturers and principals. The core focus of the company is in the areas of storage, distribution, order processing and related administration. The company has invested heavily in information technology and one of its key success factors is the ability to provide total visibility of sales and stock information at all times. Principals have full access to their respective business areas and they can capture sales data at transaction level and produce and design reports to their own standards and parameters. The software is user friendly and facilitates trend analysis and performance by time periods. The benefit of such services to principals comes in the form of increased transparency and visibility of stock flows through their respective pipelines. In effect, information has eliminated unwanted inventory.

In the wholesale area of the business, pharmacies are served through the company fleet of vans from three main hubs located in Dublin, Ballina and Limerick. The target market is individual pharmacies and, with support from customer service and sales representatives, business is largely conducted online via modems. The system allows for two-way exchange of information. Pharmacists drop orders automatically by scanning product out at the point and time of sale. The mid-range servers which receive the orders search the inventory management system and acknowledge orders subject to stock availability. In the event of stock being available, a pick ticket and associated invoice is generated and the order is assembled and dispatched to the appropriate van route.

It is a very dynamic system that supports a very demanding logistics model and shows e-business and real time provision of information can reduce inventory in the pipeline. The pharmacist is constrained by space and needs to have low stock levels continuously turning over. United Drug needs to stock a broader range and a higher quantity of high turnover products. Information is the key and real time provision of two-way information is the primary success factor.

16.7 E-BUSINESS AND SUPPLY CHAIN COLLABORATION

The need for trust and collaboration as a basis for competitive advantage is one of the most challenging aspects of e-business. In the past, it was those organisations that were adept at keeping information, in the form of exclusivity, which were considered successful. However, it is now companies who are skilled at sharing the right information with the right people that are reaping the rewards. A lack of visibility into supply chain activities creates uncertainty across the chain. The results are often unwanted time buffers, such as increased cycle times and unwanted material buffers, such as large inventory piles. Currently, there is an increased recognition of the need for greater transparency and improved synchronisation with trading partners across the supply chain in order to identify more mutual revenue enhancing opportunities.

The most widely adopted technology for collaboration between trading partners is the Internet because it enables cost effective and real time communications regardless of platforms. Organisations are therefore beginning to compete on the basis of the responsiveness of their respective micro-networks. Increased leveraging of the Internet, coupled with integration technologies, is creating seamless inter-organisation processes that increase the overall velocity of the supply chain. In 'best of breed' organisations, customers can even access the supplier's sales configurator via the World Wide Web and configure the desired product. The configurator can check material and manufacturing capacity availability not only within its own organisation, but also within that of suppliers providing key components. It can go even further by confirming the delivery date. This concept is embodied in Dell's model of "Virtual Integration".

Dell: Customer and Supplier Partnerships

Dell has established one of the most advanced manufacturing systems in the world through it's "Virtual Integration" model. It takes Dell only four days from order acceptance of PC products with respective configurations to final customer delivery from its base in Limerick to its customer base across EMEA. Dell builds every machine to order and, in the process, cuts out dealers and distributors while providing mass customisation. The thousands of combinations and permutations of potential product features are planned and handled through Master Scheduling and advanced Material Requirements Planning (MRP) closed loop systems. Phantom bills of materials are incorporated into planning techniques and they are converted in a timely manner through effective communication to real and tangible features specified by the customer through the normal manufacturing process. The requirement is to ensure that product features are available to satisfy customer demand. The skill is to ensure that stock levels remain in control and JIT manufacturing prevails. The key is real time provision of information. E-business has increasingly become the mechanism for the provision of this real time information.

Dell is very focused on inventory levels within the pipeline and only tolerates warehouses as locations for order merging and final assembly of parts. This is spectacular when one appreciates that monitors built in the Far East for a particular batch of PCs manufactured in Ireland are only transhipped through a warehouse and are never stored at cost to Dell. In order to implement such programmes, interfaces between respective legacy systems and collaboration through e-business technology with limited and approved suppliers and customers are necessary.

In an effort to accommodate e-business communication and its implications within the supply chain, organisations are increasingly changing their hierarchical structures. They are deconstructing and building leaner and flatter organisations and, in some cases, entire sections of the business are being cut out, merged or expanded to fit the new formats. In the same way, new types of managers are emerging, as specialist top-down departments cannot deliver in the connected environment of e-business. Organisations, which are less defined, favour generalists who can forge new partnerships inside and outside the business.

Chrysler, the US automobile manufacturer, has recorded savings of $2.5 billion through its customer supplier relationships. It has reduced its supplier base to those companies that rated highest in sharing information relating to cost reduction and quality initiatives. It has built interfaces with its suppliers legacy systems to understand the best way of ordering sufficient volumes on a just in time basis.

16.8 E-BUSINESS – POTENTIAL IMPLICATIONS FOR CUSTOMERS AND SUPPLIERS

E-business means a new age of customer self-service. There are the examples of Fedex, TNT, DHL and UPS customers using the net to track their own products through the respective networks of their distribution suppliers. In all cases these distribution companies, which specialise in high volume parcel deliveries, install their proprietary software and supporting hardware in the premises of their respective customers. The system produces a consignment note for each shipment and this reference is used to track the shipment until final delivery.

The shipment is scanned in at the local hub of the customer and transported to its final destination after it is routed through the European hubs in Stanstead, Liege, Brussels and Cologne. In all of these locations, break bulking occurs for thousands of shipments that converge from both the road and air networks. The logistical operations in each of these centres are impressive and highly focused but, as expected, they are operations rather than customer- focused. Packages must be sorted at high speed and in a reliable manner into the right containers in order to connect with the right scheduled flight or truck. The system, which enables tracking of shipments through barcode technology, is the customer service portion of this complex logistical operation. The sheer volume of shipments which passes through the network makes the tracking system on the Internet a very cost effective service offering to all of these integrator companies.

Banks and insurance companies increasingly give online access to their customers to query their respective pension and financial accounts, etc. IBM does business with thousands of companies, processes over 3 million invoices a year and disburses more than $25 billion to suppliers every year. Accordingly, IBM opted for an Internet-based invoicing solution and suppliers worked with IBM to create customised business forms that are posted on a website. Using a standard Internet connection and web browser, authorised trading partners may access the site, fill in the form online and submit it electronically. The same phenomenon of getting customers to do more work and simultaneously offering them improved service could also happen with suppliers.

The addendum to this IBM initiative is an even more spectacular low cost subscription service for suppliers. Purchase orders are now online and can be turned into invoices automatically. The online invoice will be pre-populated, based on the purchase order and the supplier will simply press the 'submit invoice' button for payment after completion of the work.

16.9 E-BUSINESS – POTENTIAL IMPLICATIONS FOR MANUFACTURING LOGISTICS

The Internet and enabling technologies are allowing companies of all types and sizes to create global markets by effective sharing of information. It is the message behind the data that enables companies to make the decisions that matter. Customer knowledge must be consolidated so that it can support every layer of business.

One of the most successful companies to exploit the Internet in both its supply chain and the way it sells direct to customers is Dell Computers. Dell views e-business and trading over the Internet as the closest thing to trading telepathically. Dell currently sells over $5 million PCs over the Internet every day. Dell believes that if the information is good enough and the supply chain is tight enough, sales can be made almost before the customer realises they want it!

Virtual Integration is a philosophy employed by Dell whereby the advantages of a tightly controlled and co-ordinated supply chain are merged with the focus or specialisation of a virtual company. Essentially, customer focus, supplier collaboration, mass customisation and just in time manufacturing are all brought together through innovative use of technology and real time sharing of information in order to achieve new levels of efficiency and productivity. Dell focuses on delivering solutions to customers and on leveraging the expertise and investments of others within the supply chain to create the most value for their customer base. In this way, capital is invested only in customer-oriented value add activities, and for this reason Dell will only partner with suppliers who can retain their leadership in quality and service. Regardless of the contractual implications, everyone has a single view of the enterprise and all partners are treated as 'equals' with real time sharing of information.

E-business and the technology available today support the philosophy of information sharing. In the case of Dell, information sharing is so complete through e-business and the sharing of design databases and methodologies with supplier partners that Dell's order fulfilment performance has been improved dramatically. In 1993 Dell had $2.6 billion in sales and $342 million in inventory. At the end of last year, it had $12.3 billion in sales and $233 million of inventory.

Dell has also reached out to its customer base via customised intranet sites, which exist securely within the customer firewalls. They give the customer direct access to purchasing and technical information about specific configurations they can buy from Dell. There is no doubt that in the case of Dell, e-business and technology have enhanced the economic incentives to share and to collaborate.

16.10 E-BUSINESS – POTENTIAL IMPLICATIONS FOR THIRD PARTY LOGISTICS

Third party logistics has arguably been influenced by Michael Porter's Value Chain Model. This model proposes that companies compete on the basis of their respective core competencies and outsource activities for which they cannot add value.

In the Irish electronics industry, the concept of outsourcing is very strong and companies like Exel Logistics and Irish Express Cargo have serviced large multinationals like 3COM, Intel, HP and IBM with distinction. IBM sees the benefit of outsourcing in terms of contracting in the expertise at minimal risk to the business. The history of IBM and its growing trend of moving the business to locations of low labour and low tax costs underlines this principle of risk. IBM, with a global labour force of 300,000 full-term contracts and a contract work force of over 200,000, refers to outsourcing as the programme of "Managing the Vendor". It acquires expertise and skilled labour without the associated risks and manpower implications.

The general basis for third party logistics services is the provision of warehouse management and distribution services. In all cases service providers must tailor their offering to the defined requirements of the customer. The range of services generally comprise off-site warehouse management of purchased and consigned stock, the JIT replenishment of manufacturing lines, the invoicing of customers and the distribution of finished product. It always requires strong communication between suppliers, third party service providers and customers. Suppliers of consigned stock need guarantees of stock accuracy, while customers need assurances of invoice accuracy along with timely replenishment and distribution of materials. The integration of systems between the respective parties is generally a feature of these programmes. The future requires further collaboration for 'win-win' situations and real time information through intranet services are considered the best way forward. The Internet is more cost effective and reliable than leased lines, which are comparatively more expensive and are comparatively more open to security violations unless they are protected by cumbersome firewalls.

The third party logistics industry is undergoing significant and rapid change. As real power continues to shift from the manufacturer end of the supply chain to the customer, distributors must adjust their business models to reflect this new balance. Failure to change may result in 'disintermediation', whereby a direct channel between manufacturer and customer emerges at the expense of the third party logistics industry. The ongoing competitive battle between Barnes and Noble, Borders and Bertlesmann AG to dominate the online bookselling business is a case in point. As a result of the 'virtual shelf space' created by online selling, there is equal opportunity for sales for all types of books. Online database search facilities make the sale of a book on Irish folklore as practical as a bestseller. And online booksellers are not standing still. They are expanding into music distribution, too. Similar changes are happening in magazine distribution where WalMart, for example, has reduced its supplier base for magazines from 305 to 3! Similar cases apply in the insurance industry, where dial direct companies are a strong threat to the local brokerage services and in the travel agency sector where larger organisations can provide a more responsive, comprehensive and cost effective package to holiday makers.

The primary force currently reshaping the industry is the prolific interconnectivity of disparate companies, virtual customer communities and networked systems. E-business and the Internet have changed the shape of the industry and speed of action has become more critical. EDI purchase orders have replaced faxed orders, which earlier replaced telephone orders that had earlier replaced mail orders. Soon, it will be the web enabled order that automatically checks credit and inventory, calculates freight charges, issues a tracking number and speeds the merchandise through an expedited logistics company. These Internet orders will have the capability of locating available inventory from any number of networked locations and can co-ordinate shipments to the customer location regardless of origin. Federal Express, for example, long considered the premier overnight package company, has transformed itself into a logistics company. It invests almost 10 per cent of its annual $10 billion revenue into information processing with the stated goal of managing information as well as packages.

The sharply proscribed boundaries of the third party logistics industry no longer exist. Distributors who want to survive and succeed are transforming themselves. They are providing additional value added services to distinguish themselves from competitors. They are providing rapid replenishment. They are managing customer inventory. They are providing their customers with new ways of entering and tracking orders. They are constantly looking for ways to add value to their service offering. They are constantly looking for ways to learn and to execute best practices and the Internet is quite clearly a source of such valuable information. Indeed, according to Bruce Merrifield of Merrifield Consulting Group Inc., a US-based consultancy firm which specialises in the wholesale distribution industry, "Any CEO who is not personally interacting with custom news filter services on the Internet is an incipient corporate liability".

Entrepreneurial logisticians may begin to organise new types of distribution services focused not on the producer as origin, with multi-drop destinations, but on the consumer as destination, with multi-pick up origins. This is known as 'just for you distribution', or 'J4U'. Late changes in orders or in destinations will be accommodated via a telecommunications link with the train or truck and by the use of product finishing facilities, which will be located not at the factory, but on the vehicle! Principles of value adding distribution have always been applied within the transport sector (e.g. sorting mail on trains) but the full potential of the delivery vehicle, given the capability of onboard computers and miniaturised manufacturing equipment, has yet to be realised.

16.11 E-BUSINESS – POTENTIAL IMPLICATIONS FOR THE TRANSPORT INDUSTRY

In the past, step changes in technology have had a detrimental impact on the transport industry. When aeroplanes replaced passenger ships there was a devastating decline in ocean liners and the railway industry suffered a similar fate with the emergence of the combustible engine. By contrast, the changes produced by e-business and advances in information and communication technologies provide the transport sector with the means to re-engineer itself and to resolve endemic issues such as congestion and difficulties in management and co-ordination.

It is said that today every business competes in two markets: the marketplace in which resources and products exist physically and require traditional freight transport services, and the marketspace, which is a virtual world of electronic commerce in which the main object of transaction is information. Transport companies that compete on the traditional basis will have to recognise that in many sectors physical goods are likely to be a decreasing portion of the modern firm's total output. Companies that compete on the customer's marketspace requirements through information conduiting will be ahead of their traditional competitors and will be comparatively stronger at predicting mobility requirements. They will be focusing less on origin to destination speed and more on coping with rapidly changing origins and destinations.

Some forecasters envisage that, in those retailing sectors which currently favour the large store format, traditional retailing involving the movement by car of a customer to a retail premises may be replaced by a channel structure in which manufacturers interact with consumers directly through telecommunications and use home delivery services to bypass conventional retail outlets. This phenomenon, known as reintermediation, may cause retail outlets to become less central in commerce, as direct distribution from electronically–triggered warehouses grows. Thus, the conversion to disintermediation offers real opportunities to the proactive and well-informed third party logistics service providers.

Most transport organisations generate and use information as a by-product of their core activity. This information may have commercial value within the marketspace and, accordingly, transport firms are expected to align themselves to ancillary markets appropriate to the era of electronic commerce. Computerised reservation systems employed by the larger airlines to co-ordinate bookings and to assist with yield management are a good example of how a service can be extended in a commercially viable manner. Initially, it was extended to smaller airlines and to travel agents but today, with the advent of e-business and the Internet, prospective customers can avail of the service.

E-business can touch virtually every department in a third party logistics company. The sales force could benefit from mobile computing, giving both themselves and the customers instant online access to inventory and order status regardless of the salesperson's location. Marketers could benefit from improved recognition of behavioural changes in account activity and could modify their campaigns accordingly. Warehouse personnel could provide better asset management if inventory stocking levels, customer demand, supplier production volume and cyclical trend indicators were available through an online query. Accounting staff might be able to reduce the days outstanding if the accounts receivable system flagged potential slow payers by matching current order volume and historical payment patterns against comparable data on similar customers. Accordingly, e-business has the potential to produce measurable savings by functioning as a cohesive information conduit that integrates disparate functional systems across the organisation. It is essential to keep abreast of this rapidly expanding technology.

16.12 E-BUSINESS – POTENTIAL IMPLICATION FOR RETAIL LOGISTICS

The majority of businesses may utilise the Internet and e-business to improve their service to customers and to reduce inventory holdings while selling from traditional shops and outlets. However, e-business can transform the supply chain and allow companies to collaborate together so that everyone gets the best forecasts and is as ready as possible for the inevitable outcome.

The concept is that in order to get the right products in the right place at the right time and at the right price, an effective supply chain operation means having the right information in a timely manner about all of those steps. There are, of course, companies who have neither transport nor warehouses and who do not even manufacture because they have reliable access to the right information.

Sainsbury's use Internet technology to employ Efficient Consumer Response (ECR) programmes. Under this collaborative arrangement, using EPOS technology, retailers share information about product performance while in turn, suppliers share information about product performance on a national level. In the case of sales promotions, which are initiated to increase customer awareness of product offerings and which inevitably give rise to dramatic skews in production and inventory levels within the pipeline, Sainsbury's communicates with its suppliers via PCs over the net and as a team. The implications of the promotions are discussed, with everyone viewing the same forecasts, planned orders, inventory levels and EPOS data. The information can be graphically displayed and updated as required for more informative decisions. Utilising the same techniques, supplies can be readily adjusted during the promotion depending on sales. The principle is to ensure logistics are right through real time sharing of information over the Internet.

The e-business opportunities for retailers are enormous. Freeing up hidden information in complex supply chains could lead to leaner pipelines and lower selling prices. The elimination of non-value added elements with their associated costs are the way to attack the 'soft buck'. Many companies have successfully squeezed down the cost of production to the lowest possible level and now there is an impetus to reduce costs that are unnecessarily spread throughout the distribution channels.

The opportunity for the retailer may be a threat to the supplier, as any hidden inefficiency may be flushed out in the full light of e-business. Each part of the supply chain will have to look retrospectively at their own processes to squeeze out costs and each supplier may have to join the technical network of the retailer so that information can be shared back and forth. The efficiencies offered by e-business are potentially so great that it's hard to see how retailers can avoid adopting it.

16.13 CONCLUSION

The Internet and its associated technologies are a major source of future competitive advantage and, even though some commentators and corporations are not comfortable with electronic business, there is no sensible option but to embrace it. Throughout the world, millions of people are involved in developing e-business and they are collectively investing enormous amounts of time, energy and money in its successful deployment. The US-based research company Forrester predicts that the value of e-business trading on the Internet will grow to $330 billion by the year 2002, while over 630,000 US companies and 245,000 European companies will be involved in fully fledged integrated business to business and business to consumer electronic commerce.

Internet standards, methods and technologies are increasingly being adopted, as they prove to be more effective and far cheaper than existing proprietary and EDI solutions. Unlike EDI, the low costs of the Internet will allow organisations of all sizes to communicate electronically with their respective business partners. Progressive organisations will move from an internally focused cost reduction strategy to an externally focused revenue enhancement strategy. Successful organisations will purge their respective micro-networks of dysfunctional processes and replace them with agile, more collaborative processes that take advantage of customers' changing wants and needs.

The critical issues for senior management to consider are the business implications and opportunities presented by the new electronic infrastructure that has emerged from the evolution of commuting and communication technologies. The successful organisations of the future will be those that have developed the mindset and models for thinking about the business areas, business strategies and business processes enabled by the emerging e-business technologies. The role of the marketing function will continue to be that of finding customers and exploring, understanding and communicating their needs; the role of manufacturing will continue to be the pursuit of low cost through technical innovation, efficiency and component standardisation; the role of logistics will be to pinpoint individual customer needs in place, time and design specifications, and to deliver the final product in a creative and economical way. The supply chain will be characterised by strong linkages between a reduced number of suppliers with materials and goods flowing under careful control to minimise inventory levels. Third party service providers will play an increased role in the final stages of production, helping to provide flexibility of destination choice, delivery timings and product presentation. There will be increased value adding services within the supply chain and this will be made possible by e-business and a heavy linkage with information technology. A far-reaching e-business solution will inevitably strip the old organisational structure to the bone and replace it with an entirely new one that is not based on old or hierarchical structures.

There is considerable evidence that organisations are beginning to understand the powerful benefits of integrating e-business into the supply chain and those organisations who already have EPOS and EDI technology have a distinct advantage because they already appreciate the strategic importance of IT. However, the real promises of e-business will only be delivered when large organisations open up their cultures and learn to share information with suppliers and customers via the Internet. E-business and information communications technology will facilitate a virtual marketplace and those companies that are proactive stand to improve their market position and their competitiveness significantly.

References and Further Reading

Cooke, James A, "Virtual Companies Need Real Logistics Support" *Logistics Management* (November 1997). Located at: http://www.manufacturing.net
Coughlan, C, "Ireland the E-Hub of Europe" *The Sunday Business Post* (September 1998). Located at: http://www.sbpost.ie
Crowley, J A, "Virtual Logistics: Transport in the Marketspace" *International Journal*

of Physical Distribution & Logistics Management (1998) Vol. 28 No. 7, pp. 547-574.

European Commission, *European Initiative on Electronic Commerce* COM(97)157 (1997). Located at: http://www.cordis.lu/esprit/src/ecomcom.htm

Fuller, J B, J O'Connor & R Rawlinson, "Tailored Logistics: The Next Advantage" *Harvard Business Review* (May-June 1993).

Hines, P, "Integrated Materials Management: The Value Chain Redefined" *The International Journal of Logistics Management* (1993) Vol. 4, No. 1.

Kalin, S, "Choose Your Medicine" *WebBusiness Magazine* (June 1999). Located at: http://www.cio.com

Thompson, I (ed.), *Electronic Commerce in Europe – An Action Plan for the Marketplace* (London: IMRG) 1998. Located at: http://www.imrg.org

General Internet Sites

http://www.ibm.com	IBM Homepage
http://www.ibm.com/services	IBM Global Services Homepage
http://www.dell.com	Dell Homepage
http://www.dell.com/uk	Dell website for the UK
http://www.forrester.com	US Consultancy Firm Homepage

Chapter 17
Education and Training in Logistics and Transport

Orla Gregory
Institute of Technology, Carlow
and
John Mangan
Irish Management Institute

17.1 INTRODUCTION

The importance of the education and training that Irish logistics and transport practitioners receive cannot be exaggerated, as it impacts directly on the efficient management of the supply chain in which they are an essential element. Within their own industry, logistics and transport practitioners are now required to take a wider strategic view rather than the previously acceptable narrow operational view. This increased role and status requires substantially different and enhanced skills, education and training.

When this is combined with increasing international competitiveness and the emerging trends in production and distribution, it is clear that logistics/supply chain management skills are essential for Irish firms to reduce both the negative impact of Ireland's relatively peripheral location and also to ensure continued firm success in increasingly competitive markets.

While location cannot be changed, the skill and expertise with which Irish logistics and transport practitioners manage the consequences of Ireland's peripheral location can be enhanced through adequate education and training. This enhancement could go a long way towards compensating for the negative impact of location and help gain competitive advantage for Irish firms. It is important to understand the forces at work in the marketplace which have created these logistics and transport sector training needs.

Relatively little published information is available concerning the education and training of Irish logistics and transport practitioners. Most material appearing in academic journals describes the education and training available to their American counterparts. In part, this is indicative of the scant regard which has been paid in the past to the critical role Irish logistics and transport practitioners play in both their organisations and in Irish industry as a whole.

This chapter reports on a recent survey by one of the authors (Gregory)[1] on the education and training of logistics executives in Ireland. Changes in logistics practices and skills requirements of the surveyed executives are re-

---

[1] A survey "Irish Logistics Executives: Their Education and Training", carried out in 1998 and resulting in 44 usable responses, by Orla Gregory, Institute of Technology, Carlow.

viewed, and future issues in this regard are considered. The survey results are also considered in the context of reported research conducted elsewhere. At the end of the chapter an inventory of training providers and information sources in the logistics and transport areas has been assembled.

17.2 CHANGES IN IRISH LOGISTICS PRACTICES

No single aspect of logistics can be identified as driving the change currently being experienced in Ireland and worldwide; rather, a combination of strategic factors have cumulated and have had a 'snowballing' effect on the logistics discipline. These trends have resulted in an increasing realisation of the importance of information flows in managing the logistics pipeline and a willingness to use the opportunity of a borderless European Market to rationalise distribution networks.

While each aspect has impacted on logistics practices in different ways and to varying degrees, the combined effect has resulted in the dynamic change currently being experienced. Some of the changes that have significantly influenced the logistics sector include:

- increased use of information technology and Electronic Data Interchange (EDI);
- increasing strategic profile of logistics and transport;
- growth in outsourcing;
- changes in purchasing practices and supplier relations systems;
- increased global logistics and global competition;
- changes in production and distribution systems;
- continuous organisational changes;
- economic growth.

The above changes in logistics practices within organisations located in Ireland were elicited from a recent survey of logistics executives (hereafter referred to as 'the survey of logistics executives in Ireland'). The survey of logistics executives in Ireland reported that almost all respondents (41) [44 was the total number of respondents] were currently subcontracting transportation and almost half (21) expected to increase their use of outside sources of transportation. A current reduction in the number of suppliers was reported by a substantial number of respondents (29) but more than half (25) expected that this reduction would be reversed. Respondents were asked to specify how their organisation's approach to logistics had changed. Increased supplier partnerships was most frequently reported. This confirmed the high number reporting a current practice of reduction in suppliers and implies an increasing emphasis on a partnership relationship with retained suppliers. Outsourcing of transport, distribution, warehousing and inventory management was frequently reported and respondents anticipated a future increase of this practice.

Many causes were given for the changes being experienced in the organisations' approaches towards logistics. The two most frequently mentioned were:

- *Cost reductions*: it would appear that Irish organisations are becoming increasingly aware that effective logistics management can lead to substantial cost reductions and improved profits.
- *Customer service/relations*: this reflects the view of Ballou (Yanacek, 1987) that "customer service ... is the reason for the logistics effort".

These new and increasingly changing requirements on the logistics function within organisations leads to the need for a corresponding rise in the level of professionalism and skills among logistics managers. Adequate education and training must be received by practitioners if they are to achieve the levels of competency, aptitude and expertise required to meet today's demands and survive the uncertain challenges of the future.

17.3 CHANGES IN SKILL REQUIREMENTS

The new direction in logistics management requires change, and those practitioners that fail to respond and acquire the necessary training will be left behind. Logistics is not a profession for those who like a static job, unchanging from day to day. Many logistics practitioners report increased job responsibilities (85 per cent of traffic, transportation and distribution professionals surveyed in America (Quinn, 1994), and similarly 68 per cent in Ireland (the survey of logistics executives in Ireland)).

With logistics attaining a strategic orientation in many firms, practitioners must possess certain necessary skills in order to manage their function effectively. The contemporary logistics and transport practitioner needs to be proficient in a range of business, logistics and management skills. A strong academic training in logistics, emphasising technical and computer skills, will be the hallmark of the successful logistics professional; this is a development from the position of logistics professionals in the past who were hired for their strong background in materials management and related areas.

Murphy and Poist (1991) suggest that logistics practitioners' skill requirements fall into three broad categories:

1. *business* skills (knowledge of the various functional disciplines such as marketing, finance, etc.);

2. *logistics* skills;

3. *management* skills (ability to plan, organise, etc.).

Previously, operational skills associated with delivering the goods were required (i.e. keeping a good warehouse, delivering on time, routing the truck fleet efficiently), but a change is occurring. There is a move from purely operational skills towards two other sets of skills. One set deals with analytical abilities – strategic vision and an ability to evaluate strengths, weakness, threats and opportunities. The second deals with relationship development – the ability to build relationships in a supply chain, to relate upstream to vendors and downstream to customers, and also the skill and ability to relate to other functions within the business, such as marketing and finance.

In the survey of logistics executives in Ireland, respondents were asked to rate the level of importance of eight listed skills in their current jobs. Three skills were identified as being of equally high importance: communications, people management and problem solving skills, with problem identification following closely. The strong emphasis respondents placed on the human resource management skills of communication and people management would suggest that these Irish logistics executives are, as Murphy and Poist (1991) noted, "Managers first and logisticians second". The results of the survey of logistics executives in Ireland reflect the emphasis on communications and people management skills identified by many authors.

When the group of Irish logistics executives in the survey were asked which were the most important skills they would require in the future, the five most important identified were, in descending order of importance:

- communications/negotiations;
- computers/information technology;
- general experience;
- logistics supply chain management;
- people management.

It is interesting to note that computer and information technology skills were ranked more highly as future than as present skills (Table 17.1).

Table 17.1   Skill Importance

Skill	Average Weighted Level of Importance (1= Low importance 5 = High importance)
Communication	4.5
People Management	4.5
Problem Solving	4.5
Problem Identification	4.1
Negotiating	3.9
Analytical	3.5
Project Management	3.5
Computer	3.4

Source: Survey of Logistics Executives in Ireland

It is notable that, according to the survey, the relative levels of importance of various skills, as perceived by the Irish logistics practitioner, are what might be expected from an executive in any functional area. This is probably function-independent. The logistics executive's self-perception is of a manager first and a logistician second.

17.4 EDUCATION AND TRAINING IN LOGISTICS

Continuing education and training is not just a matter of keeping pace – it is a survival issue. It is essential that Irish logistics practitioners actively seek to obtain the necessary skills if they wish to meet the changing demands of their profession. According to LaLonde (1990), "things are moving so fast that it is probably safe to say that if you do not invest 10 per cent of your time in building your skills, you will be obsolete in four or five years". It would appear that Irish practitioners are attempting to invest time into building their skills, according to the results of the survey.

Qualifications Held and Types of Training Received

A high level of education among practitioners was reported – 50 per cent held a certificate or diploma, and almost 25 per cent held a degree. All respondents had received some form of education and/or training in the previous two-year period (1996-1998). The most common types of training received during this two-year period were:

- formal college – received by 30 respondents;
- in-house training – received by 25 respondents;
- seminar/workshop – received by 24 respondents;
- 'on the job' – received by 23 respondents;
- in-house training with an external trainer – received by 14 respondents.

Effectiveness of Types of Training

Those surveyed were asked to rank the effectiveness of the training received. These are listed below in descending order:

- seminars/workshops;
- in- house training;
- in-house training with an external trainer;
- formal College;
- 'on the job' training.

It is interesting to note the apparent low perceived level of effectiveness of 'on the job' training, even though it is identified as being received by 52 per cent of respondents to this question. Also, while formal college training was the type received most frequently, it was ranked only fourth in effectiveness. These results are almost a complete reversal of those of a survey of American logistics executives reported by Quinn (1994). Perhaps these results reflect a cultural difference, with Irish logistics executives appreciating more off site, subject-specific forms of training.

Reasons Given for Course Effectiveness

As well as identifying the most effective type of training, respondents were also asked to justify their number one ranking of the effectiveness of the training received (Figure 17.1). The most frequently stated reasons for effectiveness of training received were:

- 'job relevance' – reported by 11 respondents
- 'material content' - reported by 6 respondents
- 'good course delivery' - reported by 5 respondents

Figure 17.1: Reasons Given for Course Effectiveness

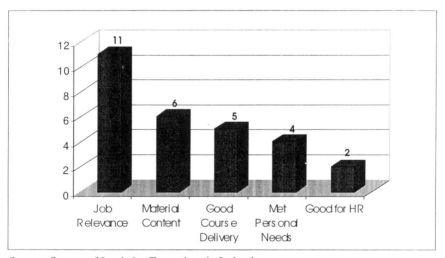

Source: Survey of Logistics Executives in Ireland

Areas of Training Received by Respondents

The six areas of training received most frequently by respondents were (Figure 17.2):

- computer/information technology – received by 30 respondents;
- safety/environmental/legal training – received by 22 respondents;
- personnel management training – received by 16 respondents;

- general management training – received by 13 respondents;
- customer service – received by 12 respondents;
- inventory management – received by 11 respondents.

The absence and low ranking of training in different aspects of logistics is notable.

Figure 17.2: Areas of Training Received

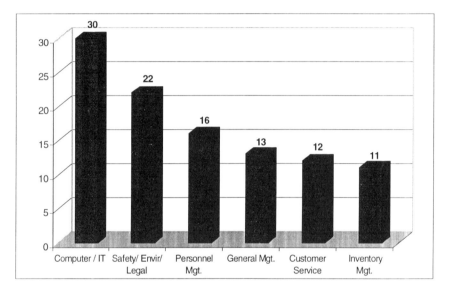

Source: Survey of Logistics Executives in Ireland

As previously mentioned in this chapter, the logistics practitioners reported that customer service/relations was the second most important reason why their organisation's approach to logistics has changed but, surprisingly, customer service ranked only fifth (twelve respondents) in the areas where training was most frequently received. Perhaps training is not always received in the most necessary areas. Similarly, the infrequent identification of inventory management as an area of training received (only eleven respondents) does not correspond with the practitioners' response elsewhere that inventory reduction was the second most important change in their organisations' approach to logistics.

Safety/environment/legal training was received by 22 respondents. This emphasis could be due to the increasing pressures being placed on Irish organisations to meet EU regulations. This was also reflected in the number of respondents who identified 'more geographic cover (national and EU)' as a significant change in their responsibilities. Personnel management is identified as an area of training received by sixteen respondents – this indicates the emphasis respondents placed on people management skills.

Reasons for Further Training

The three reasons for further training identified by the logistics executives were (Figure 17.3):

- 'personal development' – 31 respondents;
- 'to obtain useful job related skills' – 30 respondents;
- 'improving career/promotion prospects' – 17 respondents.

Salary improvement was not reported as a particularly significant reason to pursue further training; only seven respondents identified it as such a reason. This response supports Honniball's (1993) finding that there was little evidence to show that education had a positive effect on salary for Irish logistics executives (see Figure 17.3 below).

Figure 17.3: Reasons for Pursuing Further Training

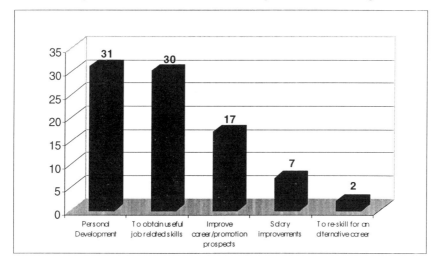

Source: Survey of Logistics Executives in Ireland

Areas for Further Training

The most significant areas identified in the survey as being of potential benefit were (Figure 17.4):

- 'logistics/supply chain management'– identified by 13 respondents;
- IT/computers – identified by 12 respondents.

Figure 17.4: Areas for Further Training

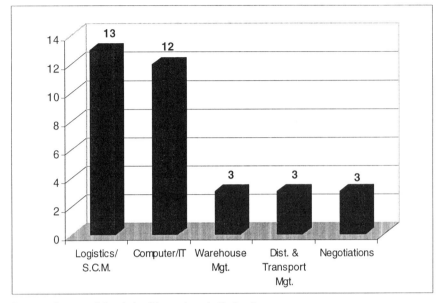

Source: Survey of Logistics Executives in Ireland

While computers/IT systems was reported by these logistics practitioners as the area of training most frequently received, it was ranked only second in the category of areas for furthur training. This corresponds with the view of many authors (e.g. Cooke (1992), Quinn (1994), Gooley (1994)) that, of all areas of education and training identified by logistics executives as being desirable, computers and information technology was given the highest priority.

Sources of Training

Responses to the question where training was available were varied – only three specific institutions were mentioned more than once:

- Cranfield University – identified by 5 respondents;
- Irish Management Institute – identified by 3 respondents;
- Institute of Logistics – identified by 3 respondents.

It is disappointing that there is so little awareness of the various other sources of training available and that so few providers of training appear to be acknowledged by respondents. It would appear to confirm the belief expressed in the Forfás (1996) report, *World Class to Serve the World*, that in Ireland the available selection of courses is not adequate and that "there is a current weakness in the provision of dedicated logistics skills in the education system".

Both authors of this chapter have spent a number of years teaching in the transport and logistics fields at a variety of institutions in Ireland. Many practitioners find it difficult to identify where training is available and what are the best sources of information in these areas. Consequently we have assembled some relevant pointers in Appendices 17.1 and 17.2, which we hope will be of some benefit to logistics and transport practitioners. This is the era of lifelong learning and so we would hope that all practitioners, regardless of their level, skills and abilities, would strive to continuously update themselves and enhance their learning in the vast, dynamic and constantly changing field which is logistics.

17.5 CONCLUSION

With the changing role of Irish logistics and transport in recent years and the wider recognition of its importance at corporate level in particular, the requirements for managing logistics have broadened. No longer is logistics divided into discreet functions: emphasis is on the integration of these functions to meet continually changing market demands in line with current thinking on supply chain management. As the contribution of logistics and transport practitioners to their organisations' competitiveness is being recognised, they are moving up the organisation hierarchy. Furthermore, the increasingly competitive environment in which organisations operate has significantly increased the pressures to improve performance and become more cost efficient.

Whether these challenges can be overcome and opportunities exploited will depend on the ability and skill of Irish logistics and transport practitioners to utilise the transport and communications infrastructures and services available to them. To achieve this successfully, it is essential that Irish logistics practitioners acquire additional skills, as existing ones will not meet the new demands placed on them.

The existing supply of education and training is not perceived as fully meeting either the present or future needs of practitioners. The evolution of logistics in Ireland to meet the requirements of the country's economic development may necessitate an enlargement of present arrangements. It may also require some modification to the portfolio of courses currently available in this area.

Appendix 17.1

Institutions which Provide Information and/or Offer Training in Logistics and Transport[2]

Carlow Institute of Technology (www.itcarlow.ie)
Diploma and Degree programmes in purchasing management, which deal to a significant extent with logistics and supply chain management.

Chartered Institute of Transport in Ireland (www.ccs.ie/citi/citi.htm)
CITI is a membership organisation for people working in the transport and related sectors. They offer a variety of short courses in the general transport area. In addition, they offer a distance education programme for those who wish to study for institute membership. Apart from this, the CITI host frequent seminars and provide a variety of information updates to their members.

Cork Institute of Technology (www.cit.ie)
CIT offers a Diploma in technology in transport management. CIT is also the national centre for seafarer training for the merchant marine.

Dublin Institute of Technology (www.dit.ie)
DIT offers a full-time, two year Certificate and a three year Diploma course in transport management. DIT, in conjunction with the National Institute of Transport and Logistics (NITL), is currently developing a suite of programmes in logistics and supply chain management. A Masters degree in tourism management, with a strong transport component, has also recently been introduced at DIT Cathal Brugha Street.

FÁS (www.fas.ie)
FÁS offers a logistics and distribution traineeship at a number of locations. The course lasts 36 weeks, with training being split between formal classroom training and workplace-based training with a host company

Institute of Logistics and Transport (www.ccs.ie/ILOG/ilog1.htm)
The ILT is a membership organisation for people working in the logistics and related sectors. The ILT was formed by the merger in the UK of the Institute of Logistics with the Chartered Institute of Transport, giving rise to the Institute of Logistics and Transport. The ILT branch in Ireland hosts regular site visits and other events.

Irish Institute of Purchasing and Materials Management (www.iipmm.ie)
The IIPMM offers a variety of short courses and seminars. In addition, they

---

[2]   Please note that this listing is not intended to be exhaustive and therefore the omission of any particular organisation is unintentional.

offer courses leading to certificates and diplomas in conjunction with various colleges throughout Ireland.

Irish Management Institute (www.imi.ie)
The IMI provides a range of programmes in all areas of management, from one-day short courses to Masters Degrees. A variety of short programmes are offered in logistics, purchasing and supply chain management. In addition, workshops are held with visiting leading experts in the logistics field.

UK Universities
A variety of undergraduate and postgraduate degree programmes in logistics, transport, and supply chain management are offered at various UK universities. It is important to note that some of these programmes can be done on a full-time or part-time modular basis. Two of the best are:

- The MSc degrees in logistics and supply chain management and transportation management at the School of Management at Cranfield University (www.cranfield.ac.uk/som)
- The MSc degrees in international transport and in lean operations, and the MBA in supply chain management at Cardiff University.

University College Dublin (www.ucd.ie)
The Graduate School of Business at University College Dublin offers a full-time one year/part-time two year Masters in Business Studies degree programme in logistics and manufacturing. In addition, supply chain management is part of the undergraduate degrees in Commerce.

It is important to note also that logistics and supply chain management usually feature at some stage in the syllabi of most MBA and related degree programmes.

Waterford Institute of Technology (www.wit.ie)
WIT offers a Certificate in business studies in transport and distribution.

Other Useful Contacts

Council of Logistics Management (www.clm1.org)
European Logistics Association (www/elalog.org)
Institute of Freight Forwarders of Ireland (www.ioff.ie)
Irish Government Departments and Government Agencies (www.irlgov.ie)
Irish Exporters Association (www.ccs.ie/exporter/iexport.htm)
Irish Road Haulage Association (☎ 01 822 4888)
Irish Ships Agent Association (☎ 021 813180)

Appendix 17.2

Published Sources of Information in Logistics and Transport[3]

Books

Benson, D, R Bugg & G Whitehead, *Transport and Logistics* (Hertfordshire: Woodhead-Faulkner) 1994.

Bowersox & Class, *Logistical Management* (New York: McGraw Hill) 1996.

Button, K, *Transport Economics* (Aldershot: Edward Elgar Publishing) 2nd edition, 1993.

Christopher, M, *Marketing Logistics* (Oxford: Butterworth-Heinemann) 1997.

Christopher, M, *Logistics and Supply Chain Management* (London: Financial Times/ Pitman Publishing) 2nd edition, 1998.

Coyle, J, E Bardi & C Langley, *The Management of Business Logistics* (St Paul, Minnesota: West Publishing) 6th edition, 1996.

Dornier, P, Ernst, R, Fender M and Kouvelist, P, *Global Operations and Logistics* (New York: Wiley) 1998.

Lambert, D, J Stock & L Ellram, *Fundamentals of Logistics Management* (New York: McGraw-Hill) 1998.

Journals

Asia-Pacific International Journal of Business Logistics
Cranfield Research Papers in Marketing and Logistics
Distribution
Handling and Shipping
International Journal of Logistics Management
International Journal of Logistics: Research and Applications
International Journal of Physical Distribution and Logistics Management
International Journal of Purchasing and Materials Management
Journal of Business Logistics
Journal of Transport Economics and Policy
Journal of Transport Geography
Logistics and Transportation Review
Logistics Europe
Logistics Information Management
Logistics Management
Maritime Policy and Management
Supply Chain Management
The European Journal of Purchasing & Supply Management
Traffic Management
Transport Reviews
Transportation and Distribution Management
Transportation Journal

---

[3] Please note again that these listings are not intended to be exhaustive and therefore the omission of any particular publication is unintentional.

Transportation Practitioners Journal
Transportation Research A, B, C, D, E
Transportation Science

In addition, it would be remiss not to also indicate some of the leading business journals, which are cross-disciplinary and leaders in the field.

Business Strategy Review
California Management Review
European Management Journal
Harvard Business Review
Sloan Management Review

References

Buxbaum, P, "The Next Generation of Logistics Managers: Fearless Communicators" *Transportation & Distribution* (1995) Vol. 36, No. 10, pp. 84-86.

Cooke, J, "A Look into the Future of Logistics" *Traffic Management* (1992) Vol. 31, No. 9, pp. 65-68.

Forfás Transport and Logistics Group, "World Class to Serve The World" February 1996 report.

Gooley, T, "Hit the books – Career Development of Logistics Managers" *Traffic Management* (1994) Vol. 33, No. 2, pp. 42-46.

Hines, P, "Integrated Materials Management: The Value Chain Redefined" *The International Journal of Logistics Management* (1993) Vol. 4, No.1, pp. 13-22

Honniball, C, "A General Profile of the Irish Logistics Executive, with Particular Emphasis on Qualifications" (University College Dublin) 1993.

LaLonde, B, "Update Logistics Skills for the Future" *Transportation & Distribution* (January 1990) p. 46.

Marien, E J & C G Evenson, "Education for Transportation Professional: Practical Help from Universities" *Defence Transportation Journal* (July-August 1986) pp. 17-19.

Murphy, P & R Poist, "Skill Requirements of Senior-Level Logisticians: Practitioner Perspectives" *International Journal of Physical Distribution and Logistics Management* (1991) Vol. 21, No. 3.

Murphy, P & R Poist, "A Comparison of Head Hunters and Practitioner Views Regarding Skill Requirements of Senior-Level Logistics Professionals" *The Logistics and Transportation Review* (1991) Vol. 27, No. 3, pp. 277-295.

Quinn, F, "You and Your Job" *Traffic Management* (1994) Vol. 33, No. 5, pp. 53-56.

Transport Policy Research Institute, "An Analysis of Training Needs in the Physical Distribution (Logistics) Sector of the Irish Economy" (University College Dublin) November 1991 report.

Yanacek, F, "The Logic Behind Logistics – Many of the Most Effective Logistics Departments in the Nation are not called 'Logistics' Departments'" *Handling & Shipping Management* (1987) Vol. 28, pp. 30-40.

Chapter 18
Overview: Logistics and Performance

John Mangan
and
Kevin Hannigan
Irish Management Institute

18.1 The Major Themes

The chapters of this book have been grouped into three distinct sections. Section 1 introduced the subjects of transport and logistics and placed both in the context of an economy experiencing rapid growth and change. Section 2 described the air, maritime, road and rail modes and, specifically, their development and role in the Irish economy; this section also explored the relationship between transport and the growth of tourism in Ireland. Section 3 progressed to a discussion of various themes within logistics and the wider, inter-company, boundary-spanning concept of supply chain management. The final chapter of the book then discussed education and training in logistics and transport. Across all of these disparate chapters three major themes became apparent, as detailed in the sections which follow.

18.2 SUSTAINED ECONOMIC GROWTH REQUIRES EFFICIENCY IMPROVEMENTS

Rapid economic growth, such as is the case presently in Ireland, requires not just a major improvement in the transport infrastructure, but also an improvement in the use of this infrastructure through better, more efficient management of resources. Such rapid growth also implies a major change in the structure of the economy, in the output produced and in the delivery mechanisms for output. With regard to efficient transport and logistics, one of the major drivers has undoubtedly been market deregulation. Competition between and within modes has intensified, generally to the benefit of the consumer. Added to this has been a more proactive, market-focused input by successive Governments into transport and related policy. Public policy debates concerning transport infrastructure in the future are as likely to focus on 'soft' issues, i.e. skills, efficiency gains and the sophisticated use of technology, as on the 'hard' issues, i.e. the provision of the physical infrastructure, which has dominated such debates to a considerable extent in the past.

Other drivers of efficient transport and logistics have included productivity improvements gained as a result of both developments in information and communications technologies and from improvements in freight handling and transportation methods. Added to this is the fact that the transport intensity of freight has decreased significantly.

The various contributions to this book have illustrated that transport and logistics are knowledge-intensive operations, the development of which require much more than the provision of fixed capital and infrastructure. When faced with input constraints, solutions that emphasise a better, rather than a greater, use of resources are to be favoured. *In summary, Ireland requires more sophisticated management of transport and logistics systems as well as modern transport infrastructure.*

18.3 COMPETITIVE ADVANTAGE IS GAINED FROM SUPERIOR LOGISTICS

Logistics and management of the supply chain has emerged as one of the key areas in which firms can attain a competitive advantage over rivals. This is particularly the case for many of the firms that are operating most successfully in the Irish economy. Peter Drucker's assertion in 1962 that distribution represented the last major frontier for significant cost reduction in the firm has evolved to an understanding that not only can effective logistics management save costs, but it can also gain competitive advantage for firms, given that firms now operate in global markets defined by hyper competition and constant, rapid change.

Professor Martin Christopher of Cranfield University has asserted that, increasingly, it is supply chains and not individual firms or their products that compete. This assertion has certainly proved true for many firms operating in Ireland, some of whom were reviewed in this book. Witness the case of Dell, detailed in Chapter 12, and described as a company that sells Intel and Microsoft technology through a highly efficient logistics operation. Within its operations, it carries less than seven day's stock at any point in time; no finished stock is held, as Dell only manufactures to order. This is truly an example of a remarkable supply chain, and one which has key nodes located in Ireland. Other examples of exceptional supply chains include the various examples in the retail logistics sector cited in Chapter 15. According to Professor Christopher the new marketplace, characterised by sophisticated and demanding customers and consumers, requires highly responsive companies, with the arena of marketing logistics becoming the essential interface. This essential interface must now facilitate product delivery in an economical, creative and customer-focused manner.

One of the key success factors for the continued prosperity of many firms located in Ireland will undoubtedly be the availability of staff skilled in best practice logistics. Training and education in the sector is thus likely to increase, indeed, *must* increase.

The trend in recent years has been for firms to concentrate on their core competencies and outsource other activities. As a result, third party service providers have been readily soaking up the non-core competencies of their clients. The current disparity in service excellence among different categories of third party logistics service providers in Ireland will, unfortunately, most likely remain. The leading Irish third party service providers are market-facing firms with reputations for technology development and high quality service delivery which are second to none. Many of these companies have become best in class not just in Ireland, but overseas as well. As well as excelling in core logistics areas such as transportation and warehousing, these firms are also successfully undertaking various value adding functions for their clients (e.g. mass customisation of products, providing repair and return channels for products, etc.) while also reducing the number of touch points in the supply chain.

Indeed, it is possible that the logistics sector may become a highly viable future export service industry. A case in point is the recently announced global partnership between Irish Express Cargo, an indigenous Irish firm, and the giant multinational Hewlett Packard. Other examples include the decision, again detailed in Chapter 12, of Microsoft to relocate their UK distribution hub to the manufacturing plant in Ireland. This shows that distribution can be effectively managed from the geographically peripheral location which is Ireland. It will be very interesting to see how Irish logistics service providers compete in the emerging era of fourth party logistics and e-business.

18.4 DEVELOPMENTS IN INFORMATION TECHNOLOGY AND INCREASED ENVIRONMENTAL AWARENESS ARE KEY DRIVERS

It was already noted above that developments in information and communications technologies have enhanced the efficiency of logistics systems. Those third party logistics service providers in Ireland who do not possess up to date information and communications technology capabilities will be increasingly relegated to the sidelines. E-business is revolutionising business practices globally and logistics will increasingly play a partnership role in delivering products marketed virtually.

Increased environmental responsibilities, reflected most notably by a 'cradle to grave' approach to manufacturing, will substantially impact logistics systems. Green supply chains, incorporating reverse loops for product and packaging recycling, will become the norm. Internalisation of externalities resulting from transport output could significantly increase logistics costs. Other issues such as congestion, accentuated by both JIT and reverse logistics practices, may also have a negative impact upon the efficiency of logistics systems.

18.5 CONCLUSION

Taken together, these themes lead to the conclusion that logistics management is an important area in which both firms and countries compete. However, many of the chapters indicate that weaknesses in the development of the management of logistics and transport in Ireland may be slowing the modernisation of the economy, with practices and modes of operation more reminiscent of earlier times still prevalent. New ideas and operational models are emerging at a phenomenal rate and the role of the logistics manager in the future will differ considerably from the past in terms of importance and scope. In the immediate future, however, the pay-off from implementing modern management practices is likely to be substantial, while any lethargy to face up to the demands of global markets would be costly indeed.

Index